Successful
Industrial
Product
Innovation

Recent Titles in
Bibliographies and Indexes in Economics and Economic History

Joseph Alois Schumpeter, A Bibliography, 1905-1984
Michael I. Stevenson, compiler

The Green Revolution: An International Bibliography
M. Bazlul Karim, compiler

Information for International Marketing: An Annotated Guide to Sources
James K. Weekly and Mary K. Cary, compilers

Telecommunication Economics and International Regulatory Policy: An
Annotated Bibliography
Marcellus S. Snow and Meheroo Jussawalla, compilers

Manpower for Energy Production: An International Guide to Sources
with Annotations
Djehane A. Hosni, compiler

Central European Economic History from Waterloo to OPEC, 1815-1975:
A Bibliography
Richard D. Hacken, compiler

International Real Estate Valuation, Investment, and Development
Valerie J. Nurcombe

Japanese Direct Foreign Investments: An Annotated Bibliography
Karl Boger, compiler

Economic Methodology: A Bibliography with References to Works in the
Philosophy of Science, 1860-1988
Deborah A. Redman, compiler

A Literature Guide to the Hospitality Industry
*Philip Sawin, Denise Madland, Mary K. Richards, and
Jana Reeg Steidinger, compilers*

Successful Industrial Product Innovation

An Integrative Literature Review

COMPILED BY
Roger J. Calantone
AND
C. Anthony di Benedetto

Bibliographies and Indexes in Economics and Economic History, Number 11

GREENWOOD PRESS
New York • Westport, Connecticut • London

Library of Congress Cataloging-in-Publication Data

Calantone, Roger J.
    Successful industrial product innovation : an integrative
literature review / compiled by Roger J. Calantone and C. Anthony di
Benedetto.
        p.   cm. — (Bibliographies and indexes in economics and
    economic history, ISSN 0749-1786 ; no. 11)
    Includes bibliographical references.
    ISBN 0-313-27571-8 (lib. bdg. : alk. paper)
    1. New products.   I. di Benedetto, C. Anthony.   II. Title.
III. Series.
HF5415.153.C35   1990
658.5'75 — dc20   90-41840

British Library Cataloguing in Publication Data is available.

Library of Congress Catalog Card Number: 90-41840
ISBN: 0-313-27571-8
ISSN: 0749-1786

First published in 1990

Greenwood Press, 88 Post Road West, Westport, CT 06881
An imprint of Greenwood Publishing Group, Inc.

Printed in the United States of America

The paper used in this book complies with the
Permanent Paper Standard issued by the National
Information Standards Organization (Z39.48-1984).

10 9 8 7 6 5 4 3 2 1

Contents

vi   Contents

Preface

      The development and marketing of new industrial products is an issue of importance to business managers, technical R&D personnel, and academics. New product development is a risky activity, and the financial stakes can be very high, so the product manager's task is to keep the amount at stake low as long as risk and uncertainty remain high. The industrial product manager is in a position to coordinate the efforts of several individuals or departments within the company in order to achieve success with a new product. Successful new product development demands a strong, healthy interface between marketing, R&D, and manufacturing. At all stages of the product development process, design, engineering, production, and marketing activities must be carried out and coordinated. Thus, effective product development requires the bridging of functional areas within the firm, as well as adequate interfacing with the "outside"--the market and external sources of new product and process ideas.

      Beyond these immediate managerial concerns, there are other reasons why success in new product development has become a key investigative issue. In many industries, successful innovation is of critical importance to the continued competitiveness of the firm, both nationally and globally. Furthermore, significant, successful innovation by North American firms in the world market is a powerful sign of economic and scientific vitality. Domestic firms can obtain an edge over foreign competition through successful innovation which results in product competitiveness in the global market.

      Successful new industrial product development depends on the coordination of skills and activities from many functional areas within the firm. Due to the very complexity of product innovation, the relevant literature is scattered throughout the marketing, business strategy, and technical/engineering journals. In fact, a journal devoted to issues in product innovation and development has recently been launched (<u>Journal of Product Innovation Management</u>). Despite the virtual information explosion on new product development which has occurred, it has been many years since an attempt was made to compile a comprehensive, annotated bibliography on product innovation. Indeed, the 1976 annotated bibliography by Robert Rothberg, published by the American Marketing Association, appears to be the most recent, and it is focused on certain topics within the product innovation/development literature. There is thus a need for an up-to-date, broad-scoped literature review in this area.

Over the past ten years, many new and exciting avenues of research in new product development and innovation have opened. These include: research on the reasons for success or failure of new products; management of the interface between marketing and R&D; assessing demand for new-to-the-world product forms; quicker, more efficient and more reliable techniques for test marketing and "pre-test-market" assessment of new products; and so on. With this increase in topical coverage some questions naturally arise. How much of the research being reported in either the business, management, or engineering literature is relevant and/or helpful to managers involved in new-product development? Furthermore, as noted above, product innovation and development are multidisciplinary, multifunctional activities. What is the quality of the scientific knowledge available on the new product process? To what extent can business managers and marketing staffs involved in the process learn from what is published in other functional areas such as engineering or technical journals?

The purpose of this study is to produce an integrative literature review on the industrial new-product development process. It will attempt to integrate the findings from the marketing, business, and engineering literatures so as to identify general, managerially oriented conclusions. This work could serve as a useful entry point into the innovation literature for both product managers and academic researchers seeking ways to improve the practice of industrial product innovation and management. What we have attempted to do is to identify the key issues and problems that practicing product managers face and to determine to what extent the academic literature addresses these concerns.

The book is structured according to topic area. Several topic areas of interest to the product development process were identified: factors influencing the extent of product and process innovation; stages of the new-product development process; forecasting of new product diffusion; the R&D - marketing interface; the encouragement of product innovation through organizational structure; and technology transfer. We did not strive to be exhaustive in our literature review; rather, we selected a reasonably complete and representative set of articles from major marketing, business management, operations research, and engineering publications and sought to organize and integrate them. Most of the articles cited are found in academic journals, some with a decidedly technical focus (Management Science, e.g.) and some with a more managerial slant (such as Harvard Business Review). Certain articles from national conference proceedings were also included. As a rule of thumb, articles from approximately 1978 to the present were included. However, several key articles from earlier years were also cited if they had a major role in the historical development of a topic area. The literature review shows that some issues have been well investigated, while others deserve more attention in the literature. We attempt to identify these areas needing more attention.

Acknowledgments

The authors gratefully acknowledge the assistance of several individuals in the preparation of this manuscript. Paulette Marino and Patricia Casey were valued assistants who helped out in all phases of library search, abstract writing, and paper organization. Lucinda Zoe and Russell Powell provided expert guidance through the management and engineering libraries respectively, and carried out the computerized library searches. Bernadette Dupont typed most of the Annotated Bibliography section. Thanks also go to Janet Cabaniss who painstakingly and professionally edited the final version of this book.

The authors would especially like to thank Diane Schmalensee, George Day and the Marketing Science Institute for their encouragement and financial support of this project.

How to Use this Book

This book is divided into six chapters, each covering a topic in product innovation. Each chapter is composed of a literature review and an annotated bibliography. The literature reviews integrate the findings of key researchers and discuss applications of these findings. The annotated bibliographies reference all articles listed in the preceding literature review as well as other pertinent research. Authors' names, title, publication specifics, and a brief abstract are presented. Heading names in the annotated bibliographies correspond to those of the literature review for easy referencing.

TO THE PRACTICING MANAGER

This review serves as an entry point into the literature on product innovation. Topics are organized into sections for easy reference. The literature reviews can stand alone as statements on the development and state of the art of each topic area. They should provide sufficient information to the practitioner for many questions that might arise. For the practitioner who requires further information or clarification, each literature review can profitably be combined with the abstracts in the corresponding annotated bibliography.

TO THE ACADEMIC RESEARCHER AND THE STUDENT

Each literature review provides summaries of the development of each topic area in a rough chronological order. The academic researcher or graduate student may thus gain insights on the ways in which research on the topic has developed. By contrast, within each subheading in the annotated bibliographies, the articles are ordered alphabetically for ease of access by the user. An alphabetical author index and subject index are also provided. The researcher or graduate student, like the practitioner, can use the literature reviews and annotated bibliographies in complementary fashion.

Successful
Industrial
Product
Innovation

1

Product Innovation

Since 1980, the literature on innovation has expanded greatly and covers a variety of disciplines--marketing, management, engineering, and decision sciences. It has been reported in both academic and practitioner journals, from Management Science, Omega, and Decision Sciences to Journal of Product Innovation Management, Business Horizons, and Journal of Business Strategy. Two major categories of interest appear in the literature: models of product and process innovation, and management perspectives and managerial implications of the innovative process.

MODELS OF PRODUCT AND PROCESS INNOVATION

An important early study of successful industrial innovations was carried out by Myers and Marquis (1969). They studied 560 commercially successful innovations, from over 100 firms in five different industry segments. Product innovations, innovations in the production process, and innovations in product components were investigated. Data such as costs, changes in the production process, and source of basic information used were obtained for each innovation. Although not many differences were found among the industry segments, this study spurred much follow-up work: for example, Utterback (1975) re-examined the same data with more powerful statistical techniques. Earlier, Utterback (1974) had examined factors that limit and determine a firm's effectiveness in the innovative process. As a result of in-depth analysis of several industries, he determined that strategies for growth and competition in an industry differ across industries: for example, in the automotive industry, sales maximization may be predominant, while in transportation and communications, cost minimization may be more important. In the chemical industry, performance maximization may dominate both of the above. The implication to management is that, in a cost-minimizing situation, production is likely to be the main source of uncertainty, while product technology would be more uncertain in a performance-maximizing industry.

Based on ideas presented in the Myers and Marquis (1969)

and Utterback (1974) studies, Utterback and Abernathy (1975) presented a dynamic model of product and process innovation. In this important model, product innovations were shown to predominate at early stages in the innovation process, when production processes were flexible and the firm seeks to gain a competitive advantage via emphasis on product performance maximization. As time passes, the competitive emphasis shifts to product variation and the production process becomes more rigid, with the formation of "islands of automation." Process innovations, required by rising volume, predominate. In the third stage, incremental innovations in both product and process predominate as competitive focus is placed on cost minimization. Production processes become rigid, efficient, and capital-intensive. Some support for the hypotheses of the model was obtained by re-examination of the Myers and Marquis (1969) data. The model is further discussed in Abernathy and Utterback (1978) and Utterback (1981), while De Bresson and Townsend (1981) and Calantone, di Benedetto, and Meloche (1988) provided further empirical tests. In the latter study, it was found that technically autonomous firms are most successful with process innovations that allow them to achieve cost savings and scale economies, and that successful internally-developed innovations developed by technically autonomous firms tended to be introduced early in the production process. Moore and Tushman (1982) linked the Utterback-Abernathy model to the product life cycle and discussed the implications for competitive advantage. They concluded that, because changes in types of innovation lead to changes in competitive emphasis, the firm must recognize that strategies, processes, and organizational structures must evolve over time as well, and must therefore be explicitly managed.

An important extension to the basic model was made by Utterback (1982), who distinguished between evolutionary and revolutionary product and process innovation. Using the automotive, transistor, and typewriter industries as examples, he showed that an industry with relatively stable market shares and little real product innovation is "ripe" for attack by an invading firm that is new to the industry, and which has a radical product. Such a discontinuous change in the industry pattern forces the incumbent firms either to make hurried improvements to the old technology, or somehow to gain access to the new technology, perhaps through acquisition (Cooper and Schendel 1976). Among their conclusions, Calantone, di Benedetto, and Meloche (1988) found that successful product innovations frequently were "revolutionary" ones originating outside the industry. That is, if a market that is receptive to a new technology can be identified, then the invading firm stands a reasonable chance of success. This is consistent with Utterback (1982). Ettlie and Rubenstein (1987) also investigated the issue of radical versus incremental innovations and found that, up to a point, larger firms with greater resources were more likely to be successful in revolutionary product innovation, but very large firms (over 45,000 employees) would not necessarily be so inclined. This premise is reasonable, as very large firms may not be able to respond as rapidly to technological change, and technologically-oriented firms with a small number of employees are not necessarily at a disadvantage in generating innovative ideas (Scherer 1980, Chap. 15).

Although the Utterback and Abernathy model has received some criticism in the literature (De Bresson and Townsend, 1981), it provides a reasonable starting point for understanding the process of innovation in industry.

Other articles have also examined the process of innovation in industry. Mansfield and Rapaport (1975), seeking to explain why some firms innovate more than others, looked at the percentage of costs devoted to R&D. Bagozzi (1983) extended previous work on consumer response models to develop a structural equation model of response to innovation; he also made recommendations to managers on how to design products and corresponding marketing mixes. Shmuel and Rothkopf (1984) created a class of models to bridge the gap between theoretical market share and dynamic forecasts. Yoon and Lilien (1985) examined the relationship between R&D and marketing activities for original and reformulative new products. Their framework was designed to help one understand the complexity of the problem of achieving high performance in the new product process. Acs and Audritsch (1988) concentrated on R&D, market structure, and the effects of both on large and small firms.

MANAGEMENT PERSPECTIVES AND IMPLICATIONS

Managerial implications are discussed in two broad categories in the literature: barriers and impediments to the innovation process, and how to improve or control the process. Although most of this literature is non technical in nature and is aimed at practicing managers (via publications such as <u>Harvard Business Review</u>, <u>Research Management</u>, and <u>Business Horizons</u>), a few of these articles present technical analyses and were published in <u>Management Science</u> or the engineering literature.

Impediments to the Innovation Process

One of the best arguments pertaining to the role of technology in the formulation of manufacturing strategy was provided by Abernathy and Wayne (1974). They acknowledged that it is difficult for a firm's production department to implement cost-reduction programs (i.e., to take advantage of the learning curve) while at the same time their R&D or marketing departments are proposing technology- or market-based changes to the product. Abernathy and Wayne concluded that "product innovation is the enemy of cost efficiency, and vice versa." This issue is conceptually linked to the dynamic innovation model of Utterback and Abernathy discussed earlier, in that a firm poised to take advantage of cost-reducing innovations tends to have instituted a highly automated and inflexible production line.

Crawford and Tellis (1981) addressed the state of technological innovation in the early 1980s in the United States. They noted that at that time, R&D expenditures, the percentage of gross national product devoted to R&D, and the

number of technological breakthroughs were all decreasing.
As a result, the U.S. share of major worldwide innovations
was declining. They sought to identify reasons for the
comparative slowdown in R&D activity in the United States,
and noted that certain governmental regulations were
oppressive to innovation (for example, that antitrust action
inhibits innovation, and that strong governmental support for
innovation was lacking). They concluded that there was
uncertainty as to the roles of government, industry and
society on technological innovation. Hayes and Abernathy
(1980) also display this sentiment when they argued that, in
the early part of the 1980s, American managers were not doing
enough to keep their firms technologically competitive over
the long run. Cohn (1980) and McIntyre (1982) identified
several obstacles to corporate innovation, including
resistance to change, organizational politics, emphasis on
short-term efficiency, negative attitudes toward   new
technologies among managers, risk aversion, and lack of
initiative by marketing departments.   Gold's 1984 study also
recognized resistance to change as the most basic impediment
to product innovation.   It recommended a new long-term
approach based on integration of product innovation and
market development and designed to help firms meet the
changing pressures they face. Other factors leading to the
decline of American innovation include excessive merger
activity into unrelated businesses, transfer of technology
to other countries, less personal contact between executives
and engineers than in other industrialized nations, and the
use of rigid financial management tools (Abernathy   1982).
Compton (1982) presented a case study of the Ford Motor
Company to illustrate other problems faced in the innovative
process, such as salary compression, and suggested how these
problems could be avoided.

Von Hippel (1988) discussed another major obstacle to
innovation in organizations: namely, the way in which
external information is gathered and used by firms.   A
manufacturing firm relies on the innovation inputs of several
organizations (research laboratories, universities, etc.), so
a key factor in the   firm's innovative endeavors is its
ability to acquire outside information. In practice, several
barriers may exist in gathering appropriate information:
salespeople may not relay information on a   potential
innovation because they fear they might not be able to sell
or   service the new product easily; salespeople may be
discouraged by the firm's compensation system from
undertaking any activity (such as information gathering) that
takes time away from selling current products; or the firm's
reward system may be oriented toward in-house innovations.
Von Hippel presented several suggestions for removing these
barriers, many of which center around how to gather
information from user groups or applications laboratories.

Improving and Controlling the Process

Improvements to and control of the innovation process
have been well documented. Innovation is an important
determinant of growth and change in the American economy and

quality of life. It can also be abused,   leading to a depletion of resources, an underutilized work force, and so on;   yet, if properly controlled, technological innovation can help provide the answers to these very problems (Hill 1981). Effective innovation requires a number of conditions: that the technical staff can provide the necessary functions for innovation; that the organizational structure must provide for an adequate flow of information; that there is a strong interface between R&D and marketing; and that technical plans must be integrated with aspects of the overall corporate strategy (Roberts, 1977).

Numerous authors have commented on the role government plays in the fostering of technological innovation. Klein (1981) suggested that if American firms are protected from foreign competition (or,   for that matter,   new domestic entrants) by legislation, the need to innovate to stay competitive is slowed.   Technological advances made by competitors act as a "hidden foot," poised to prod the firm to take more risks in innovation. The threat of the "hidden foot"   may be as effective as the invisible hand in encouraging innovative activity by American firms.   Graham (1981)   concurred with this sentiment by noting that stimulation of domestic technological innovation would help America's international competitive position.   Schnee (1978) commented on the success of certain high-technology industries in the United States (notably the space and   defense industries) and the role of the government in supporting these industries.   Horwitz (1981),   Hollomon (1979, 1981) and Utterback (1981) all made recommendations on the specific sorts of government assistance that ought to be provided to improve American technological innovation. Among these are supporting and stimulating basic technology research, promoting competition among firms, lowering entry barriers to new competitors, and financing projects that might be too risky for bank financing.   Other ideas for improvement of American economic growth are   provided by Peck and Goto (1981). These authors draw upon the Japanese experience with technology importation and indicate how American firms might learn from the Japanese, for example, by emulating the institutions and policies implemented in Japan which encourage the effective use of technology for innovative growth.   Hill and Utterback (1981) stated the government's objective best: The government should encourage innovation by increasing the firm's risk, "not by increasing the risk of failure of new technology, but by increasing the risk that a firm will fail if it does not innovate!" (Hill and Utterback, 1981).

In addition to examining the role of government, several articles have addressed other factors which contribute to improving or controlling the innovative process. The issue of how to manage actively the interdepartmental communication flows in R&D laboratories is explored by Tushman (1979). Nadler and Tushman (1980) presented a general approach for analyzing the functioning of an organization. They suggested that an organization is composed of its required task, its individuals, and its formal and informal organizational structure, and proposed a model that explored the relationships or "fit" among these components. Communication patterns within the organization that facilitate the exchange of information greatly enhance the innovative process (Ebadi, 1984). A supportive top management and efficient interfunctional teamwork (Zmud, 1984; Johne and Snelson, 1988) have also been shown to contribute positively to this process. Other positive influences include effective organization and efficient implementation (Quinn, 1985; Price, 1987). The use of formal planning and controlling mechanisms such as budgets, periodic reviews, and postmortems also have made positive contributions to innovative effort (Rinholm and Boag, 1988). Other literature is focused on the role of key players such as the R&D manager (Foster, Linden, Whiteley, and Kantrow, 1985) and the entrepreneur (Foxall and Johnston, 1987).

PRODUCT INNOVATION: ANNOTATED BIBLIOGRAPHY

MODELS OF PRODUCT AND PROCESS INNOVATION

1.1   ABERNATHY, W.J. AND J.M. UTTERBACK (1978), "Patterns of Industrial Innovations," Technology Review, 80 (June-July), 2-9.
Expands upon the Utterback and Abernathy (1975) model of dynamic product and process innovation. Depicts, via a graphical model, how the character of a successful innovation changes as the enterprise matures, and shows how other companies may change themselves to foster innovation as they grow and prosper.

1.2   ACS, ZOLTAR AND DAVID B. AUDTRESCH (1988), "Innovation in Large and Small Firms: An Empirical Analysis," American Economic Review, 78(4), 678 - 690.
Presents a model suggesting that innovative output is influenced by R&D and market structure characteristics. Based on a new and direct measure of innovation, they found that: 1) Total number of innovations is negatively related to concentration and unionization and positively related to R&D, skilled labor and the degree to which large firms comprise the industry; 2) These determinants have different effects on large and small firms.

1.3   BAGOZZI, RICHARD P. (1983), "A Holistic Methodology for Modeling Consumer Response to Innovation," Operations Research, 31(1), 128-176.
The author presents a general structural equation model for representing consumer response to innovation, extending an earlier model of Hauser and Urban. The model accounts for measurement error, estimates intercorrelations exogenous factors, finds a unique solution and tests hypotheses on the measurement of consumer responses and their impact on actual choice behavior. The paper presents the development of four generic response models for determining how consumers behave and how managers might better design products, appeals and programs.

1.4   BUSKIRK, B.D. (1986), "Industrial Market Behavior
        and the Technological Life Cycle," Industrial
        Management and Data Systems, (November-December),
        8-12.
Products in the industrial market depend on their
underlying technology for their competitive advantage. Low-
cost production of generic goods puts the technological life
cycle at the production rather than market level, but still
the factors will be much the same. The product life cycle
has often been criticized; however, this has not stopped the
PLC from being one of the most used concepts in consumer
marketing. The author suggests a six stage TLC: cutting edge;
state of the art; advanced; mainstream; mature and decline.

1.5   CALANTONE, ROGER J., C. ANTHONY DI BENEDETTO AND
        MARTIN S. MELOCHE (1988), "Strategies of Product and
        Process Innovation: A Loglinear Analysis,"
        R&D Management, 18(1), 13-21.
Applies loglinear regression to the Bolton Enquiry Data
Base to test empirically the Utterback-Abernathy Dynamic
Process model. Conclusions: 1) Successful product innovations
occur earlier in the model than to successful process
innovations; 2) Technically autonomous firms are successful
with process innovations which allow them to achieve cost
savings/economies of scale; 3) Successful product innovation
frequently comes from outside the industry; 4a) Successful
product innovation development by technically autonomous firms
are introduced in early stages of the production process; 4b)
Successful product innovations developed outside the industry
are typically introduced early in the innovative process.

1.6   COOPER, A.C. AND D. SCHENDEL (1976), "Strategic
        Responses to Technological Threats," Business
        Horizons, 19(2), 61-69.
Several industries threatened by major technological
innovations are studied, and conclusions are drawn which have
implications for other firms confronted with new technologies.
Firms tend to defend themselves by improving the old
technology and by making major commitments to utilize the new
technology. Acquisition is posited as a means to acquiring
both the technical capabilities and the organization attuned
to the new field.

1.7   DE BRESSON, C. AND J. TOWNSEND (1981), "Multivariate
        Models for Innovation--Looking at the Abernathy-
        Utterback Model with Other Data," Omega, 9(4), 429-
        436.
The contribution of the Utterback and Abernathy (1975)
model of product and process innovation is reviewed from the
point of view of methodology. Then, its feasibility is tested
with United Kingdom multivariate data on innovation covering
many industries. Some aspects of innovation are confirmed,
yet some facts do not fit the model. Thus, the Utterback-
Abernathy model might be a useful starting point but it fails
to give an integrative framework to industrial innovation.

1.8   DEWAR, ROBERT D. AND JANE E. DUTTON (1986), "The
        Adoption of Radical and Incremental Innovations: An

Empirical Analysis," Management Science, 32(11),
1422-1433
Proposes and empirically tests whether different models are
able to predict the adoption of technical process innovation
that contain a high degree of new knowledge (radical
innovations) and a low degree of new knowledge (incremental).
Results suggest that extensive knowledge depth is important
for the adoption of both innovation types.

1.9   ETTLIE, JOHN E., WILLIAM P. BRIDGES AND ROBERT D.
        O'KEEFE (1984), "Organization Strategy and
        Structural Differences for Radical Versus
        Incremental Innovations," Management Science, 30(6),
        682-695.
Evaluates a general model of the innovation process in
organization that suggests that the strategy-structure causal
sequence is differentiated by radical versus incremental
innovation--unique strategy and structure required for radical
innovation.   More traditional strategy and structure
arrangements tend to support new product introduction and
incremental process adoption--large, complex decentralized
organizations that have market dominated growth strategies.

1.10   ETTLIE, JOHN E. AND ALBERT H. RUBENSTEIN (1987),
        "Firm Size and Product Innovation," Journal of
        Product Innovation Management, 4(2), 89-108.
The authors report the results of a study which
distinguishes between radical and incremental technology.
They hypothesize that up to a certain point, large firms with
greater resources are more likely to commercialize radically
new products successfully.   Findings generally support this
theory but refinements to the model are now possible.   For
example, small firms need not be excluded from radical product
introduction if they resolve critical funding and research
problems.   Very large organizations are unlikely to introduce
radically new products.   Large firms were much more likely
than small firms to adopt ambitious new processing
technologies.

1.11   MANSFIELD, EDWIN AND JOHN RAPAPORT (1975), "The
        Costs of Industrial Product Innovations," Management
        Science, 21(12), 1380-1386.
To better understand the factors resulting in large
differences among innovations in the percent of innovation
costs devoted to R&D, detailed data were obtained on a sample
from the chemical industry.   An econometric model was used to
test a number of tentative hypotheses developed to explain
these differences.

1.12   MYERS, S. AND D.G. MARQUIS (1969), "Successful
        Industrial Innovations," National Science
        Foundation, Report # 69-17, Washington, D.C.
An early study of successful technological innovation in
five different industry segments.   Over 560 commercially
successful innovations were studied, including product,
process and component innovations.   Examined costs and impact
on the production process of each innovation.

1.13   RAISBECK, GARY R. (1982), "Systems Development:
         Technology-Push, User-Pull, or Producer-Motivated,"
         Interfaces, 12(4), 108-112.
    Presents a conceptual model of the relations among users,
producers and R&D in technological innovations.

1.14   SCHERER, F.M. (1980), Industrial Market Structure
         and Economic Performance, 2nd edition, Chicago, IL:
         Rand-Mc Nally (Textbook).

1.15   UTTERBACK, JAMES M. (1974), "Innovation in Industry
         and the Diffusion of Technology," Science, 183, 620-
         626.
    Examines factors that limit and determine a firm's
effectiveness in innovation and the phases in the innovation
process.   Phases are idea generation, problem solving,
implementation and diffusion.   Environmental factors are a
primary influence on innovation, as 60-90 percent of
innovation stems from market or production needs, not
technical opportunities.   Strategies for growth and
competition in an industry (sales maximization, cost
minimization, or performance maximization) may be used on a
basis for drawing distinctions across industries.

1.16   UTTERBACK, JAMES M. (1975), "Successful
         Industrial Innovations: A Multivariate Analysis,"
         Decision Sciences, 6(1), 65-77.
    Re-examines Myers and Marquis (1969) data on successful
industrial innovations using multivariate hypotheses.

1.17   UTTERBACK, J.M. (1981), "The Dynamics of Product
         and Process Innovation in Industry," in C.T. Hill
         and J.M. Utterback (eds.), Technological Innovation
         for a Dynamic Economy, New York: Pergamon Press.
    The theme of this paper is that the conditions necessary
for rapid innovation are much different from those required
for high levels of output and efficiency in production. The
pattern of change observed within an organization will often
shift from innovative and flexible to standardized and
inflexible under demands for higher levels of output and
productivity. Different creative responses from productive
units facing different competitive and technological
challenges may be expected.

1.18   UTTERBACK, J.M. (1982), "The Innovative Process:
         Evolution Versus Revolution," in The Innovative
         Process: Evolution Versus Revolution, Proceedings of
         a Symposium for Senior Executives, Cambridge, MA:
         Massachusetts Institute of Technology.
    An extension of the Utterback and Abernathy (1975) model
which explicitly differentiates between evolutionary and
revolutionary product and process innovation. Supported by
empirical evidence in the automotive, transistor, and
typewriter industries, the author hypothesizes that an
industry marked by very stable market shares is "ripe" for a
discontinuous product change. The invader will likely be new
to the industry in the uncoordinated, adaptive stage. The new
product ultimately takes over the market, leaving the

established forms no alternative but to make improvements to the established product or take over the invading firm. Similarly, differences between evolutionary and revolutionary process change are explicated.

1.19   UTTERBACK, J.M. AND W.J. ABERNATHY (1975), "A Dynamic Model of Product and Process Innovation," Omega, 3(6), 639-656.
Reports results from empirical tests of relationships between patterns of innovation within a firm and several firm characteristics: stage of development of its production process and chosen basis of competition. Synthesizes two complementary models of innovation: the relationship between competitive strategy and innovation, and the relationship between production process characteristics and innovation. Empirically tests results using the data from the Myers and Marquis (1969) study.

1.20   YOON, E. AND G.L. LILIEN (1985), "New Industrial Product Performance: The Effects of Market Characteristics," Journal of Product Innovation Management, 2(3), 134-144.
This article provides a framework to understand the complex relationships between R&D activity, marketing activity, and product success. The authors differentiate original from reformulated new products, and determine the relationships between patterns of R&D and marketing activities and ultimate success.

MANAGEMENT PERSPECTIVES AND IMPLICATIONS

Impediments to the Innovation Process

1.21   ABERNATHY, WILLIAM J. (1982), "Competitive Decline in U.S. Innovation: The Management Factor," Research Management, 25(5), 34-41.
Examines consumer electronics and auto industry. Key to stemming decline in U.S. competitive performance is in the hands of management. Causes of problem: 1) excessive merger activity into unrelated business, 2) transfer of technology abroad, 3) origins and experience of management personnel, personal contact between CEO and engineers (common in Japan, not so here), use of financial management tools which can be too rigid, 4) marketing research relied upon for confirmation if setting goals for innovative programs (survey research in the area of new technology is treacherous).

1.22   ABERNATHY, WILLIAM J. AND KENNETH WAYNE (1974), "Limits of the Learning Curve," Harvard Business Review, 52 (September-October).
The role expected of technology is critical in the formulation of manufacturing strategy. Management must realize that a shift in strategy has a pervasive effect across the organization's functional areas. The production department cannot follow a program of cost reduction along the learning curve at the same time that R&D or marketing are

going into new ventures that may change the nature of the product.   The authors conclude that "unfortunate(ly),... product innovation is the enemy of cost efficiency, and vice versa."

1.23   ALBERTS, WILLIAM W. (1989), "The Experience Curve
        Doctrine Reconsidered," Journal of Marketing, 53(3),
        36-49.
The author studies the relationship between advantaged cost position and the decision to build market share. He first offers a rebuttal of the experience curve doctrine. The rebuttal counterargues that the key to generating a cost advantage is innovation. The author then makes a case that in most market circumstances, rate of return buinding (not share building) is the most profitable way for a unit to exploit an innovation-caused cost-advantage.

1.24   BELL, ROBERT R. AND JOHN M. BURNHAM (1989), "The
        Paradox of Manufacturing Productivity and
        Innovation," Business Horizons, 32(5), 58-64.
The paradox of instability in the midst of stability must be solved in order for U.S. manufacturing to compete in today's environment. Instability in production environments fosters innovation, flexibility and creativity. Several needs are identified in order for instability to exist in the midst of stability, including the need for: top management understanding, commitment and initiatives, orientation across the entire plant, better communications pathways, recognition that change involves education, training and involvement, avoiding intrusions (the quick fix), assuring that people understand and support change and are not fearful of it, and others.

1.25   COHN, STEVEN (1980), "Industrial Product Adoption in
        a Technology Push Industry," Industrial Marketing
        Management, 9(2), 89-95.
Survey study of the adoption behavior of fifty firms and case studies in decision making in five firms.   Results indicate that firms whose decision makers are more favorable to change, less favorable to traditional technologies and less verse to risk are more likely to adopt new techniques. It is also shown that unfavorable attitudes toward new technologies among total managerial staff can impede adoption--the author criticizes the role of lower level managers in superintending the integration of innovation into the firm's production process.

1.26   COMPTON, DALE (1982), "Leading R&D Toward Greater
        Productivity," Research Management, 25(1), 17-21.
Challenges facing the R&D manager are identified: a) establishing appropriate objectives; b) fostering innovation and creativity; c) competing for a declining number of qualified people.   Examples from Ford: how they conduct research, setting objectives for research by top management, salary compression problems and suggestions for how to solve them

1.27   CRAWFORD, C. MERLE AND GERALD J. TELLIS (1981), "The

Technological Innovation Controversy," <u>Business
Horizons</u>, 24(4),76-88.
Extensive literature review. Asks: a) what is the recent
rate of technology innovation: b) if the rate is declining,
why? c) are there contrary observations?   Results: 1. R&D
expenditures, R&D as percent of GNP, number of technological
breakthroughs, all slipping.   Productivity in R&D is
declining.   American R&D as a percentage of GNP slipping
relative to other countries.   American share of major
innovation declining. 2. Governmental regulations oppressive.
Anti-trust action inhibits innovation. Regulatory process in
U.S. creates uncertainty--it is an enemy of technological
innovation. Lack of overall government push for innovation.
Policy of caution, within industry. Shortage of appropriately
trained personnel. 3. Conflicts on the state of technology,
and the roles of government, industry and society.

1.28   GOLD, BELA (1984), "Integrating Product Innovation
        and Market Development to Strengthen Long-Term
        Planning," <u>Journal of Product Innovation Management</u>,
        1(3), 173-181.
A new long-term approach to planning, actively integrating
product innovation and market development, is required for
heavy industries to meet changing pressures. Example given:
steel industry. Most basic impediment: resistance to change.

1.29   HAYES, ROBERT H. AND WILLIAM J. ABERNATHY (1980).
        "Managing Our Way to Economic Decline," <u>Harvard
        Business Review</u>, 58 (July-August).
What is the cause of the sluggish American economic
performance in the 1980s?   These authors argue that
responsibility rests not only with general economic forces,
but also with the failure of American managers to keep their
companies technological competitive over the long run.   They
conclude that the key to long-term business success is "to
invest, to innovate, to lead, to create value where none
existed before. [This] requires leaders, not just controllers,
market analysts, and portfolio managers. In our preoccupation
with the braking systems and exterior trim, we may have
neglected the drive trains of our corporations."

1.30   MC INTYRE, SHELBY (1982), "Obstacles to Corporate
        Innovation," <u>Business Horizons</u>, 25(1), 23-28.
Several obstacles to corporate innovation were identified,
including: resistance to change, conservative subordinates,
product/market boundary charters, separation of power,
politics (organizations), emphasis on short-run efficiency,
marketing departments that follow rather than lead.

1.31   VON HIPPEL, ERIC (1988), "The Sources of
        Innovation," <u>The Mc Kinsey Quarterly</u>, Winter, 72 -
        79.
A manufacturer is an orchestrator of innovation inputs by
many organizations. Barriers to accepting information from
outside the firm: 1) "Field Service Filter": sales personnel
may not report on a potential innovation for fear they
couldn't service it or use it well, so may provide poor
evaluations. 2) "Sales and Marketing Research Filter": These

personnel are NOT trained to do innovation gathering job. Financial reward system may discourage any activity that reduces sales of current products. 3) "R&D Filter": If reward system is geared to in-house innovation. Makes suggestions for taking down these barriers, e.g., applications, laboratories, customer product groups, user groups.

Improving and Controlling the Process

1.32   BOAG, DAVID A. AND BRENDA L. RINHOLM (1989), "New Product Management Practices of Small High-Technology Firms," Journal of Product Innovation Management, 6(2), 109-122.
This article studies the use of formal management procedures and structured frameworks, and determines their impact on control and success of new product development activities. The authors report the results of an empirical study of high-tech companies, in which they found that new product development success was higher for more formalized companies than for less formalized or informally-structured companies.

1.33   EBADI, YAR M. (1984), "The Effects of Communication of Technological Innovation," Management Science, 30(5), 572-585.
Empirical study of the patterns of communication among researchers and among organizations and the effect of these patterns on the success of innovation. Data gathered from the principal investigators of 117 Sea Grant projects funded in 1975.

1.34   FERNELIUS, W. CONRAD AND WILLIS H. WALDO (1980), "The Role of Basic Research in Industrial Innovation," Research Management, 23(4), 36-40.
78 case histories, with empirical analysis. Factors that stimulate and hamper innovation process are examined. Findings and factors examined: There are many patterns of innovation. Research and innovation are predominantly incremental. Importance of teamwork. Source of ideas (market need versus technology push). Type of innovation (product versus process). Time required from original concept to completion of innovation. Effects of management support, presence of product champion, and interfirm communication.

1.35   FOSTER, RICHARD N., LAWRENCE H. LINDEN, ROGER L. WHITELEY AND ALAN M. KANTROW (1985), "Improving the Return on R&D--I." Research Management 29(1), 12-17.
An analytic framework identifies the key factors which can improve the contribution of technological advances to corporate profits. The R&D director in the modern large corporation has a complex, multifaceted and, in some ways, ill-defined job.

1.36   FOXALL, GORDON AND BRIAN JOHNSTON (1987), "Strategies of User-Initiated Product Innovation," Technovation 6(2), 77-102.

This article identifies further research into the strategic, managerial and organizational issues pertaining to the expansion of the entrepreneurial role of the user-initiator in the commercialization of his invention.

1.37   GRAHAM, E.M. (1981), "Technological Innovation and the Dynamics of the U.S. Comparative Advantage in International Trade," in C.T. Hill and J.M. Utterback (eds.), Technological Innovation for a Dynamic Economy, New York: Pergamon Press.
The options for technological innovation that would improve America's international position fall into three categories: 1) those which would serve to increase rates of domestic technological innovation; 2) those which would lower barriers imposed by foreign governments; and 3) those which would help the U.S. economy adjust to changing world conditions.

1.38   HENRY, DONALD F. (1983), "Degrees of Product Innovation," Journal of Business Strategy, 3(4), 3-14.
Innovation is used here as a spectrum against which one can compare product innovation: from New Products/New Markets to aesthetic features of current products. Good discussion of considerations in each product type. In the second part, a PIMS study finds that factors (non-organization) influencing profitability are subtle and complex. But innovation is more profitable if pursued by business with strong competitive positions, and when managers can leverage the experience of others.

1.39   HILL, C.T. (1981), "Technological Innovation: Agent of Growth and Change," in C.T. Hill and J.M. Utterback (eds.), Technological Innovation for a Dynamic Economy, New York: Pergamon Press.
Discusses the impact of technical innovation on the U.S. economy and society. Innovation is a key agent of economic growth, productivity, inflation, employment, nature of work, international trade, and quality of life. However, technology can also be abused in that it may result in the exhaustion of resources, mismatch of job opportunities and worker skills, release of toxic materials, and so on. Paradoxically, technology can also contribute to solving these problems.

1.40   HILL, C.T. and J.M. UTTERBACK (1981), "Introduction," in C.T. Hill and J.M. Utterback (eds.), Technological Innovation for a Dynamic Economy, New York: Pergamon Press.
Policy towards technological innovation is coming to be viewed as a key element in the long-term economic and social policies of the United States. The government should take steps to encourage innovation by increasing the risks that firms face: not by increasing the risk of failure of new technology, but by increasing the risk that a firm will fail if it does not innovate.

1.41   HOLLOMON, J.H. (1979), "Government and the Innovation Process," Technology Review, 81 (May), 30-41.

This article investigates what the federal government can do to encourage socially desirable innovation. The relationships of U.S. government programs to technological innovation are examined. Based on this, and the experience of other countries, recommendations are offered to Congress, including: support for broadly applicable technology, reassessing the role of national laboratories, and lowering barriers of entry to individual inventors and small firms.

1.42   HOLLOMON, J.H. (1981), "Policies and Programs of Governments Directed Toward Industrial Innovation," in C.T. Hill and J.M. Utterback (eds.), Technological Innovation for a Dynamic Economy, New York: Pergamon Press.

West Germany and Japan have successfully promoted technological innovation and adaptation of new technologies in both new and existing firms, and have de-emphasized the support of R&D in well-advanced technologies such as defense and space programs. The author implies that for America to remain competitive with these highly advanced innovating nations, it should proceed similarly.

1.43   HORWITZ, PAUL (1981), "Direct Government Funding of Research and Development: Intended and Unintended Effects on Industrial Innovation," in C.T. Hill and J.M. Utterback (eds.), Technological Innovation for a Dynamic Economy, New York: Pergamon Press.

Encourages the U.S. federal government to support basic technology research, to maintain close contact with the users of the new technologies, to promote competition between firms, to facilitate new entrants, and to sponsor risky projects (banks tend to support less risky ones).

1.44   JENSEN, RICHARD (1988), "Information Cost and Innovation Adoption Process," Management Science, 34(2), 230-239.

In product development, the question sometimes arises: should a firm adopt an innovation of uncertain profitability or obtain additional information and make a later decision on adoption or rejection? Further, information can be costless information or expensive; and the pattern of optimal behavior is sometimes complex. This article examines this complexity of managerial decision-making regarding innovations of uncertain profitability in the presence of costless or costly information.

1.45   JOHNE, A. AND P. SNELSON (1988), "Auditing Product Innovation Activities in Manufacturing Firms," R&D Management, 18(3), 227-233.

This article describes the processes involved in developing products quickly and efficiently. Businesses which have successfully pursued product innovation strategies tend to view development work in a more comprehensive manner than just efficient technical project management. The authors present the results of an empirical study of product development procedures in manufacturing firms in the U.K. and U.S. Support from top management and teamwork across functions are key factors in short- and long-run success.

1.46   KLEIN, B.H. (1981), "The Slowdown in Productivity
        Advances: A Dynamic Explanation," in C.T. Hill and
        J.M. Utterback (eds.), <u>Technological Innovation for
        a Dynamic Economy</u>, New York: Pergamon Press.
Productivity is related closely to dynamic competition or
rivalry among firms.   Risk-taking is encouraged by the
"invisible hand" (the opportunity to prosper and grow) and
also by the "hidden foot" (the threat that one's rivals may
make an advance if one does not take risks).   Technological
innovation and productivity are slowed in American firms are
protected from new entrants and foreign competition.

1.47   MOORE, WILLIAM L. AND MICHAEL L. TUSHMAN (1982),
        "Managing Innovation Over the Product Life Cycle,"
        in M.L. Tushman and W.L. Moore (eds.), <u>Readings in
        the Management of Innovation</u>, Marshfield, Mass.:
        Pitman, 131-150.
There are predictable patterns in the amount and type of
innovation over the product life cycle.   Changes in type of
innovation can lead to differences in competitive outlook,
suggesting that organizational structures must also change.
Thus, new strategies, structures and processes must be
developed through time, and also the transition from old to
new needs to be managed.

1.48   MORTON,   MAXWELL   R.   (1983),   "Technology   and
        Strategy: Creating a Successful Partnership,"
        <u>Business Horizons</u> 26(1), 44-48.
Innovation Quotient: a strategy development tool helping
companies incorporate technical innovation into their process
of developing corporate strategy.   It is based on four
innovation quotients: business, technical, attitudinal and
economic.

1.49   NADLER, DAVID A. AND MICHAEL L. TUSHMAN (1980), "A
        Model for Diagnosing Organizational Behavior,"
        <u>Organizational Dynamics</u> (Autumn).
The authors recommend a general approach for organizational
functioning   and   a   "congruence   model"   for   analyzing
organizational problems. They conceptualize four components
to   the   organization: tasks,   individuals,   formal
organizational arrangements, and the informal organization.
The model explores the relationships across the components.

1.50   PECK, MERTON J. AND AKIRA GOTO (1981), "Technology
        and Economic Growth: The Case of Japan," <u>Research
        Policy</u>, 10.
Technology importation requires that institutions seek out
foreign technology. This paper describes: Japan's technology
transfer process, Japan's domestic R&D in relation to the
importation of technology, and its institutions and policies
that are favorable to the effective use of technology for
economic growth. The concluding section provides some lessons
for the U.S.: Americans can borrow from the Japanese example
to increase their use of technology for economic growth.

1.51   PRICE, R. (1987), "Creativity and Innovation in

Engineering Organizations," IEEE Conference on Management and Technology: Management of Evolving Systems, <u>Proceedings</u>, 156.

The author recommends a strategy for managing innovation which comprises three components: 1) vision for the future; 2) effective organization; 3) efficient implementation. Despite the popularity of such terms as intrapreneuring and skunkworks, the author argues that these concepts really can only help to improve innovation in a small fraction of engineering organizations.

1.52   QUINN, JAMES BRIAN (1985), "Managing Innovation: Controlled Chaos," <u>Harvard Business Review</u>, 63 (May-June), 78.

This article is an in-depth discussion of an on-going study. Results: Big companies stay innovating by acting like small entrepreneurial ventures. The author discusses characteristics of inventors and bureaucratic barriers. Examples of how several large companies innovate: 1) clear long-term visions; 2) practical orientation to innovate; 3) small flat organization (6 to 7 in group); 4) multiple approaches; 5) developmental shortcuts; 6) skunkworks; 7) interactive learning. To innovate, the firm must: 1) have top level commitment; 2) be committed to customers; 3) use portfolio strategy; 4) offer a flexible entrepreneurial atmosphere; 5) offer incentives.

1.53   RINHOLM, BRENDA L. AND DAVID A. BOAG (1988), "Controlling Innovation: Ready, Aim, Fire," <u>Proceedings</u>, First International Conference on Technology Management, Special Publication of the International Journal of Technology Management.

This study of new product development investigates the procedures used by high-technology firms to control the development process. Performance appears to be improved by control mechanisms such as written long-range R&D plans, budgets, development policies and screening and selection procedures, periodic development reports, and formal project postmortems. Companies that actively plan their R&D activities in the light of scarce company resources and marketplace realities outperform companies that do not perform all of these activities in a satisfactory way.

1.54   ROBERTS, EDWARD B. (1977), "Generating Effective Corporate Innovation," <u>Technology Review</u>, 80 (October-November), 26-33.

Effective corporate innovation requires the planned integration of staffing, structure and strategy. The critical areas are: 1) the staffing of technical organizations must provide the functions necessary for innovation; 2) organizational structure must enhance the flow of technical and market information; 3) strong links with marketing must be maintained; 4) strategic planning must improve integration of top management's technical plans with other aspects of overall corporate strategy.

1.55   ROEHRICH, ROLAND L. (1984), "The Relationship Between Technology and Business Innovation," <u>Journal</u>

of Business Strategy, 5(2), 60-73.
Argues, with numerous examples and data support, that
business and technological innovation must be more closely
linked. The success of one may depend on the success of the
other. Each industry has a characteristic envelope of margins
and turnovers, and with new ventures the industry may develop
in many simultaneous directions. Thus technology should be
focused in the direction of business innovation. Discusses
three generic winning strategies based on market segmentation
for an innovation. Also discusses mergers and acquisitions of
technological firms into big jigsaw conglomerates.

1.56   SCHNEE, JEROME R. (1978), "Government Programs and
         the Growth of High-Technology Industries," Research
         Policy, (January), 2-24.
Large government programs can play an important role in the
growth of high-tech industries such as the space and defense
programs. In these programs, in fact, American computer and
semiconductor firms were able to initially assume the leads
in their respective fields, and retain those positions. There
has, however, been some criticism of governmental involvement.
For example, some critics have maintained that such high-tech
programs created imbalances in the nation's supply of
scientific and technological manpower.

1.57   TUSHMAN, MICHAEL L. (1979), "Managing Communication
         Networks in R&D Laboratories," Sloan Management
         Review 20 (Winter), 37-49.
The article examines the problem of how to manage
communication networks for research and development. Several
studies comparing the communication networks of high- and low-
performing projects are summarized. The results are linked
with the larger literature of the management of R&D, and lead
to a contingent approach to managing communication. The
author presents a communication design model and process as
a framework for managing these networks.

1.58   ZMUD, ROBERT W. (1984), "An Examination of 'Push-
         Pull' Theory Applied to Process Innovation in
         Knowledge Work," Management Science, 30(6),
         727-738.
This article assesses certain key propositions from the
organizational innovation literature involving process
innovation for knowledge work. The study examines the
validity of 'push-pull' theory, importance of top management
values and member receptivity toward change in an
organization's use of process innovation.

2

Stages in New-Product Development

A large volume of the literature on product innovation is
concerned with the individual stages in the new product
development process: what each stage involves, how it can be
carried out more effectively, and what implications there are
for management. This chapter begins with a discussion of
articles which present an overview of the new-product
development process. Then the remainder of this chapter
presents a deeper discussion of the development process
stages, which include idea generation, screening, concept
testing, pre-test marketing, financial analysis and risk
reduction, product development and testing, test marketing
and launch.

OVERVIEWS OF THE PRODUCT DEVELOPMENT PROCESS

Most articles on product development focus on one of the
specific stages listed above. However, a few take a broader
perspective. These fall into one of two categories: those
which present an overview of the stages in the product
development process, and those which evaluate the practice of
new-product development in industry. Such articles are
generally non technical and are written for the practicing
product manager. Often these topics appear in managerially
oriented publications such as the Journal of Product Innovation
Management and Industrial Marketing Management.

The most commonly cited overview article is that of Booz,
Allen and Hamilton (1968) which, although quite dated, is a
good place to start. It describes the stages in the product
development process: idea generation, screening, business
analysis, development, testing, and launch. At the time of
this study, Booz, Allen and Hamilton found that 58 new-product
ideas were required for each product successfully brought to
market. Clearly, risks are high, especially at early stages
of development. As a project passes careful evaluation at the
end of each stage, risk of commercial failure is reduced and
a greater financial commitment can be made. (Good discussions
of relevant evaluation criteria at various stages in the
process are given in Ronkainen, 1983 and 1985). The 1968 Booz,
Allen and Hamilton study showed that many of the problems

faced in new-product development could be traced to organizational factors. A later study (Booz, Allen and Hamilton, 1981) showed that the number of new-product ideas needed for a successful launch had been reduced to 7, indicating perhaps that some improvements had occurred in the efficiency of the product development process. Clearer specification of the steps in the process may also have explained some of the improvement. The later study acknowledged that the process could be consumer driven, competition driven or technology driven, and it outlined a sequence of stages for each of these situations. More recently, Crawford (1986) provided an expanded overview of the process, from preconceptualization to rollout, together with a discussion of ideas and decision models relevant to each stage.

Differences between the new-product and new-service development processes are discussed in Cowell (1985) and Easingwood (1986). In the latter study, for example, the author found the role of test marketing to be different for services than for products--a test market would more likely be used to check for proper functioning of a service than to project nationwide sales levels.

Cooper (1976), in his book Winning the New Product Game, discussed three industrial product development case histories (milk pouches, the Contempraphone, and a turboprop engine) and depicted the actual development process used in each case. He categorized the stages of the process into technical and market activities. This is one of the earliest extensive studies to imply that both kinds of activities must be carried out adequately to increase the chances of product success. Many of the articles on product screening (described below) address this issue. Cooper (1976) also suggested that different constituencies or work groups in the firm are apt to view the process quite differently.

A related literature compares normative principles of new-product development with managerial practice. In some cases the studies reveal that great discrepancies exist: product strategies are frequently not clearly spelled out, and available marketing research techniques are often not employed (Feldman and Page, 1984). On the other hand, many stages in the process are carried out quite completely (Feldman and Page, 1984; Cooper and Kleinschmidt, 1986; Moore, 1987). Moore, for example, found that at least an informal understanding of the principles of new-product marketing was apparent in many situations, and that steps such as idea screening, financial analysis, and product testing were carried out in most firms in some fashion. Crawford (1980) suggested the development and use of the Product Innovation Charter to provide a directional mandate for managers involved in the product development process and to ensure coordination of efforts throughout the process. Wind and Mahajan (1988) provided a set of strategic guidelines for improving the practice of new-product development. These included: balancing the focus on internal and external product development, focusing on consumer benefits, taking a multidisciplinary approach (research, marketing, manufacturing, financial), and balancing low-risk and high-risk projects (i.e., portfolio analysis).

IDEA GENERATION

Where should an innovating firm look for new-product ideas? A broad literature, generally appearing in publications aimed at practicing managers such as <u>Industrial Marketing Management</u>, <u>Business Horizons</u>, and <u>Harvard Business Review</u> has addressed the idea-generation stage. Some articles define and discuss the implications of the marketing concept on idea generation; others explore alternative sources of new-product ideas, attempting to classify, for example, innovative concepts as "technology-push" versus "market-pull" ideas.

Idea Generation and the Marketing Concept

While definitions of the marketing concept differ, most involve the notion of understanding the customer's wants and needs, then fulfilling them while satisfying organizational goals. The implication of this is that the marketplace ought to be a valuable source of ideas for new products. Indeed, there is some evidence for this in the literature. Banting (1978) reported that a frequent cause of failure in new-product development was the lack of a customer orientation--in other words, a "production" rather than a "marketing" orientation. Cooper and Kleinschmidt (1988) examined both successful and unsuccessful new industrial products and found that a strong marketing orientation was frequently absent, especially in the case of product failures. Further, marketing activities (such as understanding market needs and providing adequate sales and promotional support) tended to have been better carried out in the cases of successful products. The literature on idea screening (presented below) discusses further the importance of adequate attention to marketing activities.

However, there is a conflicting viewpoint to consider. Bennett and Cooper (1979, 1981) argued that strict adherence to the marketing concept could actually hinder significant product innovation in the long run, since it may encourage the firm to concentrate on minor line extensions and adjustments to the marketing mix and not to support "true" R&D adequately. Really innovative ideas tend to come from technology-push innovation, which often must proceed without a clearly defined customer need. Similar concerns are voiced in Tauber (1979) and Reisz (1980). (Note: other authors have argued that the marketing concept itself is not entirely at fault: that it is still valid but should not be viewed as the only way to conduct business. This issue is outside the scope of this book.) The remaining parts of this section examine two new-product idea generation sources available to the firm: those growing from the market and those originating in the laboratory.

Market-Pull Ideas

Von Hippel (1978, 1986) and Urban and von Hippel (1988) made one of the strongest cases for relying on product users as an important source of new-product ideas. In product categories marked by rapid change, likely future users (he used the term "lead users") are probably the best source of ideas.   von Hippel argued that current market research methodologies focused too much on current heavy users, while the researcher was likely to be most interested in the future needs of lead users. The key step, he contended, is to identify an important technological or marketing trend, and to identify who the likely lead users were based on that trend. Tauber (1975) suggested "problem inventory analysis" as a way of eliciting market needs. In this procedure, customers would be provided a list of problems and asked to state what products come to mind. The results could serve as clues for further study.

Technology-Push Ideas

Technology push is potentially an important source of new-product ideas, especially with respect to radically new technologies. In the development of heart pacemakers and similar high-tech innovations, it was shown that adequate attention to technological variables, such as recognition of technical opportunities, was essential to product success (Globe, Levy and Schwartz, 1978). Leaf (1978) described how product teardown analysis and other methods could be used to generate ideas from competitive products. Hise, Futrell and Snyder (1980) discussed how affiliated research centers could provide needed external assistance in obtaining and developing new technical ideas, while Roberts and Peters (1982) commented on the role of technical university faculty in the generation of ideas of commercial value. The conditions for success of a technology-push product idea were listed by Paul (1987) as that the technology must meet unmet market needs; the product's price must be low enough; the firm must educate the customer as to the benefits of the technology; and the firm must be prepared to face slow acceptance of its innovative product. An interesting group of articles by Craig (1987), Galt (1987) and Boyce (1987) discussed market-pull versus technology-push and the implications of R&D spending and governmental assistance. Finally, Rothwell and Gardiner (1988) suggested that the market-pull/technology-push dichotomy is inappropriate, and that firms engaged in product development should focus on robust versus lean designs, that is, on innovative ideas likely to produce families of products, not just single products.

SCREENING

Concepts and ideas for new products must be evaluated on a number of key dimensions: feasibility of manufacture, likely cost of further development, expected production and marketing costs, fit with company goals, and likelihood of acceptance in the marketplace, among others. Concept evaluation, or screening, seeks to identify which concepts ought to be considered further. Much work has been devoted to analyzing new-product launches of the recent past, identifying factors which tended to lead to product success or failure. This information can be (and has been) developed into models for predicting likely market success for new-product ideas. Models that possess many of the features which led to past successes are candidates for further development.

Most of the articles in this category were found in the product development/industrial marketing literature (Journal of Product Innovation Management, Industrial Marketing Management, Research Management). A few articles were in mainstream marketing journals such as Journal of Marketing or Journal of the Academy of Marketing Science. Although there is substantial overlap in coverage, the articles may be broadly classified into three subcategories: those that simply identify success factors in product development, those that propose methodologies for idea screening, and those that stress managerial or strategic implications.

Success Factors

A few articles published prior to 1975 examined new-product failures and identified reasons for failure (National Industrial Conference Board, 1964; Konopa, 1968; Hopkins and Bailey, 1971; Hlavacek, 1974). The Conference Board study isolated several factors leading to product failure, including: inadequate market analysis, product deficiency, high costs, poor timing, strength of competing firms, and inadequate distribution or marketing effort. (The other studies cited above produced similar findings.) Most of these failure factors were found to have resulted from deficiencies in marketing activities, an indication of the crucial role of marketing in successful product introduction. The earliest major investigative study that compared product failures to successes was Project SAPPHO (Rothwell, 1972).

Using the results of these and other studies, Cooper initiated Project NEWPROD, an in-depth analysis of factors that influence product success (Cooper, 1979, 1980a-c, 1981). Managers of recently launched successful and unsuccessful industrial products in Canada (about 100 of each) responded to a questionnaire which probed specific production, marketing, financial, and management issues related to new-product development. Factors making a difference between success and failure included, among many others, proficient launch execution, meeting customer needs better than competitors, high product quality, good test marketing and prototype testing, and understanding the customer's purchase decision process. Barriers to success included setting a high price on a product with no economic advantage, entering a dynamic market with many product introductions, and trying to sell in a market whose customers were already well-satisfied. Cooper concluded by observing that product success depends upon a) having a unique product, b) having adequate marketing effort, and c) having adequate technical and production skills. Similar results were found in later studies by Cooper (1982, 1983); but in these studies it was also found that R&D spending and new-product program effectiveness were not directly related to success. How the research dollar was spent, and how the product was subsequently marketed, were more important determinants of success than how much was invested.

Cooper and Kleinschmidt (1987a,b) conducted the NEWPROD

II study, designed to extend the original Project NEWPROD. NEWPROD II sought to identify components of success and included a variety of possible success measures (profit, payback, market share, relative sales, etc.). They found the major success factors to be a superior product, good performance of activities prior to actual development (such as preliminary market and product testing), the presence of a "protocol" (or project definition), and certain key proficiencies and synergies. In a similar vein, Cooper (1988) noted that, in many cases, new-product success or failure was decided in the very early stages of the development process (idea generation, screening, preliminary assessment, and concept definition), and he discussed how managers can improve their practice at these stages.

A number of other recent empirical studies on product success and failure tend to support the findings of NEWPROD and NEWPROD II (Hopkins, 1981; Cooper and de Brentani, 1984; Link, 1987; Davis, 1988). In a study of industrial manufacturing companies, Calantone and di Benedetto (1988) developed an integrative model of the new-product decision process and showed that marketing, technical, and launch activities specific to the new product were direct determinants of success and failure, while possession of marketing and technical skills and resources by the firm had indirect effects. A different approach was taken by McDonough and Spital (1984), who examined new-product development undertaken in response to a competitive threat. Successful product projects tended to have high visibility, to be closely controlled by management, and to have business-oriented engineers in charge.

For an interesting perspective on buyer and seller perceptions of reasons for product failure, see Folkes and Kotsos (1986). Johne and Snelson (1988) provided an extensive review of the literature on success factors in new-product development.

Methodologies for Screening

Articles in this classification typically used empirical success/failure data to build a screening model or categorization scheme which could be used to predict the likelihood of success of new-product ideas. Typical of these are the studies of Calantone and Cooper (1979, 1981), which used cluster analysis (a computer program which groups together similar objects) to identify prototypical scenarios of new-product success and failure. Cooper (1985) briefly discussed how a product manager might be able to build his or her own firm-specific screening model. For another methodology based on information theory, see Dillon, Calantone and Worthing (1979).

Strategic Implications for Management

Strategies that managers can use to help a new product succeed are the topic of the articles in this section. Balachandra (1984) provided a useful set of warning signals that should be considered in deciding whether to develop a new-product idea further. Certain signals, such as low subjective estimates of probability of technical success, reestricted availability of raw materials, and managerial concern over continued existence of a market, are critical and must not be ignored.   Other indicators, such as the lack of a project champion, anticipated high level of competition, the overall profitability of the company developing the product, and a discouraging probability estimate of commercial success, may or may not indicate project termination.

Empirical articles by Cooper (1984a, 1985a) showed that the strategy chosen by management for its product development program was correlated with the results achieved by the firm. These studies indicated that management can follow two strategic paths, both leading to favorable chances for product success: a technologically aggressive stance coupled with a strong marketing orientation, and a conservative stance in which management chooses line extensions on the basis of synergy and focus.   Related articles (Cooper 1984b, 1985b) showed that firms which chose a "balanced strategy," that is, a combination of technological and marketing aggressiveness with conservative fit and focus, stood the greatest chance of success.

Newness of the technology, of the target market, or of the product increases risk. A few articles have discussed how management can evaluate and deal with the high risks of product development.   Abetti and Stuart (1988) listed four factors determining new-product project risk.   They formulated a scoring model based on these factors to be used in screening product ideas. They suggested, however, that the most serious evaluative steps occur after concept screening and testing, before more costly steps were undertaken.   More (1982) identified five dimensions of new-product risk (high development cost, low marketing synergy, development complexity, a low level of competitive advantage, and high buyer risk) and discussed how government could provide "risk-reducers" for managers in the form of dollar incentives.

Other recommendations for product managers which may be useful at this stage of product development include those from the European Industrial Research Management Association (1982) and Lee, Fisher and Yau (1986).

CONCEPT TESTING

Once a product idea or concept has passed the screening stage, a new set of decisions faces product management. A concept, such as an idea for a new carpet cleaner, may potentially be developed into any one of dozens of products: products having different shapes and sizes of containers, different brand names, different guarantees and so on (Green and Wind, 1975). Not all of these potential products will be equally preferred by customers. The manager must choose the physical form(s) of the product concept which will be most acceptable to consumers. A sizable literature has emerged describing the use of methodologies, such as conjoint analysis, that aid the manager in evaluating and selecting from among alternative product forms. The majority of these articles are technical, and appear in quantitative research journals such as Journal of Marketing Research, Marketing Science, and Management Science. A few describe the managerial use of analytical techniques and are written in less-technical language. These appear in the Journal of Product Innovation Management or Harvard Business Review.

Conjoint analysis, or tradeoff analysis, is a method which has been used in measuring the perceived values of various possible product designs (Hargreaves, Claxton, and Silber, 1976). respondents are presented with a number of variations on a product concept (as in the carpet cleaner example above) and are asked to rank their preferences. Computer analysis of their responses identifies the utility associated with each of the attributes evaluated by the respondents, and ultimately can identify the combination of attributes that consumers would prefer the most. An advantage of the methodology is that not all combinations need to be ranked by the respondent, thus making his or her task much easier. (If there were six container shapes, six brand names, and two possible guarantees, there would be 72 possible product forms to choose from, but the respondent might be asked to rank a sample of about only 20.) A further advantage is that this step can be taken before any product manufacturing expense is incurred: cards, pictures or verbal descriptions may be provided for ranking.

Early articles on the use of conjoint analysis are those of Green and Wind (1975) and Hargreaves, Claxton, and Silber (1976). An early application paper is that of Wind, Grashof, and Goldhar (1978), who applied conjoint analysis to scientific and technical information services. More technical articles on the topic include those of Pekelman and Sen (1979), who provided an analytical procedure which improves upon the prediction of product acceptance and concept choice. Green, Carroll, and Goldberg (1981) described POSSE (Product Optimization and Selected Segment Evaluation), a procedure that uses inputs derived from conjoint analysis to develop "consumer choice simulators" modeled using response surface techniques. Corstjens and Gautschi (1983) discussed and investigated empirically the robustness of the conjoint analytic method. Kohli and Krishnamurthi (1987) proposed a dynamic-programming heuristic to find the highest-utility new-product profile using conjoint or hybrid-conjoint analysis. A real-life application was described in Page and Rosenbaum (1987), and a related technique and a sample application is provided in Rabino and Moskowitz (1984).

A useful methodology for modeling consumer response to innovation was described in Hauser and Urban (1977). This technical article urged the integration of psychometrics, utility theory, and stochastic choice theory in the design of new products; it also included a discussion of applications to real situations. A later, related article by Hauser (1984) discussed in less technical style how consumer theory, market research and quantitative analysis can improve effectiveness of new-product research and development. Hauser proposed a useful model describing the relationship between consumer behavior and its antecedents: product characteristics, psychosocial cues, perceptions, and preferences.

An excellent review of the concept generation and testing literature up to 1978 was presented by Shocker and Srinivasan (1979). They compared a number of approaches to concept testing on several criteria: how well each approach accounted for the relevant product market, how well each modeled individual (or segment) decision making, how well they evaluated alternative concepts, and so forth. However, the authors did not select any of the models as being the "best" or strongest predictor of ultimate sales levels. For a good discussion of some of the techniques used in consumer and industrial product concept testing (such as focus groups, employee panels, central location testing, and use testing), see McGuire (1973).

PRE-TEST MARKET MODELS

Pre-test marketing can provide the product manager with critical information on the likely success of a new product before it goes into mass production and nationwide launch. A pre-test market evaluation of a new product has many advantages over full-scale test marketing. It can reduce further costs of development and introduction; it can provide more timely data than test marketing (within weeks rather than months or years); it can be hidden from competitors; and it can allow the product manager to make modifications of the marketing mix (Shocker and Hall, 1986). Since it is also inexpensive as compared to a test market ($15,000 to $100,000 as of 1986), pre-test marketing is a useful risk-reduction technique in the product development process.

A number of different models have been proposed to carry out pre-test marketing. Among these are ASSESSOR (Silk and Urban, 1978), TRACKER (Blattberg and Golanty, 1978), NEWS (Pringle, Wilson, and Brody, 1982), COMP (Burger, Gundee, and Lavidge, 1981), and LITMUS-II (Blackburn and Clancy, 1982). These models differ in some of the submodels and assumptions, and also in what data are required and how they must be obtained. Most are based on Awareness-Trial-Repeat models (models of the process by which customers learn about, buy, and adopt products). Pre-test market models usually rely on data easily obtained from mall intercepts, via phone surveys, or in lab facilities at shopping centers. Results (that is, assessments of the likely acceptance of a new product if it were to be launched nationally) are usually obtainable within three or four months.

A number of the pre-test market models are presented in great detail in the literature. ASSESSOR (Silk and Urban, 1978) is one of the earliest models. It is particularly useful because it uses both management input (positioning strategies and marketing plans) and consumer research input (laboratory and post-usage measures) to develop forecasts of brand share, draw, and cannibalization. Product managers are interested in knowing what portion of a new product's sales is draw (sales obtained from competitors' brands) and how much is "cannibalized" or siphoned from other brands in their own product line. ASSESSOR also aids the manager in deciding among alternative advertising, price, and packaging options, at relatively low cost. ASSESSOR has stimulated additional research (Urban, Katz, Hotch, and Silk, 1983; Urban and Katz, 1983).   Urban and Katz (1983) showed empirically that two-thirds of products scoring well in an ASSESSOR pre-test were successful in test marketing;   these authors concluded that both pre-test and test marketing are essential steps in almost all product development processes.

Another commercially successful pre-test market procedure is LTM,   or Laboratory Test Market (Yankelovich, Skelly and White, 1981).   This method finds the relationship between laboratory store sales results and such factors as usage, repeat rate, novelty of the product form, and relative "clout" or intensity of promotional effort.   LTM has been shown to predict the results of subsequent test markets very well in real-life applications.   The TRACKER model (Blattberg and Golanty, 1978) is discussed in detail in the section below on test marketing.

Most of the other articles on pre-test market models describe one model in rather technical detail, and appear in technical journals such as <u>Journal of Marketing Research</u> or <u>Marketing Science</u>.   Two exceptions are the review articles of Shocker and Hall (1986) and Robinson (1981).   Shocker and Hall discussed in nontechnical language the strengths and weaknesses of four of these models (NEWS, ASSESSOR, LITMUS and BASES). They also provided a cost justification for pre-test marketing based on likelihood of acceptance of new products, and they showed that product development is cheaper in the long run if the firm weeds out questionable products by pre-test marketing before test marketing.   Finally, the authors compared each model according to model characteristics, assumptions, cost, time required, and other attributes.   Robinson (1981) compared a number of pre-test market models on the basis of dimensions such as test product configuration, test marketing plan, test environmental conditions, and measurement of consumer behavior. A related article by Tauber (1977) reviewed laboratory test markets as well as concept tests, product tests. and other forecasting systems.

A more technical comparison of pre-test market models was presented by Mahajan, Muller, and Sharma (1984a) (see also Golanty, 1984; Pringle, Wilson, and Brody, 1984; and Mahajan, Muller, and Sharma, 1984b).   This article selected only one part (the submodel describing the relationship   between advertising and awareness) of each of five pre-test market models (NEWS, TRACKER, LITMUS, Dodson and Muller, and Claycamp and Liddy) and compared them. The authors concluded that, despite differences across models, all   were adequate representations of the actual advertising-awareness relationship for both brand and product category data. (Note: the Dodson and Muller, 1978 and Claycamp and Liddy, 1969 models are discussed in other sections of this paper.)

Product positioning is an important step in product design.   It has   been more than adequately discussed in articles and books written for the practicing business manager (such as Aaker and Shansby's "Positioning Your Product," 1982). New conceptual issues in product positioning such as "surrogate" positioning and psychological meaning of products have been discussed in recent articles by Crawford (1985) and Friedmann and Lessig (1987).   The remaining few articles cited here   focus on methodologies for product positioning, are

written in more   technical language, and are aimed at the
marketing researcher or management scientist.

PERCEPTOR was described in an important early article
(Urban, 1975). Urban proposed a model and a methodology for
measurement to aid in product design.   Product attributes
(characteristics) are linked in this model to trial and repeat
probabilities through multidimensional scaling.   Later,
alternative positioning methodologies were proposed by Albers
and Brockhoff (1977), Gavish, Horsky, and Srikanth (1983), and
De Sarbo and Rao (1985).   The Gavish, Horsky, and Srikanth
methodology is interesting in that they developed and tested
an efficient heuristic (or rule) for solving large sample
problems in which exact solution procedures could not be used.
In addition, they assumed a two-stage (consumer and firm)
decision process.   An alternative product design model is
LINMAP   (Shocker and   Srinivasan, 1974), which is a
linear-programming procedure based on conjoint analysis and
is particularly useful for the design of consumer durable
goods. Its basic consumer-choice assumption, like many other
positioning models, is that the individual's preferred brand
is a function of distance from that individual's ideal. The
LINMAP procedure is used to derive these individual ideal
points.

FINANCIAL ANALYSIS AND RISK REDUCTION

Of course, screening, concept testing, and pre-test
marketing are all designed to reduce the risk and expense of
new-product failure. But in addition, the product manager must
assess the financial risk of new-product development,
preferably early in the development process   before large
amounts of money are committed.   As might be expected, a
literature discussing the models of financial analysis has been
developed, some of which draw from financial portfolio theory.
This is a very diverse literature, composed of quantitative
articles (in Management Science, TIMS Studies, and Omega) as
well as practitioner-oriented articles (in the Journal of
Product Innovation Management and Research Management). (Note:
there is an extensive literature on product portfolio models
including the Boston Consulting Group growth-share matrix and
the General Electric market attractiveness-business position
model.   These are outside the scope of this book and will not
be discussed here.)

Two good articles applying financial portfolio theory to
the product development problem are Cardozo and Smith (1983)
and Rabino and Wright (1985). Cardozo and Smith showed that
portfolio theory has promise as a tool for analyzing and
planning the product portfolio. The authors recommend how
financial portfolio theory ought to be modified for studying
new products. Rabino and Wright addressed the issue of risk
directly by suggesting the use of a measure they called
"project beta." Their measure is similar in concept to the
"beta" used in financial analysis and can be interpreted as
the impact of risk of an individual product on the risk of
the product portfolio. They provided a particularly clear and
easy-to-read illustration of the use of "project beta" in
evaluating three product ideas, and they showed that

incorporating risk into the project evaluation might change the desirability of certain projects. They concluded by suggesting other ways by which financial analysis could help to fine-tune marketing evaluation of new-product projects.

Another perspective on risk and uncertainty was provided by Cochran, Patz, and Rowe (1978). Their article used real examples of commercial and military projects to support their contention that uncertainty, and the urgency of capitalizing on new technology, must be recognized for the innovating firm to develop realistic estimates of cost and delivery time. The impact of uncertainty and urgency on marketing strategy development was also discussed.

One should recognize, however, that balancing the financial riskiness of projects is only one way in which managers can reduce the risks of the product development process. Significantly, one of the important roles of the product manager is to manage actively the development processes in order to reduce the probability of failure. Thus, a complete discussion of risk reduction in the context of new-product development should include more than just financial risk. In the face of relatively high probabilities of failure, the product manager must evaluate and control the process as it proceeds, thereby reducing the risk of commitment of funds. For example, the manager who is actively managing the process may realize that the project cannot be allowed to continue as is, and that steps must be taken to make it conform better to market needs. The actively engaged manager will, in the course of the project, face questions on where the company should seek ideas (Should the firm go to an outside plant? Should they lease the technology?), development and testing procedures (Is it worth committing to a full-scale test market?), and so on. The manager develops alternatives as time progresses, allowing him or her to make decisions that reduce risk.   Methods for reducing the risk of new-product development are a major subject in recent new product textbooks. Crawford (1987, Ch. 8, pp. 177-197) presents a good discussion of concept evaluation. In it, he discusses evaluation tasks which occur at several points in the new product development program, as well as several evaluation techniques appropriate to each step.

PRODUCT DEVELOPMENT AND TESTING

A large and diverse body of literature has addressed the issue of how to manage the development and testing stage and how to focus research support at this stage for optimum effectiveness. This literature is scattered throughout general business (Harvard Business Review, Sloan Management Review), quantitative management (Management Science, European Journal of Operations Research), and engineering (IEEE Transactions) publications.

Management of Product Development

An interesting issue occasionally discussed in the literature is the need to customize product development

management. Souder (1978) studied 18 large American firms and
their product development programs and suggested that
effectiveness of new-product management methods depended upon
the nature of the technological and market environments.
Takeuchi and Nonaka (1986) identified six management
characteristics related to product development (stability,
self-organizing units, overlapping phases, multilearning,
exercise of subtle control, and organizational transfer) and
concluded that each firm must develop its own management style
to promote new-product development. Krubasik (1988) noted that
speed of product development and risk reduction were mutually
conflicting objectives, and that a firm ought to choose the
development strategy appropriate to the situation. He offered
the IBM Personal Computer and the Boeing 767 as interesting
case studies in product development. Finally, some authors
have addressed the issue of how to accelerate the product
development process: through relying on external sources
(licensing, acquiring firms); through intensifying internal
R&D (providing higher rewards for successful R&D); or through
initiating innovative R&D management strategies (using peer
review or integrating R&D with other company functions) (Gupta
and Wilemon, 1987; Gold, 1987).

Research Support for Product Development

Crawford's (1977) article on marketing research
highlighted the importance of research support throughout the
new-product development process. He proposed a set of
hypotheses on why new products fail, including the following:
managers do not define the decision process clearly; the role
of market research in the process is not well understood; the
researchers themselves do not adequately "sell" their
services; and marketing research and product development
systems work contrary to each other. His article is a clear
testament to the importance of the integration of marketing
research throughout the entire process.

Some of the screening articles mentioned above (Cooper,
1982, 1983a) noted that the dollar amount spent on R&D is less
important in determining new product success than how the
dollar is spent. Much the same is true in market research.
Armistead (1981) proposed a methodology to help a firm decide
how much to spend on R&D, based on published financial
information. He found that the normal range of R&D spending
is between 20 and 33 percent of available earnings, with
emerging high-tech industries being at the high end of this
range. More (1984, 1985) examined the issue of the timing of
market research expenditures in industrial product development
and found that significant differences, dependent upon the
particular situation faced (payoffs, uncertainty, risk, etc.).
Raelin and Balachandra (1985) discussed the issue of when to
terminate investment in a high-cech R&D project.

Product Testing

Klompmaker, Hughes, and Haley (1976) provided a good
starting point for a discussion of the product-testing stage.

Their overview article discussed the issues of timing a test market, what information can be gained from it, and how this information can be used. A number of business-press articles have reviewed the recent technological advances available to the manager conducting a test market (such as Neilsen's ERIM and IRI's FASTRAC); a good reference is Paskowski (1984).

The more technical articles dealing with product testing discuss ways in which the statistical information obtained can be improved. Dutka (1984) noted that frequently more than one test market is carried out for a product; he explained how the results of several test markets can be combined to yield stronger results. Watkins (1984) explored the use of predictive models in product testing. Finally, Buchanan and Morrison (1985) discussed two types of product tests (repeated paired comparisons and triangle tests) and indicated how the researcher can determine which test format is best for the issue being investigated.

TEST MARKETING

Test marketing is a category of sales forecasting. Specifically, it is an attempt to forecast sales of a new product based on national projection of actual sales in a limited geographical area.   This section discusses sales-forecasting models that are driven by data obtained from test marketing, as well as articles and books that review these models.

Some of the early test market models are DEMON (Learner, 1968), Parfitt and Collins (1968), STEAM (Massy, 1969), the Ayer model (Claycamp and Liddy, 1969) and SPRINTER (Urban, 1970). All of these are based on the notion that awareness of a brand leads to trial, which in turn leads to repeat (an A-T-R or Awareness-Trial-Repeat model). Advertising and promotional levels are usually included as determinants of awareness (or product knowledge) levels, while awareness level and distribution intensity are antecedents of trial. Most of these models require data on purchase intentions, advertising recall, and so on, obtained usually via questionnaire. The Parfitt and Collins model employs panel data. The Ayer model represents product purchase as a function of packaging, product satisfaction, and category usage, in addition to promotion and distribution, and reportedly has high accuracy in prediction of trial (Claycamp and Liddy, 1969). SPRINTER (Urban, 1970) deserves some added attention because there are a number of versions of it. The basic Mod I version models the A-T-R process as a function of promotion effectiveness and distribution level. The more advanced Mod II and Mod III versions explicitly incorporate many more variables including, for example, word-of-mouth effects. This model has been used in test market planning, charting preliminary sales results, and projecting local results to national sales levels.

An interesting test market model appearing later in the literature is TRACKER (Blattberg and Golanty, 1978). This is a dynamic A-T-R model that estimates the number of new triers in any one period as a fraction of the people who became aware of the brand during that period, plus a fraction of the people who were previously aware but had not tried the brand yet.

It recognizes that these fractions may not be the same and in fact estimates them separately using regression techniques. It can also be used in a pre-test-market application. Lilien, Rao, and Kalish (1981) proposed a model for forecasting new product sales which incorporates Bayesian procedures for updating and estimation of model parameters. They focused particularly on the effect of the detail sales force, and not advertising or sales promotion. Other models of note are NEWPROD (Assmus, 1975) and Eskin's (1973) model.

Mesak and Mikhail (1988) presented a model which utilized trial models, repeat-purchase models, and entry market share models, and operationalized the model using actual historical data from a particular industrial-product case study. They demonstrated how this approach could help a firm make a good strategic decision on whether to enter a new product in the industrial marketplace.

Several articles have compared and critiqued these and other test market models. Larreche and Montgomery (1977) compared STEAM, SPRINTER, NEWS, Ayer, and several other test-market and pre-test-market models on the basis of structure adaptability, completeness, ease of use, and so on. In fact, the results they presented were part of the outcome of a Delphi probe into the use of marketing models. On the criteria chosen for comparison, the NEWS and Ayer models scored the highest. Mahajan and Muller (1982) compared only one portion (the adoption-diffusion submodel) of each of several test-market and pre-test-market models including STEAM, Ayer, NEWPROD, SPRINTER, and TRACKER. SPRINTER was found to rate highly on the characteristics studied. Finally, an article by Narasimhan and Sen (1983) compared several test-market models on the dimensions of level of complexity handled, likelihood of acceptance by product managers, and so on. On the basis of this very complete analysis, NEWS and TRACKER were found to be superior to other models.

This area has been well documented in the marketing and management science literature. Many of the articles discussed above appeared in either Journal of Marketing or Journal of Marketing Research. The interested reader can consult review articles in the forecasting literature, or one of several product management books which discuss the issue of new product forecasting in detail. Assmus (1984) wrote a very good review article, focusing on recent forecasting models, comparing their benefits and costs, and discussing trends for forecasting in the future. Mahajan and Wind (1988) evaluated strengths and weaknesses of test-market models as well as pre-test-market models, concept testing models, and new product diffusion models. (This paper is discussed later under diffusion forecasting.) Finally, the topic of new-product forecasting is covered in depth in several textbooks for product management courses (Urban and Hauser, 1980; Wind, 1981; Wind, Mahajan, and Cardozo, 1981; and Crawford, 1987, to name a few).

PRODUCT LAUNCH

Research on launching new products covers practical issues in launch planning (in Harvard Business Review and other practitioner journals), as well as economic decision models (in <u>Management Science</u> and <u>Marketing Science</u>), a very broad range. This discussion divides the literature into two categories: articles on pioneering advantages and launch timing; and articles on policy decisions at launch.

Pioneering Advantages and Timing

An extensive empirical analysis of new products was carried out by Urban, Carter, Gaskin, and Mucha (1986). They determined that the pioneering brand (first brand of a product form) had advantages which allowed it to maintain highest market share as other competitors entered. In their model, market share was related to entry, time between entries, and effectiveness of positioning. The authors find empirical support for their model, and conclude by discussing managerial implications for both pioneers and followers. Schnaars (1986), in an in-depth look at 12 well-known consumer product classes, showed that the pioneer did not always emerge as the market share leader. Both pioneering and "poaching" can be risky, and under certain prevailing market conditions, either could be advantageous. Olleros (1986) discussed another of the risks faced by pioneers: that of "burnout" encountered after commercialization of radically new technologies. Eliashberg and Robertson (1988) studied preannouncing (or signaling) of new products and identified conditions that would cause firms to preannounce new product introductions (for example, opportunity for image enhancement, distribution advantages, or demand stimulation).

The related issue of launch timing was investigated by Kalish and Lilien (1986). The pioneering studies indicated that early launch may be beneficial. This article addressed the opposite issue: what if the product is rushed to market prematurely? Kalish and Lilien developed a market diffusion model which accounted for the possibility of negative word-of-mouth arising from new-product failure. They concluded that substantial penalties can arise if launch is mistimed.

Policy Decision Issues

Many articles have addressed the issue of pricing for new products. Dean's (1976) article discussed the impact of price on the strategic position of a product throughout its life cycle. A mathematical approach to this issue was presented in Wernerfelt (1985). Advanced methodologies for price selection are found in Thomas and Chkabria (1975), who used Bayesian updating of prior estimates of demand for pricing new products; Kalish (1983) and Bass and Bultez (1982), who modeled dynamic pricing by firms facing changing demand and cost functions; and Smith (1986), who used a mechanism involving customers maximizing consumer surplus. Other launch policy issues receiving attention in the literature include distribution (Montgomery 1975), communication (Andrews 1986), optimization of both pricing and advertising (Thompson and Teng, 1984), brand name (Moore and Lehmann, 1982 and Zinkham and Martin 1987), and product warranty and manufacturer reputation (Bearden and Shimp, 1982).

STAGES IN NEW-PRODUCT DEVELOPMENT: ANNOTATED BIBLIOGRAPHY

OVERVIEWS OF THE PRODUCT DEVELOPMENT PROCESS

2.1   BOOZ, ALLEN AND HAMILTON (1968), Management of New
        Products, Chicago, Illinois: Booz, Allen and
        Hamilton.
Describes the stages in the product development process:
idea generation, screening, business analysis, development,
testing and launch. At the time of this study, 58 new product
ideas were required for every one successful new product
launch.

2.2   BOOZ, ALLEN AND HAMILTON (1980), New Products
        Management for the 1980s: Phase I, Chicago, Illinois:
        Booz, Allen and Hamilton.
Shows that, since the 1968 study, the number of new product
ideas needed for a successful launch had been reduced from 58
to seven. Processes for consumer-, competition- or technology-
driven new product development are outlined.

2.3   CALANTONE, ROGER J., C. ANTHONY DI BENEDETTO AND
        ROBERT G. COOPER (1986), "Variations in New Product
        Development Management: A Clustering Approach,"
        Proceedings, 1986 Summer Educators Conference, Series
        No. 52, Chicago: American Marketing Association,
        231-236.
This paper explores the management of the new product
development (NPD) process.   Several different kinds of
activities, of both a marketing and a production/technical
nature, make up the NPD process.   These activities must be
coordinated to improve chances of successful commercialization.
Describes six scenarios of NPD and shows that the most
successful ones maintain a balance between marketing and
technology activities.

2.4   COOPER, ROBERT G. (1976), Winning the New Product
        Game, Montreal: Centre Quebecois d'Innovation
        Industrielle.
Discusses three industrial product development case
histories: plastic milk bags, contempraphone, turboprop

engines. Depicts actual development process used in each case. Categorizes stages of the process into technical and market activities.

2.5   COOPER, ROBERT G. (1983), "The New Product Process: An Empirically-Based Classification Scheme," R&D Management, 13(1), 1-13.

Examined a total of 58 industrial product launches (30 successes, 28 failures) in Canada. In each case, respondents reported which marketing activities (e.g. market investigation, research, marketing plan development, market launch) and technical activities (e.g. technical feasibility assessment, prototype construction and testing, trial production) were undertaken, and how much time was allotted to each activity. Cluster analysis was applied, and the cluster with the highest probability of success was that which had the most adequate balance between marketing and technical activities.

2.6   COOPER, ROBERT G. AND ELKO J. KLEINSCHMIDT (1986), "An Investigation into the New Product Process: Steps, Deficiencies and Impact," Journal of Product Innovation Management, 3(2), 71-80.

Shows that project success is related to the completeness of the development process. Operational subactivities in the new product development process include: initial screening, preliminary market and technical assessment, market research, financial analysis, product development, in-house testing, customer tests, test market, trial production, precommercialization business analysis, production startup and market launch.

2.7   COWELL, DONALD W. (1988), "New Service Development," Journal of Marketing Management, (Spring), 296-312.

A list of differences between new service and new product development is identified. Among these are the following: Services are often produced in fixed systems (hotels, air travel). Service developments are often easy-to-accomplish changes such as near line extensions and product/style improvements. There is greater ease of concept generation, due to closer contact with end user, and less thorough screening. Field testing is difficult: some services cannot be made in pilot plant; prototype process. Product evaluation is more difficult because service is produced and consumed at same time. Factors also include: fewer inhouse tests, less patenting, less up-front R&D investment, more opportunity to observe actual consumption of services.

2.8   CRAWFORD, MERLE C. (1980), "Defining the Charter for Product Innovation," Sloan Management Review, 22(1), 3-12.

This paper reports on a study of new product planning in 125 American firms. Based on information obtained from both the business press and personal interviews, Crawford identified a key element in this planning: the Product Innovation Charter. The paper outlines a composite charter which can provide a comprehensive activity and directional mandate for managers and can ensure a coordinated and integrated plan for any new product function.

2.9   CRAWFORD, C. MERLE (1986), "Evaluating New Products:
         A System, Not an Act," Business Horizons, 29
         (November-December), 48-55.
This is an expanded overview of the new product system from
preconceptualization to rollout. Incorporates a wide scope of
concerns and ideas with the newest testing methods, screening
models, etc., at each stage.   (Details of models not
discussed.) Step 1, preconceptualization; step 2, concept
testing; step 3, screening; step 4, early product testing; step
5, field product testing; step 6, market testing; step 7,
rollout.

2.10   EASINGWOOD, CHRISTOPHER J. (1986), "New Product
         Development for Service Companies," Journal of
         Product Innovation Management, 3, 265-275.
This study compares new service development to new product
development in the U.K. New product introductions by service
companies may be limited by customer and staff confusion
arising from a proliferation of product offerings. Test
markets are also used differently: in a more post-hoc way to
ensure proper functioning rather than for a priori sales
projections.

2.11   EASINGWOOD, CHRISTOPHER J. AND VIJAY MAHAJAN (1989),
         "Positioning of Financial Services for Competitive
         Advantage," Journal of Product Innovation Management,
         6(3), 207-219.
Two major objectives of this study are: 1. To show how the
special characteristics of services give rise to different
positioning possibilities for financial services organizations
(e.g., an "extra service" position versus a "performance"
position). 2. To demonstrate the use of the positioning
framework. Examples from the insurance sector are provided.
Several recommendations for financial institutions are also
included.

2.12   FELDMAN, LAURENCE P. AND A.L. PAGE (1984),
         "Principles Versus Practice in New Product Planning,"
         Journal of Product Innovation Management, 1(1), 43 -
         55.
Product planning practices at nine large companies in the
electronics industry are described, and substantial differences
between these practices and theoretical principles of new
product development are found. These deviations result from
the complex nature of the new product development process and
the need for its effective management. The authors propose
recommendations for improving product planning performance.

2.13   GOMORY, RALPH E. (1989), "From the 'Ladder of
         Science' to the Product Development Cycle," Harvard
         Business Review, 67 (November-December), 99-105.
The article discusses two concepts of innovation: the
"ladder" or step-by-step process and the product cycle, viewed
by the author as being less dramatic but more critical to
profitable commercialization of technology.   It is
characterized by incremental improvement, not breakthrough.
The author suggests that the U.S. is only now learning that

product leadership can be built without scientific leadership if companies excel at design and the management of production.

2.14   GOMORY, RALPH E. AND ROLAND W. SCHMITT (1988), "Step-By-Step Innovation," <u>Across the Board</u> (November),52-56.

The step-by-step "ladder" approach to innovation is no longer adequate for today's business. Cyclical or repeated incremental innovation, used in Japan and other countries, needs to be stressed. As an example, a "ladder" discovery made in manufacturing ought to be followed immediately by incremental research in the laboratory. The benefits to a "ladder" approach include speed of innovation and launch. unfortunately it relies on outside as well as internal ideas so sometimes it suffers from "not-invented-here" barriers to adoption.

2.15   MOORE, RICHARD A. (1984), "Control of New Product Development in UK Companies," <u>European Journal of Marketing</u>, 18(6/7), 5-13.

Preliminary explanation of new product development in U.K. Average maximum time to introduce new product is 32 months, average minimum time being 10 months. Article lists several planning techniques used; frequency of review of a new product project by senior management; types of product management techniques. Includes a preliminary attempt at creating a revised new product development model.

2.16   MOORE, WILLIAM L. (1987), "New Product Development Practices of Industrial Marketers," <u>Journal of Product Innovation Management</u>, 4(1), 6-20.

Formal new product strategies and sophisticated quantitative market research techniques are lacking in most companies (consistent with Feldman and Page). However, many other stages in the NPD process are carried out more completely than previously reported: for example, sensitivity to informal understanding of new product strategies. Less sophisticated qualitative research methods may be more appropriate than the quantitative methods. Compares companies' performance at each step in the NPD process. Compares results to Feldman and Page, and Cooper and Kleinschmidt and discusses reasons for the discrepancies.

2.17   RONKAINEN, ILKKA, A. (1983), "Risk in Product Development Stages Management," <u>Industrial Marketing Management</u>, 12, 157-165.

Product development process is composed of these steps: concept, feasibility, product and process development scaleup, standardization. Article suggests that risk perceptions increase over the cycle, while cost perceptions escalate over the cycle.

2.18   RONKAINEN, ILKKA A. (1985), "Criteria Changes Across Product Management Development Stages," <u>Industrial Marketing Management</u>, 14, 171-178.

Same model as in 1983 paper. Decision makers use three groups of criteria in making go/no go decisions at major points in the product development process: Market, Product,

Financial. Of these, Market is most important in concept and feasibility stages; Product most important in product/practical development   stage;   Financial   important   in scaleup/standardization stages.

2.19   ROSENAU, MILTON D., JR. (1988), "Faster New Product
        Development," Journal of Product Innovation
        Management, 5(2), 150-153.
        The author discusses a number of methods and techniques not often mentioned in studies relating to the NPD process: short, focused development phases; management involvement and support;   procurement   and   productivity   improvements; multifunctional   teamwork;   distraction   reduction;   frozen specifications;   and   micro-computer-based   project   management software.

2.20   TINKER, EUGENE F. (1983), "Developing and Managing
        New Products," Journal of Business Strategy, 3(4),
        39-46.
        Rules of thumb, discussion of causes and effects in new product   process   discussed   to   help   firms   improve   their performance.   There are two types of new market approaches: technology push (appropriateness) and market need/demand pull (less risk).   There are several expenditure escalation points: conception, feasibility, development, pilot, commercialization. Article   also   discusses   organizational   relationships   of manufacturing process development to new product development, physical location and isolation, positioning new products in company, market share considerations, timing and portfolio.

2.21   WIND, Y. AND V. MAHAJAN (1988), "New Product
        Development Process: A Perspective for Re -
        Examination," Journal of Product Innovation
        Management, 5(4), 304-310.
        Thirteen strategic guidelines for the development of new or modified products: 1. Balance focus on internal and external development efforts.   2. Broaden range of product and service offerings, focus on common benefits. 3. Multidisciplinary focus (R&D,   marketing,   manufacturing,   financial).   4.   Focus encompasses   inputs   from   all   stakeholders   (distribution, suppliers). 5. Integrate planning of communication process with NPD activity. 6. Balanced portfolio: low and high risk and return; short and long term payoff. 7. Have champion for each project.   8.   Have   a   global   focus.   9.   Use   a   flexible manufacturing process. 10. Process facilitates development of products with short product life cycle. 11. Focus on both generation and evaluation research. 12. Evaluate under dynamic marketing conditions. 13. Integrate economic evaluation system: assess value creation.

2.22   WOODSIDE, ARCH G. AND WILLIAM G. PEARCE (1989),
        "Testing Market Segment Acceptance of New Designs of
        Industrial Services," Journal of Product Innovation
        Management, 6(3), 185-201.
        The article investigates the designing of a new industrial service   to   compete   successfully   against   two   established competitors.   The authors report the results of an empirical study of engineers and managers.   Respondents were asked to

solve a series of service problem scenarios. The study recommended that the service marketers create four specific, segment-based marketing strategies. The results were implemented, and resulted in modest improvement in company position in three of the four segments.

IDEA GENERATION

Idea Generation and the Marketing Concept

2.23   BANTING, PETER M. (1978), "Unsuccessful Innovation in the Industrial Market," Journal of Marketing, 42(1), 99-100.
One of the most prevalent causes of failure in both new product and marketing innovation is a product orientation rather than a customer orientation.

2.24   BENNETT, ROGER C. AND ROBERT G. COOPER (1979), "Beyond the Marketing Concept," Business Horizons, 22(3), 76-84.
See article by same authors (1981).

2.25   BENNETT, ROGER C. AND ROBERT G. COOPER (1981), "The Misuse of Marketing: An American Tragedy," Business Horizons, 24(6), 51-61.
Blind adherence to the marketing concept contributed to the death of new product innovation in North America. Too much attention is placed on minor tinkering with the marketing mix and not enough on R&D which is needed for long run competitive advantage. The result of this is proliferation of consumer products, while major needs like alternative energy and housing go unmet. Firms must not be guided exclusively by consumer needs, since consumers tend to express them in terms of the familiar. Bold new ideas (electric light, xerography, transistors, laser etc.) come from technical breakthroughs. Moral: Science must often progress without a clearly defined consumer need.

2.26   CHRISTENSEN, JENS FROSLEV AND FINN VALENTIN (1988), "Technology Strategy and Product Innovation in Small Scale Industry," Proceedings of the First International Conference on Technology Management, special publication of the International Journal of Technology Management.
This study reports the results of an analysis of 200 successful product developments from small and medium enterprises. Technological improvements and user needs were both seen as important precursors to innovation. In the case of user-need-driven innovations, required resources and risk levels were lower. Success in product innovation is related to company strategy stressing user benefits and not technological features. Paradoxically, this strategy also predisposes small firms to remain small.

2.27   COOPER, R.G. AND E.J. KLEINSCHMIDT (1988), "Resource Allocation in the New Product Process," Industrial

Marketing Management, 7, 249-262.
Compares how well activities were performed for both successful and failing new products. Major findings: A strong market orientation is missing in the typical industrial new product project. Managers of successful projects committed far more dollars and manpower to marketing activities than failing projects. Also spent considerably more on front end stages (predevelopment activities). Failing projects were characterized by illogical and difficult-to-explain spending patterns.

2.28   LAWTON, LEIGH AND A. PARASURAMAN (1980a), "So You Want Your New Product Planning to be Productive?" Business Horizons, 23(6), 29-34.
Interesting conclusion to a study on impact of product source ideas on the nature and success of new products and the role of marketing research. Results of survey listed. Conclusions: Industrial new products come more from R&D. Competitive goods analysis for commercial new products. Industrial products more innovative. The more innovative a product, the more highly profitable if successfully commercialized. The more imitative a product, the greater the need of marketing research benefits.

2.29   LAWTON, LEIGH AND A. PARASURAMAN (1980b), "The Impact of the Marketing Concept on New Product Planning," Journal of Marketing, 44(1), 19-25.
This study was designed to test the following hypotheses: The greater the extent of adaption of the marketing concept by a firm, a) the more likely it is that it will use customer oriented sources for new product ideas; b) the greater the utilization of marketing research, better idea generation and commercialization stages; c) the less innovative its new products will be. Results failed to support any of the three hypotheses.

2.30   REISZ, PETER C. (1980), "Revenge of the Marketing Concept," Business Horizons, 23(3), 49-53.
Emphasis on "market pull" instead of "science push" R&D has caused decreases in creativity, technological purity, thoughtful product strategy and market position for U.S. firms. The most damaging consequence is not consumers' inability to generate ideas for new products, lack of response to technological breakthroughs, or the lack of connection to the international scientific community, but rather the effects on overall corporate strategy.

2.31   SAMLI, A. COKSUN, KRISTIAN PALDA, AND A. TANSU BARKER (1987), "Toward a Mature Marketing Concept," Sloan Management Review (Winter), 45-51.
The marketing concept has been attacked for paying insufficient attention to the long term. This paper argues that the problem is not due to the concept itself, but its narrow application. The marketing concept can generate imitative and innovative product ideas via better understanding of consumer needs and strategically focused R&D.

2.32   SHAPIRO, BENSON P. (1988), "What the Hell is

'Market-Oriented'?", Harvard Business Review, 66
(November-December), 119-125.
Author argues that being "market oriented" represents a set
of processes touching all aspects of the company, and is a lot
more than the cliche of "getting close to the customer." Three
characteristics make a company market driven: 1. Information
on all important buying influences permeates every corporate
function. 2. Strategic and tactical decisions are made
interfunctionally and interdivisionally. 3. Divisions and
functions make well-coordinated decisions and execute tham with
a sense of commitment.

2.33   STAR, STEVEN H. "Marketing and its Discontents,"
        Harvard Business Review, 67 (November-December), 148
        -189.
Marketers say they give people what they want. Critics say
marketers get people to want what they don't need and often
can't have. This article examines these two opposing points
of view with particular attention to issues of consumer
satisfaction and discontent.

2.34   TAUBER, EDWARD M. (1979), "How Market Research
        Discourages Major Innovation," Business Horizons,
        22(3), 22-26.
Market researchers assume that early attitudes or behaviors
of consumers are valid predictors of adoption behavior. In the
case of innovative products, this assumption may not hold.
Measurement of consumer need or purchase interest may be valid
for screening "continuous" innovations, but customers may not
recognize or admit they need products that are unusual.

2.35   WEBSTER, FREDERICK E., JR. (1988), "Rediscovering
        the Marketing Concept," Marketing Science Institute,
        Report #88-100, Cambridge, MA: Marketing Science
        Institute.
Tracks how the marketing concept as originally formulated
in the 1950s has been interpreted in intervening years;
examines how today it appears to be making a comeback; provides
management guidelines for making a business customer-focused
and market-driven. Basic requirements include: 1. A system of
customer-oriented values must have support of top management;
2. Both market and customer focus must be integrated into
strategy-planning process; 3. Strong marketing managers and
programs needed; 4. Market-based measures needed for gauging
performance; 5. Organization-wide commitment to the customer
must be instilled.

Market-Pull Ideas

2.36   DURGEE, J. (1987), "New Product Ideas from Focus
        Groups," Journal of Consumer Marketing, 57-65.
Focus groups provide important marketing data on: product
usage, users' subjective experiences, object of product's use.

2.37   FOXALL, GORDON (1986), "Conceptual Extension of the
        Customer-Active Paradigm," Technovation, 4(1), 17 -
        27.

This paper presents a critique and extension of von Hippel's customer-active paradigm of industrial innovation. Users may initiate product innovation, not only by producing ideas and designs but through risk-reducing marketing intelligence. Thus, the customer-active paradigm, which views the user in a largely passive role, may underestimate the real contributions of the user. The customer-active paradigm should thus be extended. This presents a frame of reference for further empirical research.

2.38   TAUBER, EDWARD M. (1975), "Discovering New Product
        Opportunities with Problem Inventory Analysis,"
        Journal of Marketing, 39(1), 67-70.
The goal of problem inventory analysis is the discovery of consumer needs or problems. The consumer receives a list of problems and is asked what products come to mind for each problem. The results of this method must be regarded as preliminary and interpreted with caution.

2.39   URBAN, GLEN L. AND ERIC VON HIPPEL (1988), "Lead User
        Analysis for the Development of New Industrial
        Products," Management Science, 34(5), 569-582.
Integrates market research within a lead user methodology and reports a test of it among lead users in the field of computer-aided systems for the design of printed circuit boards. New product concepts generated on the basis of lead user data were strongly preferred by a representative sample of product users.   The article presents strengths and weaknesses of the empirical test of this methodology.

2.40   VON HIPPEL, ERIC (1978), "Successful Industrial
        Products from Customer Ideas," Journal of Marketing,
        42(1), 39-49.
Describes and compares "manufacturer-active paradigm" and a new "customer-active paradigm". Proposes a test which will allow determination of how well each paradigm fits actual conditions in the industrial market.

2.41   VON HIPPEL, ERIC (1986), "Lead Users: A Source of
        Novel Product Concepts," Management Science, 32(7),
        791-805.
Marketing research techniques currently popular tend not to be reliable for product categories characterized by rapid change. Companies should identify and study lead users as they can indicate the future needs of the marketplace, rather than simply heavy users who may not be able to think of novel attributes and uses. Lead user analysis requires the firm to: 1) identify an important market or technical trend (should be related to need for product); 2) identify users who lead trend in terms of experience and intensity of need and are best able to convey that understanding to market researchers; 3) analyze lead user data (user developed product solutions); 4) project lead user data onto general market of interest.

Technology-Push Ideas

2.42   BONNET, DIDIER C.L. (1985), "Integrating Marketing

Variables in the Early Stages of the New Product
Process to Support the Design and the Development of
Technologically Advanced New Industrial Products,"
Quarterly Review of Marketing, 11 (Autumn), 7-11.
This paper presents the results of an analysis of twenty-
three projects across ten firms. It draws conclusions about
the effects of a lack of marketing and R&D integration.

2.43   BOYCE, D.T. (1987), "Market Pull and Technology Push
        III. The Necessary Government Environment,"
        Information Technology and Public Policy, 5(2), 93 -
        95.
This paper discusses how government can improve the economic
environment associated with stimulating the information
technology industry in Great Britain. Central government can
influence industries and thus create an environment which
attracts a high volume of R&D investment, enabling high-tech
companies to meet international competition.

2.44   CRAIG, I. (1987), "Market Pull and Technology Push I.
        One Company's Experience," Information Technology and
        Public Policy, 5(2), 88-89.
Northern   Telecom,   manufacturer   of   fully   digital
telecommunications systems, successfully uses both market pull
and technology push. They have a sustained commitment to R&D,
driven by customer needs and demands. Their strategy, which
has been successful, is to study market demands and to develop
products meeting those demands.

2.45   GALT, B. (1978), "Market Pull and Technology Push
        II. Research and Development," Information Technology
        and Public Policy, 5(2), 90-92.
Design, development and manufacturing must work together as
a team, with customer experience as the main focus. The article
discusses the approach for design and development used at BNR
Ltd. in Britain, and advocates its adoption elsewhere.   The
approach helps bring good new ideas to profitable production.

2.46   GESCHKE, H. (1983), "Creativity Techniques in Product
        Planning and Development: A View from West Germany,"
        R&D Management, 13(3), 169-183.
This paper categorizes idea generation techniques and
suggests that successful idea generation requires the
following: 1. an exact formulation of the problem; 2.
multifunctional participation; 3. avoidance of experts; 4.
correct selection of methods for particular problem.

2.47   GLOBE, SAMUEL, GIRARD W. LEVY AND CHARLES M. SCHWARTZ
        (1978), "Key Factors and Events in the Innovation
        Process," Research Management, 21 (July), 8-15.
For innovations applying radically new technologies (such
as pacemakers), technological variables (recognition of a
technical opportunity, management of R&D, sufficient
development funds, and presence of a technical entrepreneur)
are the most important determinants of success or failure.

2.48   HISE, ROBERT T., CHARLES FUTRELL AND DONALD SNYDER
        (1980), "University Research Centers as a New Product

Development Resource," <u>Research Management</u>, 23(3),
25-28.
  University Affiliated Research Centers (UARCs) are viable
external sources that industry should consider when choosing
outside assistance in the NPD process.   They offer skilled
expertise with a full-time staff, and additional competence
obtained from outside consultants.

2.49   LEAF, ROBIN (1978), "How to Pick Up Tips from Your
         Competitors," <u>Director</u>, (February), 60-62.
  Corporate performance in the marketplace can be improved by
studying how competitors make, test, distribute and promote
their products.   This article exemplifies the use of teardown
analysis and other product testing techniques which provide
information on competitive activity that can be used in product
development.

2.50   PAUL, RONALD H. (1987), "Improving the New Product
         Development Process: Making Technology Push Work,"
         <u>Journal of Business and Industrial Marketing</u>, (Fall),
         59-61.
  Distinguishes technology driven NPD process from customer
driven process.   In a technology driven process, the firm
identifies   technology-driven   attributes   and   creatively
identifies possible customer/application for that technology.
Examples provided: digital readout devices, overnight package
delivery services.   Conditions for success: technology must
meet current customer needs, price level must be low enough,
marketing must educate the consumer about the technology, and
marketing must be patient as adoption might be slow.

2.51   ROBERTS, EDWARD B. AND DONALD H. PETERS (1982),
         "Commercial Innovation from University Faculty,"
         <u>Research Management</u>, 25(3), 24-30.
  Technical university faculty can be expected to generate
ideas of commercial value: industry must help establish
effective transfer relationships.   Discusses MIT--Route 128
relationships.   Hundreds of technically-based new enterprises
coming from university-generated ideas. "Idea-Havers" are
different in personal characteristics from "Idea-Exploiters."
Exploitative   behavior   seems   linked   to   background
characteristics of person -- most able to be predicted by
earlier occurrence of related behavior by individual.

2.52   ROTHWELL, ROY AND PAUL GARDINER (1988), "Re-
         Innovation and Robust Designs: Producer and User
         Benefits," <u>Journal of Marketing Management</u> (Spring),
         372-387.
  Distinction between technology drive and marketing drive is
simplistic   and   inappropriate.   Instead,   firms   should
distinguish between robust and lean designs. Robust refers to
designs that are forerunners of families of products. Redesign
can take place at the conceptualization stage or prototype
stage.

2.53   ZARECAR, WILLIAM D. (1975), "High-Technology Product
         Planning," <u>Harvard Business Review</u> 53 (January-
         February), 108.

The product planning process consists of market analysis and product definition. The paper presents an interesting but brief discussion. "A good strategy produces good results but a good product might be a bad strategy." Both taken in context of company and established as a separate unit. The author believes that organizational status is secondary to procedures for evaluation and approval.

SCREENING

Success Factors

2.54   ALT, MICH AND STEVE GRIGGS (1986), "A Theory of Product Success," Journal of the Market Research Society, 28, 235-267.
Describes a theory for explaining why certain products are successful. Also develops an analytical technique with which to test the theory. Central to both theory and analytical technology is the concept of an ideal product. Provides parameters and guidelines for new product development by revealing market gaps and defining perceived strengths and weaknesses of existing and new products.

2.55   CALANTONE, ROGER J. AND C. ANTHONY DI BENEDETTO (1988), "An Integrative Model of the New Product Development Process: An Empirical Validation," Journal of Product Innovation Management, 5(3), 201-215.
Demonstrates complex relationships existing among marketing and technical variables which are determinants of new product success. The article presents and discusses an integrative model of the new product decision process. The model is tested empirically using three-stage least squares analysis of data from sample of industrial manufacturing companies. Marketing and technical activities, launch, and new product quality are found to be direct determinants of success/failure; while marketing resources, technical resources and marketing intelligence have indirect effects.

2.56   CALANTONE, ROGER J. AND C. ANTHONY DI BENEDETTO (1990), "Canonical Correlation Analysis of Unobserved Relationships in the New Product Process," R&D Management, 20(1), 2-21.
Previous studies of success and failure in new product development have examined the effect of numerous variables upon new product outcomes. In this study, the authors use the method of canonical correlation analysis to investigate the nature of the interactions within and between two sets of variables (controllable and environmental) in the new product process, and present implications for new product management.

2.57   COOPER, ROBERT G. (1979), "The Dimensions of Industrial New Product Success and Failure," Journal of Marketing, 43(3), 93-103.
Keys to success in new product development: a) Product uniqueness and superiority; b) Marketing knowledge and

proficiency;   c)   Technical   and   production   synergy   and
proficiency.   Barriers to success: a) High priced products
relative to competition, with no economic advantage to
customer;   b)   dynamic   market   with   many   new   product
introductions;   c)   competitive   market   where   customers   are
already well-satisfied. Contributors to new product success:
a)   marketing   and   managerial   proficiency;   b)   strength   of
marketing communication and launch effort; c) market need,
growth and style; d) newness of firm; e) source of ideas and
investment magnitude.

2.58   COOPER, ROBERT G. (1980a), Project NEWPROD: What
        Makes a New Product a Winner? Montreal: Centre
        Quebecois d'Innovation Industrielle.
   The topic of this book, and of Project NEWPROD, was to
discover what makes a new product a winner.   Project NEWPROD
was an extensive research investigation into new product
success and failure, and its results are insightful for
managers who want to improve new product success rates.   The
article below (Cooper 1980b) provides information on some of
the basic findings of Project NEWPROD, which is extensively
discussed in this book.

2.59   COOPER, ROBERT G. (1980b), "How to Identify Potential
        New Product Winners," Research Management, 23
        (January), 10-19.
   Article reports the results of Project NEWPROD, a study of
factors making differences between new product winners and
losers.   These factors include: a) properly executing the
launch; b) meeting customer needs better than competitor; c)
higher quality new product; d) good prototype test with
customer; e) sales force and distribution effort well targeted;
f) proficient test market/trial sell; g) proficient startup of
full   scale   production;   h)   knowledge   of   customer   price
sensitivities;   i)   good   execution   of   NPD   process;   j)
understanding customer's purchasing decision process; k)
reducing customer's cost; l) good company-product fit in terms
of sales force and distribution; m) good company-product fit
in terms of marketing research; n) company did good job of idea
screening;   o)   firm   understands   customer   needs,   wants   and
specifications.

2.60   COOPER, ROBERT G. (1980c), "Project NEWPROD: Factors
        in New Product Success," European Journal of
        Marketing, 14(5/6), 277-292.
   See Cooper (1980a, 1980b) for complete discussion.

2.61   COOPER, ROBERT G. (1981), "The Components of Risk in
        New Product Development: Project NEWPROD," R&D
        Management, 11(2), 47-54.
   See Cooper (1980a, 1980b) for complete discussion.

2.62   COOPER, ROBERT G. (1982), "New Product Success in
        Industrial Firms," Industrial Marketing Management,
        11, 215-224.
   Most industrial new products do succeed. Dispels myth that
every firm is unique.   Nature of the firm, industry, size,
ownership, did not have impact on performance. No direct link

found between R&D spending and effectiveness of firms' new product programs. Success/failure and "kill" rates not related to R&D inputs (consistent with PIMS studies which showed no simple direct link between R&D spending and profitability). Marketing (not technological) variables were key to effectiveness and efficiency, increasing returns to R&D and success rate.

2.63   COOPER, ROBERT G. (1983), "Most New Products Do
        Succeed," Research Management, 25(6), 20-25.
    Extension of Cooper (1982) article above.

2.64   COOPER, ROBERT G. (1984), "How New Product
        Strategies Impact on Performance," Journal of Product
        Innovation Management, 1(1), 5-18.
    The strategy chosen by a firm for new product development is related to the performance results that firm will achieve. Performance of a new product may be viewed three ways: impact on company sales and profits, success rate of program (track record, kill rates), and performance relative to objectives, competitors, and profits. If high success rate is objective, a conservative strategy is appropriate: seek high technical and production synergy; deliver visible benefits to the customer. For other performance objectives, a more aggressive program is appropriate: innovative higher risk, technically complex products, state-of-the-art technology, strong R&D orientation.

2.65   COOPER, ROBERT G. (1988), "Predevelopment Activities
        Determine New Product Success," Industrial Marketing
        Management, 17, 237-248.
    Presents evidence that new product success and failure is often decided before the project enters the product development phase. Discusses how managers can improve effectiveness of early stages of innovation process. In the idea stage: listen to the customer and utilize sales and service groups. Screening: should be a formal step in new product process. Preliminary assessment: both marketing and technical assessment should be done. Concept definition: identification, development, testing and evaluation. Attributes, features and product design contribute to the bundle of benefits that provides value to the customer.

2.66   COOPER, ROBERT G. AND ULRIKE DE BRENTANI (1984),
        "Criteria for Screening New Industrial Products,"
        Industrial Marketing Management, 13, 149-156.
    Factor analysis of 86 screening dimensions produced the following dimensions: a) Product Differences/Advantages; b) Corporate Synergy; c) Technical and Production Synergy; d) Financial Potential; e) Project Financing; f) Size of Market; g) Diversification Strategy; h) Marketing Maintenance Strategy; i) Product Life; j) Rational Market; k) Domestic Market. The first four factors are the dominant screening criteria for managerial decision behavior.

2.67   COOPER, R.G. AND E. KLEINSCHMIDT (1987a), "New
        Products: What Separates Winners from Losers?"
        Journal of Product Innovation Management, 4(3),

169-184.
A study of characteristics of new product (NP) successes
and failures. Hypotheses supported by study: a) NP success
related to product advantage; b) NP success related to
marketing potential for product; c) NP success negatively
related to level of competitiveness; d) NP success related to
marketing synergy or fit; e) NP success related to technology
synergy or fit; f) NP success related to project definition
(protocol); g) NP success related to proficiency of predevelopment activities; h) NP success related to proficiency
of marketing activities; i) NP success related to proficiency
of technical activities; j) NP success related to degree of
top management support. Key success factors identified: a)
product advantage; b) proficiency of predevelopment activities;
c) protocol; and others. Implications for managers: a) product
superiority is #1 factor in success; b) project definition of
"up front" activities vital for success; c) synergy, both
marketing and technical, is important; d) controllable, non-
situational variables are dominant factors in success.

2.68   COOPER, ROBERT G. AND E.J. KLEINSCHMIDT
        (1987b), "Success Factors in Product Innovation,"
        Industrial Marketing Management, 16, 215-224.
Article presents results of Project NEWPROD II. How can
new product success be measured? What are the components of
success when success is viewed in different ways? 200 new
product case histories (successes and failures). Success
defined in terms of profit level, payback, domestic and foreign
market share, relative sales and profit, sales and profit
objectives, window on new categories or markets. The key
factors of success were found to be financial performance,
opportunity window, and market impact.

2.69   DAVIS, JOHN STEPHEN (1988), "New Product Success and
        Failure: Three Case Studies," Industrial Marketing
        Management, 17, 103-110.
Three case studies are presented: photovoltaic houses,
computer systems and hotels. They are chosen to illustrate
factors in new product success. Borrows on "conservative
strategy" model. Success was identified as market newness,
product fit and focus, and production and technology synergy.
Cooper's process model idea of success had seven elements:
idea, preliminary assessment, concept, development, testing,
trial and launch.

2.70   FOLKES, VALARIE S. AND BARBARA KOTSOS (1986),
        "Buyers and Sellers Explanations for Product Failure:
        Who Done It?" Journal of Marketing, 50, 74-80.
Buyers and sellers read descriptions of a product failure
and were asked to explain why it occurred; sellers explained
failures of products they themselves offered. They tended to
find fault with the product itself less often than did
consumers. Discrepancies between buyer and seller opinions
were related to estimates of how commonly the product fails,
thus consensus information may be one source of buyer-seller
differences.

2.71   HLAVACEK, JAMES D. (1974), "Toward More Successful

Venture Management," Journal of Marketing, 38(4),
56-60.
Examines failures of product ventures which were terminated
before the commercialization stage. Major factors leading to
product failure were identified as: inadequate market size,
distribution problems, internal conflicts, resistance and
impatience, and poor marketing research. Relatively small
sample size used.

2.72   HOPKINS, DAVID S. (1981), "New Product Winners and
        Losers," Research Management, 24(3), 12-17.
Examined about 150 companies in the U.S. Reasons for product
failures included: poor marketing, technical problems, timing,
senior company executives not involved (or too involved),
straying from technical/marketing expertise, overlooking
competition, "me-too" entries, not educating the customer, not
enough care or quality in product positioning, not integrated
with product line, costs, profit margins, or return on
investment not checked.

2.73   HOPKINS, DAVID S. AND E.L.BAILEY (1971), "New
        Product Pressures," The Conference Board Record, 8,
        16-24.
Provided further empirical support in favor of the NICB
(1964) conclusions: that marketing-related reasons were often
the major cause of product failure in the marketplace.
Marketing activities such as timing of product launch are
crucial factors in determining ultimate product success. Over
100 companies were surveyed.

2.74   JOHNE, F. AXEL AND PATRICIA A. SNELSON (1988),
        "Success Factors in Product Innovation: A Selective
        Review of the Literature," Journal of Product
        Innovation Management, 5(2), 114-128.
This article reviews the factors associated with achieving
new product success. The authors address the following
questions: To what extent can product innovation be planned?
Should development tasks be scheduled sequentially or in
parallel? What is the proper degree of formality in effective
new product decision making? What are the optimal
organizational arrangements?

2.75   KLEINSCHMIDT, ELKO J. AND ROBERT G. COOPER (1988),
        "The Performance Impact of an International
        Orientation on Product Innovation," European
        Journal of Marketing, 22, 56-70.
This study sought to answer these questions: if a firm
deliberately targets world markets, incorporates world needs
into product design, or does both, would the resulting new
products be more successful? Empirical results from industrial
firms supported all these points. Success rates for
internationally designed products were far superior to those
for domestically designed products. Further, both foreign and
donestic market shares were better if international products
aimed at export markets were developed.

2.76   KONOPA, L.J. (1968), "New Products: Assessing
        Commercial Potential," Management Bulletin #88, New

York: American Management Association.
Examined failures of products which survived early screening stages. Key reasons for product failures were identified as: bad estimates of market potential and general lack of market information. Provides partial support to the NICB (1964) report which suggested that marketing and not technical or production deficiencies are major determinants of product failure.

2.77   LINK, PETER L. (1987), "Keys to New Product Success and Failure," Industrial Marketing Management, 16, 109-118.
1985-86 study of success and failure (s/f) in new industrial products that reached commercialization. Paper identifies underlying factors for success and tests whether perceived s/f factors vary with new product "expensive" levels and/or with degree of innovation in company's new product program. The conclusion was that the companies with more innovative/high-tech new product programs have significantly different s/f factors than do lower technology/less innovative firms. The six most important causes (contributors) of new product failure are: market too competitive, insufficient marketing research, product not novel to market, product offered negligible savings/benefits to users, product inadequate and advertising inadequate. The six most important causes (contributors) of new product success are: new product synergy with marketing skills, new product synergy with technical and manufacturing skills, product quality high, product offered significant user benefits, appropriate targeting and pricing strategies, and distribution channel support.

2.78   MC DONOUGH, EDWARD F. III AND FRANCIS C. SPITAL (1984), "Quick-Response New Product Development," Harvard Business Review 62 (September-October), 52.
Results of interviews with 100 persons about success or failure of responses for new product development when a competitor has threatened to steal market share. Successful projects had high visibility (mission urgent and high priority, rewards established, updates, audit); closely controlled (well defined specifications to the competition, keep engineers on task, managers monitor personally); engineers had a business outlook (were able to perform make or buy decisions).

2.79   MELLOW, CRAIG (1988), "Successful Products of the Eighties," Across the Board (November), 40-49.
Describes and discusses five case studies: Dupont's Stainmaster, PIG corporation, Hormel Top Shelf entrees, Estraderm drug patch system, American Express Optima card. Conclusions: 1. Every product was "designed by the marketplace." 2. Each firm had to part with a long-standing belief or practice. 3. All firms stuck to businesses they knew a lot about. 4. Entrepreneurship needn't come in garages: four of the five case histories required the resources of large organizations. 5. All five items required an emotional commitment.

2.80   NATIONAL INDUSTRIAL CONFERENCE BOARD (1964), Why New Products Fail, New York: National Industrial

Conference Board.
An early study assessing reasons for new product failure. Key reasons included: inadequate market analysis, product deficiency, higher costs, poor timing, competitive strength, insufficient marketing effort, and inadequate sales force or distribution. Most of these reasons are market or marketing research deficiencies, thus indicating the importance of careful execution of marketing activities.

2.81   ROTHWELL, ROY (1972), "Factors for Success in Industrial Innovation," Project SAPPHO--A Comparative Study of Success and Failure in Industrial Innovation, Brighton, U.K.: Science Policy Research Unit, University of Sussex.
One of the first studies to compare successful and unsuccessful new products, and to uncover what characteristics made them different. Five underlying factors were uncovered which differentiated them: understanding of users' needs; efficiency of development; characteristics of management; effectiveness of internal and external communications; magnitude of marketing efforts. This was an empirical study of firms in the chemical and instrument industries.

2.82   TAYLOR, JAMES W., JOHN J. HOULAHAN AND ALAN C. GABRIEL (1975), "The Purchase Intention Question in New Product Development: A Field Test," Journal of Marketing, 39(1), 90-92.
Results of a field test of the "intent-to-purchase" question suggest that there is a positive relationship between buying interest and purchase behavior; purchase intention questions are likely to be quite useful in identifying "losers."

Methodologies for Screening

2.83   BAKER, KENNETH G. AND GERALD S. ALBAUM (1986), "Modeling New Product Screening Decisions," Journal of Product Innovation Management, 3(1), 32-39.
The authors compare the performance of several types of screening models using the actual evaluations of 86 new product managers. The results show that a fairly simple model, using a minimum number of evaluative criteria, might be useful for decision making at the Idea Evaluation stage.

2.84   CALANTONE, ROGER AND ROBERT G. COOPER (1977), "A Typology of Industrial New Product Success and Failure," in A. Greenberg and D. Bellenger (eds.), Proceedings, National Educators Conference, Chicago: American Marketing Association.
A preliminary study on new product failure. Suggests that a typology of industrial new product failures is feasible, and that a small number of scenarios can categorize most new product failures. Proposes a preliminary typology, extended and empirically tested in a later article by the same authors (1979).

2.85   CALANTONE, ROGER AND ROBERT G. COOPER (1979), "A Discriminant Model for Identifying Scenarios of

Industrial New Product Failure," <u>Journal of the
Academy of Marketing Science</u>, 7(3), 163-183.
Six clusters of product failures were identified: 1) "Better
mousetrap that no one wanted" -- 28% of failures; 2) "Me-Too
product meeting competitive brick wall" -- 24%; 3) "Competitive
one-upmanship" -- 13%; 4) "Environmental Ignorance" -- 15%; 5)
"Technical dog product" -- 15%; 6) "Price crunch" -- 13%.

2.86   CALANTONE, ROGER AND ROBERT G. COOPER (1981), "New
        Product Scenarios: Prospects for Success," <u>Journal
        of Marketing</u>, 45(2), 48-60.
Examines almost 200 industrial new product introductions in
order to identify the ingredients of new product success.   A
categorization scheme, involving scenarios of new products, is
developed from the data and proves useful in assessing the
merits and dangers of various types of new product projects.

2.87   COOPER, ROBERT G. (1985), "Selecting Winning New
        Product Projects: Using the NEWPROD System," <u>Journal
        of Product Innovation Management</u>, 2(1), 34-44.
Review of various approaches to new product screening.
Article also presents basics of NEWPROD model and shows how
managers can build their own screening models. Outlines how
such models can contribute to better new product selection
decisions. Good review of screening models provided.

2.88   COOPERS AND LYBRAND (1986), <u>Evaluating R&D and New
        Product Development Ventures: An Overview of
        Assessment Methods</u>, Washington, DC (January).
Techniques to assess the business potential of technology
projects are introduced.   The principles involved are
applicable to all those involved in the process of
technological innovation: investors, financial intermediaries,
individual entrepreneurs and other personnel who screen
projects for possible commercial application. Assessment
techniques include: checklist analyses, constraint analysis,
environmental scoring model, profitability measures,
sensitivity analysis, risk analysis, decision analysis and
decision trees, and assessment of profitabilities.

2.89   DILLON, WILLIAM R., ROGER CALANTONE AND PARKER
        WORTHING (1979), "The New Product Problem: An
        Approach for Investigating Product Failures,"
        <u>Management Science</u>, 12, 1184-1196.
Use of a discrete variable selection procedure in assessing
the factors which seem to be associated with new product
success or failure.

2.90   RAM, SUNDARESAN AND SUDHA RAM (1989), "Expert
        Systems: An Emerging Technology for Selecting New
        Product Winners," <u>Journal of Product Innovation
        Management</u>, 6(2), 89-98.
The authors descrobe INNOVATOR, an expert system for
assessment of success potential of new financial services.
The authors present how knowledge is collected from experts
and encoded; how a user interacts with the system to obtain
recommendations on specific new products; and how the inference
engine of the system arrives at the final recommendation.

Strategic Implications

2.91   ABETTE, PEIR A. AND ROBERT W. STUART (1988),
          "Evaluating New Product Risk," Research Technology
          Management, (May-June), 40-43.
Four factors which determine risk in new product projects:
1) How new is technology? Lower risk if result is better value
to customer; 2) How new is specific function or application the
product is designed to aid? Corresponds to risks of new
markets; 3) How new to the firm are the customers in that
application? 4) How innovative is the product in the
marketplace? Recommendations: 1) Most serious evaluation after
conclusive testing and screening, before significant technology
and marketing efforts undertaken; 2) Multifunctional panel of
peers for product evaluation; 3) How risk evaluation should be
made: use scoring model containing the four factors mentioned
above.

2.92   BALACHANDRA, R. (1984), "Critical Signals for Making
          Go/No Go Decisions in New Product Development,"
          Journal of Product Innovation Management, 1(2), 92 -
          100.
List of critical signals that warn of danger ahead. These
will help managers make tough decisions about project
continuation. "Red light" variables: check for significant
adverse change in any one of these: 1) subjective probability
of technical success; 2) availability of raw materials; 3)
continued existence of market; 4) government regulations.
"Yellow variables: may not indicate termination: 1) probability
of commercial success; 2) commitment of personnel; 3) smooth
technical route; 4) number of end uses; 5) project champion;
6) number of projects in R&D portfolio; 7) anticipated
competition; 8) profitability of company.

2.93   COOPER, ROBERT G. (1983), "The Impact of New Product
          Strategies," Industrial Marketing Management, 12,
          243-256.
170 firms contacted (industrial product developers). The
ten most important strategies for high overall performance were
found to be: 1) have an offensive new product program, (seek
to increase market share); 2) have an active new product idea
search effort; 3) identify market needs proactively; 4) locate
new product program as leading edge of corporate strategy; 5)
possess synergy with R&D skills and resources; 6) develop
highly innovative products; 7) meet consumer needs better than
competitors; 8) have a market oriented new product program; 9)
develop products that offer unique benefits or features; 10)
employ complex, sophisticated technology in development of new
products.

2.94   COOPER, ROBERT G. (1984), "New Product Strategies:
          What Distinguishes the Top Performers?" Journal of
          Product Innovation Management, 1(3), 151-164.
Clusters firms into five general types of new product
strategies: 1) technology driven firm; 2) balanced strategy
firm -- superior in all success measures; 3) defensive,

focused, technology deficient firm; 4) low-budget, conservative; 5) high-budget, diverse. Characteristics of balanced strategy firms: 1) technologically-sophisticated orientation; 2) strong marketing orientation; 3) chose high-potential, large and growing markets; 4) noncompetitive markets. Conclusion: Managers can positions the strategies of their own firms and compare their results with those listed in the article.

2.95   COOPER, ROBERT G. (1985a), "Industrial Firms' New
        Product Strategies," Journal of Business Research,
        107-121.
   Nineteen factors of strategy are discussed, including: 1) technical sophistication; 2) production and technology synergy; 3) market newness; 4) market potential and growth; 5) technical synergy etc. The most successful strategies call for the union of technological aggressiveness and market orientation. An alternative successful strategic option is a conservative strategy, where management wants new products with maximum fit and focus (line extensions).

2.96   COOPER, ROBERT G. (1985b), "Overall Corporate
        Strategies for New Product Programs," Industrial
        Marketing Management, 14, 179-194.
   Empirical study, extending Cooper 1984. Article identifies major types of innovation strategies that firms pursue: "strategy scenarios." These are technical driven, balanced and focused (the most successful), technically deficient, low budget conservative, high budget diverse.

2.97   COREY, E. RAYMOND (1975), "Key Options in Market
        Selection and Product Planning," Harvard Business
        Review, 53 (September-October), 119.
   Looks at how Crown Cork and Seal Company remained profitable although they had a narrow breadth of scope. These were related to key management choices in four areas. 1) What markets should be served; 2) What form should the product have; 3) What should the product do for the user; 4) For whom is product most important. Planning and market selection are shown to be integrally related.

2.98   EUROPEAN INDUSTRIAL RESEARCH MANAGEMENT ASSOCIATION
        (1982), "Ten Recommendations for R&D Managers,"
        Research Management, 15(4), 13-15.
   The ten recommendations are: 1) Industries should establish open relations with authorities, legislative bodies and consumer organizations. 2) R&D should anticipate changes in consumer and legal trends and implement appropriate actions. 3) Check that oppositions and constraints are taken into account in new product specifications. 4) Analyze relationship between worth and cost of quality levels. 5) R&D must carry out adequate tests during NPD for safety. 6) New design reviews should be formal and systematic. 7) Firms should plan for safe reuse or disposal of worn-out or obsolete products. 8) Check that process capability meets requirements. 9) R&D is responsible for technical content of instructions for proper use of products. 10) R&D should take active part in analysis of defects and failures obtained in production.

2.99   LEE, T.M., J.C. FISHER AND T.S. YAU (1986), "Is Your
        R&D On Track?" Harvard Business Review, 64(1), 34.
Introduces a simple framework for evaluation and managing
R&D projects through consideration of five key issues.
Examples of decision models (matrixes, worksheets), one for
each issue, are covered.   Emphasis is placed on use of
framework in industry's context and use of managerial
judgement. Six issues: 1) project strength -- prioritize; 2)
project timing -- when to move to next stage; 3) project fit
-- does it fit organization; 4) project responsiveness --
funding profiles; 5) program robustness -- environmental
stability.

2.100   MORE, ROGER A. (1982), "Risk Factors in Accepted and
        Rejected New Industrial Products," Industrial
        Marketing Management, 11, 9-16.
Supports hypothesis that rejected new product opportunities
tend to have greater downcycles and situational uncertainties
than selected products. Most significant dimensions of risk
(higher risk): 1) higher development cost and higher loss; 2)
lower similarity of marketing task; 3) more development
complexity; 4) less competitive advantage; 5) higher buyer
risk.   Public policy implications: government incentives for
R&D. "Risk-reducers" for managers are incentives directed at
reducing different dimensions of risk.

2.101   NEW, D.E. AND J.L. SCHLACTER (1979), "Abandon Bad
        R&D Projects with Earlier Marketing Appraisals,"
        Industrial Marketing Management, 8(4), 274-280.
Firms must practice the marketing concept early in the
product development cycle to prevent marketplace failure. This
article presents framework for accomplishing this.   Product
Development cycle: marketing concept can be used to bridge the
gaps between idea development, product development and
marketing development.   Early assessment of market potential
must not be neglected.   84% of failures fail beyond the
relatively cheap early phases of idea development.

2.102   SCHEWE, CHARLES AND JAMES L. WILK (1977),
        "Innovation Strategies for Improving MIS
        Utilization," Academy of Management Review, 2(1),
        138-142.
Importance of developing a marketing plan thoroughly geared
to user's needs, psychological, as well as informational, and
finally technical. Must understand the customer if a marketing
plan is to be effective.   General discussion is geared to
technically based MIS personnel.

CONCEPT TESTING

2.103   ACITO, FRANKLIN AND THOMAS P. HUSTAD (1981),
        "Industrial Product Concept Testing," Industrial
        Marketing Management, 10, 157-164.
Hypothetical example given. Technique: 1) define relevant
set of competitive products; 2) develop new product concept
and its constituent elements; 3) select experimental design.

Technique offers direct estimates of market share impacts of changes in product attributes; can study products; can obtain brand substitution and cannibalization patterns. Answers questions like: What current brands will be most affected? How will new product be affected if competitors introduce a similar new product?

2.104   BERKOWITZ, MARVIN (1987), "Product Shape as a Design Innovation Strategy," Journal of Product Innovation Management, 4(4), 274-283.
Article discusses the use of product shape as an element of innovation strategy in food processing. Design cues, like shape, are used by consumers to infer other, but less obvious attributes like taste, softness, comfort and speed, which can be much more important. Good product design encourages the customer to trade up, provides a basis for market segmentation, and helps broaden the product line.

2.105   CORSTJENS, MARCEL L. AND DAVID A. GAUTSCHI (1983), "Conjoint Analysis: A Comparative Analysis of Specification Tests for the Utility Function," Management Science, 29(12), 1393-1413.
Paper discusses determinations of appropriate combination rules for idiosyncratic ordinal utility functions in conjoint measurement. Presents empirical results which compare selection of combination rules based on axiomatic tests and empirical fitting procedures for combinations of factors.

2.106   FAUKER, EDWARD M. (1979), "Why Concept and Product Tests Fail to Predict New Product Results," Journal of Marketing, 39(4), 69-71.
Concept testing and product testing fail to predict new product sales results because they cannot predict adoption behavior and frequency of purchase.

2.107   GREEN, PAUL E., J. DOUGLAS CARROLL AND STEPHEN M. GOLDBERG (1981), "A General Approach to Product Design Optimization via Conjoint Analysis," Journal of Marketing, 45(3), 17-37.
Describes some of the features of POSSE (Product Optimization and Selected Segment Evaluation), a general procedure for optimizing the approach uses input data based on conjoint analysis methods. The output of consumer choice simulators is modeled by means of response surface techniques and optimized by different sets of procedures, depending upon the objective function.

2.108   GREEN, PAUL E. AND YORAM WIND (1975), "New Way to Measure Consumers' Judgments," Harvard Business Review, (July-August), 107-117.
Discussion of conjoint analysis, and its use in helping the product manager determine which product attributes are most important to the consumer. Simple example involving alternate forms of a carpet cleaner product is provided. Shows usefulness of conjoint analysis in choosing how best to develop a given product concept into a product.

2.109   HARGREAVES, GEORGE, JOAN D. CLAXTON AND FREDERICK H.

SILBER (1976), "New Product Evaluations: Electric Vehicles for Commercial Applications," *Journal of Marketing*, 40(1), 74-77.

Addressed the question of new product evaluation in a relatively mature market: electrically powered delivery vans in commercial fleet application. The use of conjoint measurement to assess attribute tradeoffs is seen as a promising methodology for addressing questions of new product evaluation: it forces the recognition of tradeoffs among product attributes and thus can be used to establish the perceived values of various possible product designs.

2.110   HAUSER, JOHN R. (1984), "Consumer Research to Focus R&D Projects," *Journal of Product Innovation Management*, 1(2), 70-84.

Case study: narrow band video telephone. Demonstrates how consumer theory, market research and quantitative analysis improve R&D effectiveness. Conceptual model of consumer analysis is proposed: PHYSICAL CHARACTERISTICS AND PSYCHOSOCIAL CUES -> PERCEPTIONS -> PREFERENCES -> BEHAVIOR. R&D task: improve physical characteristics. Perceptions (consumer's subjective evaluation of product) influenced by physical characteristics and also psychosocial cues. Consumer forms preferences for specific technologies (ranking or scaling). Behavior (choice of technology) is mediated by budget, availability and other situational constraints.

2.111   HAUSER, JOHN R. AND GLEN L. URBAN (1977), "A Normative Methodology for Modeling Consumer Response to Innovation," *Operations Research*, 25(4), 579-619.

Proposes a methodology that interprets knowledge in the fields of psychometrics, utility theory, and stochastic choice theory to improve the design of new products or services. Methodology consists of a consumer response and a managerial design process. Design process is idea generation, evaluation and refinement; consumer response is based on consumer process and aggregation of prediction of individual choices. Various techniques are introduced and described. Selected techniques are demonstrated based on survey data collected at MIT to support design of an HMO and in the consumer market to evaluate a new deodorant.

2.112   HISE, RICHARD T., LARRY O'NEAL, JAMES U. MC NEAL AND A. PARASURAMAN (1989),"The Effect of Product Design Activities on Commercial Success Levels of New Industrial Products," *Journal of Product Innovation Management*, 6(1), 43-50.

This study examines 195 new industrial products and concludes that new product developers may lessen the success potentials of new industrial products if specific design steps are not performed. The use of a complete design/development agenda is also critical. Further, it is important for researchers to examine technically-oriented aspects of the new product development process and not just the nontechnical dimensions as the marketing-R&D interface problem.

2.113   JAGETEA, LAL C. AND EDWARD J. MARIEN (1974), "Evaluating New Product Decisions," *Omega*, 2(3),

379-388.

Identifies an efficient algorithm for solving the sequential decision process in the development of a new product. The algorithm utilizes the dynamic programming solution approach.

2.114   KOHLE, RAJEEV AND RAMESH KRISHNAMURTI (1987), "A Heuristic Approach to Product Design," Management Science, 32(12), 1523-1533.

The authors find approximate solutions to the problem of identifying which multi-attribute product profile produces the highest share-of-choices in a competitive market via a dynamic-programming heuristic. The model incorporates cannibalization rates. A simulation is presented and shows the proposed heuristic to dominate an alternative lagrangian relaxation heuristic and was shown to closely approximates the optimal solution.

2.115   MC GUIRE, E. PATRICK (1973), "Concept Testing for Consumer and Industrial Products," in Evaluating New Product Proposals, New York: Conference Board, Publication # CBR-604, 33-75.

Discusses the various approaches management can take to evaluate the relative merits of proposed new products at early stages in their development. Concept testing methods for consumer products include focus-group testing, employee panels, central location testing and use testing. Methods for industrial products are also presented.

2.116   MYERS, JAMES H. (1976), "Benefit Structure Analysis: A New Tool for Product Planning," Journal of Marketing, 49(4), 23-32.

Benefit Structure Analysis: 1) was developed especially for finding new product opportunities in very broad product/service categories; 2) determines consumer reactions to a large number of relatively specific benefits or physical characteristics of the product/service; 3) provides reactions in terms of both desire for and perceived deficiencies in each benefit and characteristic; 4) provides relatively complete information as to ambient conditions surrounding use of product; 5) provides complete cross-sectional view of current usage patterns.

2.117   PAGE, ALBERT L. AND HAROLD F. ROSENBAUM (1987), "Redesigning Product Lines with Conjoint Analysis: How Sunbeam Does It," Journal of Product Innovation Management, 4(2), 120-137.

Application of conjoint analysis to product design: identifies key attributes for each of two segments of mixer buyers.

2.118   PEKELMAN, DOV AND SUBRATA K. SEN (1979), "Improving Prediction in Conjoint Measurement," Journal of Marketing Research, 16, 211-220.

Conjoint analysis is proposed for prediction of overall value of alternative new product concepts. Typically, linear interpolation is used to predict utilities for new attribute levels (other than the original discrete levels). However, linear interpolation may lead to poor predictions and poor concept choice. Authors propose the estimation of a utility function: they provide an analytical procedure and some numerical results.

2.119   RABINO, SAMUEL AND HOWARD MOSKOWITZ (1984), "Detecting Buyer Preference to Guide Product Development and Advertising," <u>Journal of Product Innovation Management</u>, 1(3), 140-150.
Presents research approach similar to conjoint measurement but focusing on continuous (not discrete) functions and interactions among variables. Allows product to be "fine-tuned" to support advertising so as to best accentuate product advantages. This is important due to the competitive nature of many packaged goods categories. It provides a "refined" view of consumer preferences. An empirical example (preferences in spaghetti sauce) is given.

2.120   RAO, VITHALA R. AND GREGORY N. SOUTAR (1975), "Subjective Evaluations for Product Design Decisions," <u>Decision Sciences</u>, 6(1), 120-134.
Presents a simple methodology to utilize subjective evaluations of a sample of potential consumers of a set of alternative product concepts in the screening stage of a new product introduction process. The Thurston Case V model was used to develop a surrogate measure of the purchase probability for each concept. An attempt was also made to develop mathematical programming models for determining the best product concept.

2.121   SHOCKER, ALLAN D. AND V. SRINIVASAN (1979), "Multiattribute Approaches for Product Concept Evaluation and Generation: A Critical Review," <u>Journal of Marketing Research</u>, 16, 159-180.
Application of multiattribute research to new product evaluation and concept generation. Excellent table contrasting top articles in concept evaluation/generation from between 1971 and 1977. Discussed: LINMAP, PREFMAP, multidimensional scaling, Kelly's representational grid, factor analysis, probabilistic choice model, many others.

2.122   SUDHARSHAN, D. (1988), "DIFFSTRAT: An Analytical Procedure for Generating Optimal New Product Concepts for a Differentiated-Type Strategy," <u>European Journal of Operations Research</u>, 36(1), 50-65.
The problem of identifying optimal multiple new product concepts may be considered in either a sequential or simultaneous fashion, and the optimal concepts generated sequentially are different from, and usually inferior to, those generated simultaneously. The author presents a new procedure, DIFFSTRAT, designed to address this problem.

2.123   WIND, YORAM, JOHN F. GRASHOF AND JOEL D. GOLDHAR (1978), "Market-Based Guidelines for Design of Industrial Products: A New Application of Conjoint Analysis to Scientific and Technical Information (STI) Services," <u>Journal of Marketing</u>, 42(3), 27-37.
The design of new products and services, and especially scientific and technical products, has often been the sole

domain of the R&D engineer and scientist. Marketing should play a major role in the design of new products through the guidelines marketing research can provide on consumers' wants, needs and unresolved problems. This article presents an application of conjoint analysis to the design of a new industrial product: a Scientific and Technical Information Services system.

PRE-TEST MARKET MODELS

2.124   AAKER, DAVID A. AND J. GARY SHANSBY (1982),
         "Positioning Your Product," Business Horizons, 25(3),
         56-62.
Discusses in non-technical language how a manager can position his product: by attributes, by price/quality, by competitor, by application, by product user, and by product class. Numerous good examples are given.

2.125   ALBERS, SONKE AND KLAUS BROCKHOFF (1977), "A
         Procedure for New Product Positioning in an Attribute
         Space," European Journal of Operations Research,
         1(4), 230-238.
This paper presents a procedure, based on mixed integer nonlinear programming, designed to help a firm develop a preferred position for a new product in attribute space. The results of some computational experiments are discussed.

2.126   ASSMUS, GERT (1975), "NEWPROD: The Design and
         Implementation of a New Product Model," Journal of
         Marketing, 39(1), 16-23.
A new product model, NEWPROD (unrelated to Project NEWPROD) was developed in cooperation with a large consumer good company. It predicts the market share for the first year after the product is introduced into the national market. The number of potential buyers who are at the various stages of the adoption process are classified as being unaware or aware of the new product, and as being triers or repeaters. Model simulates the weekly flows from one category to another.

2.127   BLACKBURN, JOSEPH D. AND KEVIN J. CLANCY (1982),
         "LITMUS: A New Product Planning Model," TIMS
         Studies in Management Sciences, 18, 43-46.
This paper discusses the theoretical development and some empirical testing of the LITMUS model: an interactive stochastic model which can be used by the marketing manager in the development of marketing strategy for product introduction. The model provides forecasts of market performance as well as diagnostics for refinement of the marketing plan. LITMUS can be effective with a small amount of consumer data, such as the output of a Laboratory Test Market.

2.128   BLACKBURN, J.D. AND K.J. CLANCY (1983), "LITMUS II:
         An Evolutionary Step in New Product Planning Models
         from Marketing Plan Evaluation to Marketing Plan
         Generation," Advances and Practices of Marketing
         Science, Providence, RI: The Institute of Management
         Science.

A trial-repeat pre-test-market analysis. Data required include the results of a simulated test market and survey as well as the company's marketing plan (advertising, promotion and distribution by period). Produces as output estimates of market share, sales volume, trial and repeat rates, number of users, profitability, etc.

2.129   BLATTBERG, ROBERT AND JOHN GOLANTY (1978), "TRACKER: An Early Test Market Forecasting and Diagnostic Model for New Product Planning," Journal of Marketing Research, 15(5), 192-202.
TRACKER: a new product forecasting model which uses survey data (not panel data) to predict year-end test market sales from early test market results (three months). Also provides diagnostic information about new product's strengths and weaknesses. Given media plan, prices, sampling level, campaigning, repeat usage estimate, model makes pre-test-market forecast of year including sales: lets managers evaluate different marketing plans to see which best meets profit or sales goals.

2.130   BURGER, P.C., H. GUNDEE AND R. LAVIDGE (1981), "COMP: A Comprehensive System for the Evaluation of New Products," New Product Forecasting: Models and Applications, Lexington, MA: Lexington Books.
A form of laboratory pre-test-market model for new products. Simulates the awareness-trial-repeat process within a controlled laboratory situation.

2.131   CRAWFORD, C. MERLE (1985), "A New Positioning Typology," Journal of Product Innovation Management, 2(4), 243-253.
Firms often use one of several approaches that are substitutes for attribute positioning. These "surrogate" positioning approaches allow a seller to communicate product attributes without having to describe them, and at the same time permit the description to be tailor-made to each individual exposed to the advertisement.

2.132   DESARBO, WAYNE AND VITHALA R. RAO (1985), "A Constrained Unfolding Methodology for Product Positioning," Marketing Science, 5(1), 1-19.
Multidimensional scaling -- "Genfold 2." An unfolding methodology for analyzing preferential dominance data that addresses product design and targeting. Relates brand and consumer characteristics to perceptual brand locations and ideal points respectively. Monte Carlo simulation example: residential communication devices.

2.133   FRIEDMANN, ROBERTO AND V. PARKER LESSIG (1987), "Psychological Meaning of Products and Product Positioning," Journal of Product Innovation Management, 4(4), 265-273.
This paper discusses the concept of psychological meaning of products. Implications regarding Crawford's (1985) new product positioning typology are presented. The authors argue that the psychological meaning of products and Crawford's typology address product positioning from converging

perspectives. Psychological meaning of products can thus be effective in planning by management.

2.134   GAVISH, BEZALAL, DAN HORSKY AND RISHANATHAM SRIKANTH
         (1983), "An Approach to the Optimal Positioning of a
         New Product," Management Science, 29(11), 1277-1297.
Procedure for optimal positioning of a new product in a finite ideal point attribute space. For small sample problems it proposed an exact solution algorithm and for large sample problems an efficient heuristic was developed and tested. Positioning approach used was tied to the profit maximization of objective by assuming a two-stage consumer and firm decision process.

2.135   GOLANTY, JOHN L. (1984), "Clarification of the
         TRACKER Methodology and Limitations," Marketing
         Science, 2(3), 203.
Rejoinder to Mahajan et al. (1984).

2.136   MAHAJAN, VIJAY, EITAN MULLER AND SUBHASH SHARMA
         (1984), "An Empirical Comparison of Awareness
         Forecasting Models of New Product Introduction,"
         Marketing Science, 3(3), 179-197.
Five awareness forecasting models are compared empirically on one submodel: the advertising-awareness submodel embedded in the new product model. This is one of the few attempts in the literature to compare empirically alternate models of a marketing process. Models included: NEWS, TRACKER, LITMUS, Dodson/Muller, AYER. Authors conclude that all the models provide reasonably good fit for both the brand and the product category data sets.

2.137   MAHAJAN, VIJAY, EITAN MULLER AND SUBHASH SHARMA
         (1984), "Reflections on Awareness Forecasting Models
         of New Product Introduction," Marketing Science,
         3(3), 205-206.
Rejoinder to Mahajan et al. (1984).

2.138   MOORTHY, K. SRIDHAR (1984), "Market Segmentation,
         Self-Selection and Product Line Design," Marketing
         Science, 3(4), 288-307.
Economic theory of marketing segmentation based on consumer self-selection. Based on third-degree price discrimination model of Pigou (1920).

2.139   PRINGLE, LEWIS H. (1984), "Issues in Comparing the
         Awareness Component of New Product Models," Marketing
         Science, 3(3), 203-205.
Rejoinder to Mahajan et al. (1984).

2.140   PRINGLE, LEWIS H., R. DALE WILSON AND EDWARD I.
         BRODY (1982), "NEWS: A Decision-Oriented Model for
         New Product Analysis and Forecasting," Marketing
         Science, 1(1), 1-29.
NEWS: A pre-test-market model. Article discusses specification of model, methods of parameter estimation, model validation. Also presents a sample application to case. Good review of other pre-test-market models: TRACKER, NEWPROD,

SPRINTER. Model based on awareness-trial-repeat (ATR); also factors in media weight/exposure. Data sources: 1) manufacturer's marketing plan provides target size, category sales, purchase cycle, maximum awareness, trial and usage volume. 2) Phone survey provides initial awareness, trial and repeat. 3) Media plan provides media weight input. 4) Trade material and company experience provide estimates of distribution and promotional conversion rate.

2.141   ROBINSON, P.J. (1981), "A Comparison of Pretest Market New Product Forecasting Models," New Product Forecasting: Models and Applications, Lexington, MA: Lexington Books.
Reviews pre-test-market models such as ASSESSOR, LTM, SPEEDMARK, and many others. Does not include all the models described in Shocker and Hall (1986). Compares them on the basis of numerous aggregate dimensions including scope of test product configuration, scope of test marketing plan, scope of test environmental conditions, measurement of consumer behavior etc.

2.142   SHOCKER, ALLAN D. AND WILLIAM G. HALL (1986), "Pre-Test-Market Models: A Critical Evaluation," Journal of Product Innovation Management, 3(2), 86-107.
A key article on pre-test marketing. States strengths of pre-test marketing as: 1) Can reduce cost of development and introducing new products; 2) provides more timely data and diagnostics than test marketing; 3) easier to keep secret from competitors; 4) allows "optimization" of certain aspects of marketing mix; 5) increases managerial understanding and involvement in NPD process. Weaknesses were stated as being: 1) do not address potential problems in implementation; 2) competitive reactions not considered; 3) some model parameterization is judgmental; 4) may lack validity (unrepresentative); 5) less applicable to minor line extensions, difficult for "new-to-world" products. Directly compares: NEWS, ASSESSOR, LITMUS, BASES.

2.143   SHOCKER, ALLAN D. AND V. SRINIVASAN (1974), "A Consumer-Based Methodology for the Identification of New Product Ideas," Management Science, 20(6), 921-937.
A four-stage procedure used in identifying new product design alternatives in accord with company objectives. It is based on LINMAP--a linear programming procedure that is used in deriving individual ideal points, and on a consumer-choice model which assumes that product choice is a function of distance from the ideal brand.

2.144   SILK, ALVIN J. AND GLEN L. URBAN (1978), "Pre-Test-Market Evaluation of New Packaged Goods--A Model and Measurement Methodology," Journal of Marketing Research, 15(5), 171-191.
Discusses development of ASSESSOR model: pre-test-market evaluation of new packaged goods that estimates sales potential before test marketing is carried out. Discusses case application of ASSESSOR as illustration. Uses intercept interviews at a "lab" facility at shopping center. The steps

of the model implementation include: Premeasurement for established trends; Exposure to ads for establishment of new brand; Measurement of reactions to advertising materials; Simulated shopping trip; Purchase opportunity; Home use/consumption; Post-usage measurement (phone interview).

2.145   TAUBER, EDWARD M. (1977), "Forecasting Sales Prior
         to Test Market," Journal of Marketing, 41(1), 80-85.
    Four systems for forecasting are reviewed. 1. Concept and product tests. 2. Historical data regression models. 3. Laboratory test markets. 4. Sales wave experiments. Three types of new products are considered: a) line extensions and ne-too items; b) new products that are not easy to classify into existing product categories but require no change in consumer usage habits; c) new product requiring a change in consumer behavior.

2.146   URBAN, GLEN L. (1975), "Perceptor: A Model for
         Product Positioning," Management Science, 21(8),
         858-871.
    This paper proposes a model (PERCEPTOR) and a measurement methodology to aid in product design for frequently purchased consumer products. The model is based on a trial and repeat process that produces an estimate of long-run share. Multidimensional scaling procedures are used to relate product attributes to trial and repeat probabilities. Several tests and recommencations for use by managers are presented.

2.147   URBAN, GLEN L. AND GERALD M. KATZ (1983),
         "Pre-Test-Market Models: Validation and Managerial
         Implications," Journal of Marketing Research, 20(3),
         221-234.
    Discusses and analyzes the pre-test-market model ASSESSOR. 63% of products tested passed pre-test screen. 66% of these were successful in test market. Bayesian decision analysis model is formulated; "typical" case shows positive value of information. Authors conclude that both pre-test-market and test-market procedures should be used in almost all cases.

2.148   URBAN, GLEN L., GERALD M. KATZ, THOMAS E. HOTCH AND
         ALVIN J. SILK (1983), "The ASSESSOR Pre-Test-Market
         Evaluation System," Interfaces, 13(6), 38-59.
    Overview of ASSESSOR pre-test-market model. Discusses market evaluation system with excerpts from frequent users of the system.

2.149   YANKELOVICH, SKELLY AND WHITE, INC. (1981), "LTM
         Estimating Procedures," New Product Forecasting:
         Models and Applications, Lexington, MA: Lexington
         Books.
    Laboratory test market procedure made available by Yankelovich, Skelly and White is described. It has been extensively used and validated: predictions made by this procedure were reliable indicators of the results of subsequent test markets. The procedure models laboratory store sales as a function of a "novelty" factor, a "clout" factor (relative intensity of promotion effort), repeat rate, usage factor and a judgmental corrective factor.

FINANCIAL ANALYSIS AND RISK REDUCTION

2.150   AYERS, F. THOMAS (1977), "The Management of
         Technological Risk," Research Management, 20(6), 24-
         28.
    Suggests applying technology forecasting, technical
assessment and alternate futures analysis to yield better
risk/return decisions.

2.151   CARDOZO, RICHARD N. AND DAVID K. SMITH, JR. (1983),
         "Applying Financial Portfolio Theory to Product
         Portfolio Decisions: An Empirical Study," Journal of
         Marketing, 47 (Spring), 110-119.
    This paper investigates the use of concepts from financial
portfolio theory in the analysis and management of product
portfolios. Financial portfolio theory can be integrated into
product portfolio analysis with some modification. The authors
discuss provides a framework for identifying and investigating
questions about organizational resource management.

2.152   COCHRAN, EDWARD B., ALAN L. PATZ AND ALAN J. ROWE
         (1978), "Concurrency and Disruption in New Product
         Innovation," California Management Review, 21(1),
         21-34.
    Cost and schedule overruns may occur for commercial and
military projects involving technical innovation, resulting in
several uncertainties. This article examines the role of
uncertainty arising from a rush to capitalize on technical
innovation. The uncertainties and level urgency must be
recognized in order for good estimates of cost and delivery
performance to be developed, as well as sound management
strategies. Examples discussed: BART, Alaska pipeline, short
range attack missile.

2.153   CONRAD, S.A. (1976), "Sampling Information in New
         Product Marketing," Omega, 4(1), 93-96.
    The traditional evaluation of a new product proposal is a
determination of the area break-even volume, without
consideration of the uncertain nature of the data. In this
paper sampling information is used to reduce uncertainty. The
optimal number of customers to be sampled is determined for a
proposal formulated in terms of an expected market share.

2.154   PESSEMIER, EDGAR A. (1982), "Strategy Development for
         New Product Introduction: Predicting Market and
         Financial Success," TIMS Studies in the Management
         Sciences, 18, 85-98.
    This paper describes the ADOPTEST model, used for evaluation
of marketing strategies for a potential new product. The
influences of policy variables on financial success are
demonstrated. The model can handle the data requirements and
structural properties of most real-life new product problems.

2.155   RABINO, SAMUEL AND ARNOLD WRIGHT (1985), "Financial
         Evaluation of the Product Line," Journal of Product
         Innovation Management, 2(1), 56-65.

Authors suggest use of "project beta" which shows the impact of risk of individual product on risk of the whole portfolio of products (related to Beta in financial analysis). Article suggests other ways to "sharpen" financial picture in marketing evaluation of new product projects.

PRODUCT DEVELOPMENT AND TESTING

Management of Product Development

2.156   CHATTERJEE, RABIKAR, JEHOSHUA ELIASHBERG, HUBERT
        GATIGNON AND LEONARD M. LODISH (1988), "A Practical
        Bayesian Approach to Selection of Optimal Market
        Testing Strategies," Journal of Marketing Research,
        25(4), 363-375.
The paper presents a methodology and decision model for selection of market testing strategies. A Bayesian decision theoretic framework is used that: 1. considers continuously distributed payoffs; 2. permits updating of information on market response to strategies that are not being tested directly; 3. incorporates managers' attitudes toward risk. The methodology provides a practical, usable tool that can support design of market tests and provide insights into the market testing problem.

2.157   CLAUSING, D.P. (1985), "Product Development Process,"
        IEEE International Conference on Communications, 2,
        896-900.
A ten-step generic product development process is described, with emphasis on activities to achieve competitive position. Special attention is given to actions that can strongly improve common United States practice.

2.158   EDOSOMWAN, JOHNSON AIMIE (1988), "Implementing the
        Concept of Early Manufacturing Involvement (EMI) in
        the Design of a New Technology," Technology
        Management I: Proceedings of the First International
        Conference on Technology Management, Special
        Publication of the International Journal of
        Technology Management.
This paper presents a procedure for implementation of EMI, which if properly applied can reduce the need for engineering changes and rework in manufacturing after the concept has been released for production.   The advantages and difficulties involved in implementing EMI are discussed. EMI organizational and leadership models are also presented.

2.159   FOX, HAROLD W. (1985), "Strategies for New Product
        Research and Development," SAM Advanced Management
        Journal, 50(1), 26-30.
This paper discusses the benefits of productive R&D.   A recent study showed that the average profit contribution was more than $4 for every $1 of R&D expenditures during the preceding eight years.   Additional benefits to the public include better products, cleaner air, improved health and greater safety.   One of the "best practices" for new product

management is to develop a company-specific strategy for all projects. New product strategies developed from this corporate strategy will obtain greater long-term commitment.

2.160   GOLD, BELA (1987), "Approaches to Accelerating
         Product and Process Development," Journal of Product
         Innovation Management, 4(2), 81-88.
This paper examines how firms can reduce the time needed to develop new products. Key objectives are early market entry, and maximization of competitive advantage. The author discusses the potentials and limitations of different approaches to acceleration of the development process and presents strategic implications.

2.161   GUPTA, ASHOK AND DAVID WILEMON (1987), "Accelerating
         the New Product Development Process in High-
         Technology Organizations," Proceedings, IEEE
         Conference on Management and Technology.
This article focuses on the acceleration of the new product development process in technology-intensive organizations. The authors used a two-step approach, starting with a review of the literature on new product development processes to assess current practices, followed by interviews with individuals involved in product development. The authors conclude that it is imperative for the U.S. to maintain a level of expertise in, and to accelerate the process of, new product development or risk continued difficulty in global markets.

2.162   KRUBASIK, EDWARD G. (1988), "Customize Your Product
         Development," Harvard Business Review (November-
         December), 46-52.
Not all product development is alike. Extremes in development might be called "crash program" versus "perfect product." The issue is development speed versus risk reduction. Example: IBM uses eight-phase process for many products but not for the PC and cut development time by 2/3 in order to get foothold in market. A counterexample: Boeing 767 could not take those kinds of chances because of possibility of massive and irretrievable cost overruns. For them, getting it right is more important than doing it fast. Other examples given. Conclusion: choose development strategies that fit the situation.

2.163   LARSON, CLINT (1988), "Team Tactics Can Cut Product
         Development Costs," Journal of Business Strategy,
         8(5), 22-25.
Discussion of Honeywell's Building Controls Division, which used a team system for product development which cut the development cycle by over 50%. The production team is a multifunctional group of people within manufacturing, involved from the very start of each project, concerned with making certain that chosen designs mesh with manufacturing capabilities. Lead times were shortened, production costs were lowered, and product quality was improved.

2.164   SOUDER, WILLIAM E. (1978), "Effectiveness of Product
         Development Methods," Industrial Marketing
         Management, 7(5), 299-307.

Examines the most effective new product management methods under various conditions (well or poorly defined technological environment; well or poorly defined market environment).   In many cases the commercial project manager (marketing person appointed to manage product development team) or commercial line management are recommended methods.

2.165   TAKEUCHI, HIROTAKA AND IKUJIRO NONAKA (1986), "The New New Product Development Game," Harvard Business Review, 64(1), 137.
Looks at nine successful innovative firms, and the progress of specific products given six characteristics in managing new product development process.   They relate to team and organization momentum by: 1) built in stability; 2) self-organizing units; 3) overlapping phases; 4) multilearning. They also use 5) subtle control and 6) organizational transfer of control: osmosis.   Proposes a holistic "rugby" like approach to product development rather than usual sequential approach.   Each company must develop management style to promote process (new mission to be speedy and flexible).

Research Support for Product Development

2.166   ARMISTEAD, WILLIAM H. (1981), "Research and Development in Large Manufacturing Corporations," Research Management, 24(6), 28-33.
Published financial information can be used to measure how much large companies spend on R&D, and to examine the relationship between these expenditures and profit/sales growth.   Normal range of R&D spending is 20 - 33% of available earnings, with mature industries at the low end of this range and emerging high-tech industries at the high end.

2.167   CRAWFORD, C. MERLE (1977), "Marketing Research and the New Product Failure Rate," Journal of Marketing, 41(2), 51-61.
The author presents a series of hypotheses on why new products fail: a) product developers fail to define their decision process concisely and completely; b) new product decision-makers really do not understand the proper role for marketing research; c) marketing researchers fail to sell their services effectively; d) organizational rigidities are hindering the type of involvement essential to a successful marketing research program; e) the project system of marketing research department works contrary to the needs of new product development; f) the typical director of marketing research has defaulted on his responsibilities as keeper of the research conscience; g) a firm with a low product failure rate is passing up profitable risk; h) the system of new product development inherently produces counter-productive behavior; i) predicting new product sales and profit is an inherently impossible task.

2.168   GUERARD, JOHN B., JR., ALDEN S. BEAN AND STEVE ANDREWS (1987), "R&D Management and Corporate Financial Policy," Management Science, 33(11), 1419-1427.

An econometric model is developed to determine the firm's research, dividend, investment and new capital issue interdependence.

2.169   MORE, ROGER A. (1984), "Timing of Market Research in New Industrial Product Situations," Journal of Marketing, 48(4), 84-94.

This article discusses the timing of market research effort during the management of the new product development process. In this study, the timing of market research resource expenditures in 112 new industrial product situations is measured, and significant differences in timing, related to seven important situational characteristics, were found. These were: payoffs, payoff uncertainty, downsides, downsides uncertainty, search, timing and risk.

2.170   MORE, ROGER A. (1985), "Patterns of Market Research Timing for New Industrial Products," R&D Management, 15(4), 271-281.

In an article related to More (1984), the patterns of timing of market research resource expenditure in 112 industrial new product situations were measured. Differences were related to seven major situational characteristics: marketing task similarity, distribution complexity, competitive advantage, buyer risk, development complexity, project downsides and project payoffs. Differences in patterns of research timing were related to marketing task similarity, competitive advantage, and buyer risk.

2.171   RAELIN, J.A. AND R. BALACHANDRA (1985), "R&D Project Termination in High-Tech Industries," IEEE Transactions of Engineering Management, EM-32(1), 16-23.

51 R&D projects in high-tech companies were examined. Discriminant analysis of the data uncovered 16 factors influencing the decision to terminate a project in the development phase. Key discriminating factors were found to be the extent to which the project conformed to corporate, economic and marketing objectives. High rates of product turnover, high market share, and small size tended to lead to continuations, while infancy stage product life cycle and innovative versus aligned strategy led to terminations. Non-high-tech projects had greater likelihood for continuation if product turnover was low and projects had limited end uses.

Product Testing

2.172   BUCHANAN, BRUCE AND DONALD MORRISON (1985), "Measuring Simple Preferences: One Approach to Blind, Forced Choice Product Testing," Marketing Science, 4(2), 93-109.

An approach to designing blind, forced choice product tests and evaluating their results. Two types of tests examined: repeat paired comparisons; and several triangle tests of a simple paired comparison. Researchers can compare product test formats to see which one most efficiently estimates a given constraint. Can also gauge sample size requirements for a product test format and estimate confidence intervals.

2.173   DUTKA, SALOMON (1984), "Combining Tests of
         Significance in Test Marketing Research Experiments,"
         Journal of Marketing Research, 21(2), 118-119.
    Usually several test markets are set up to reflect different
marketing environments within which to test new product or
program. The author discusses how to use all the statistical
information available from such test market experiments. For
example, four tests may all come out non-significant but three
of them "lean" in one direction: these may be combined to get
overall significance using a chi-squared distribution test.

2.174   KLOMPMAKER, JAY E., G. DAVID HUGHES AND RUSSELL I.
         HALEY (1976), "Test Marketing in New Product
         Development," Harvard Business Review (May-June), 128.
    A good overview of new product development process in
general and relating it to test marketing. Answers: when to
conduct a test market, what can be learned from a test market,
how to use information from a test market. Brief discussion
of simulation models and test markets in the laboratory
setting.

2.175   PASKOWSKI, MARIANNE (1984), "New Tools Revolutionize
         New Product Testing," Marketing and Media Decisions,
         19(11), 76-78, 128-134.
    Electronic minimarkets and simulated test markets (SYM),
Behavior Scan, Nielsens's ERIM, IRI's FASTRAC. Pluses of these
tools are speed and accuracy in gathering information and
projecting winners. Minuses are inability to measure trade
response.

2.176   WATKINS, TREVOR (1984), "The Practice of Product
         Testing in the New Product Development Process: The
         Role of Model-Based Approaches," European Journal of
         Marketing, 18(6/7), 14-29.
    Examines the potential role of predictive models in the
product testing stage of new product development in the U.K.
confectionery industry. Evidence shown of two major types of
approaches to new product development: qualitative research
based and quantitative research based of which modeling was
one possibility. A universal belief (with agencies) in tailor-
made approach to market research in NPD (not standard
approach). Difficult to establish the validity of market
research methodologies.

TEST MARKETING

2.177   CLAYCAMP, H.J. AND L.E. LIDDY (1969), "Prediction of
         New Product Performance: An Analytical Approach,"
         Journal of Marketing Research, 6(11), 414-420.
    An approach to sales forecasting which models explicitly
the steps involved in the acquisition process: product
knowledge leads to trial which leads to repeat purchase.
Reportedly high predictive accuracy in prediction of trial.
Initial purchase model represents purchase as a function of
advertising recall (itself a function of advertising

variables), distribution, packaging, promotion, product satisfaction and category usage.

2.178   CRAWFORD, C. MERLE (1987), <u>New Products Management</u>, second edition, Homewood, IL: Irwin (Textbook).

2.179   ESKIN, G.J. (1973), "Dynamic Forecasts of New Product Demand Using a Depth of Repeat Model," <u>Journal of Marketing Research</u>, 19(5), 115-129.
A repeat purchase model used in market share forecasting. Like STEAM (Massy 1969) it uses the notion of "depth of repeat."

2.180   JAMIESON, LINDA F. AND FRANK M. BASS (1989), "Adjusting Stated Intention Measures to Predict Trial Purchase of New Products: A Comparison of Models and Methods," <u>Journal of Marketing Research</u>, 26(3), 336-345.
The authors, examining a set of data on purchase intention and behavior, compared several models of behavioral prediction for accuracy. Among the conclusions was that the researcher can improve predictive accuracy by using perceptions that modify the relationship between intentions and purchase.

2.181   LARRECHE, J.D. AND D.B. MONTGOMERY (1977), "A Framework for the Comparison of Marketing Models: A Delphi Study," <u>Journal of Marketing Research</u>, 19(11), 487-498.
Compares pretest and test market models on the basis of structure, adaptability, completeness, ease of use, etc. Test market models included are STEAM and SPRINTER. The article discusses part of the results of a Delphi probe into the use and evaluation of marketing models. It reports on the "likelihood of acceptance" of each of the models tested and rates the NEWS and Ayer models highest.

2.182   LEARNER, D. (1968), "Profit Maximization Through New Product Market Planning and Control," <u>Applications of the Sciences in Marketing Management</u>, New York: Wiley.
DEMON: Decision Mapping via Optimum "Go/No-Go" Networks. A model designed to help managers evaluate alternative plans for new product introductions. Assesses impact of advertising, promotion and distribution levels on awareness, trial and use. Uses this information to build a usage function. Helps managers search for an "optimal" path through a total information network. Management may add constraints on payback period, minimum acceptable profit levels, marketing research budget available, etc.

2.183   LILIEN, G.L., A.G. RAO AND S. KALISH (1981), "Bayesian Estimation and Control of Detailing Effort in a Repeat-Purchase Diffusion Environment," <u>Management Science</u>, 27(5), 495-506.
The article develops a model and estimation procedure for forecasting and controling rate of new product sales. A repeat purchase diffusion model is used, incorporating the effect of marketing variables (detailing force effects in particular) as

well as a word-of-mouth effect. Bayesian procedures are used
to estimate and update the parameters of the model.

2.184   MAHAJAN, V. AND E. MULLER (1982), "Innovation
         Behavior and Repeat Purchase Diffusion Models,"
         Proceedings, AMA Educators Conference, Chicago, IL:
         American Marketing Association, 456-460.
     Compares the adoption-diffusion submodels in each of a
number of pre-test and test market models including STEAM,
Ayer, NEWPROD, SPRINTER, TRACKER and others. Does not examine
implementation issues nor does it identify which is the "best"
model, although SPRINTER did rate highly on most of the
characteristics studied.

2.185   MASSEY, W.F. (1969), "Forecasting the Demand for New
         Convenience Products," Journal of Marketing Research,
         6(11), 405-412.
     STEAM: A repeat-purchase model which is based on the "depth
of repeat" notion. It is quite complex and detailed and
assumes heterogeneous tastes in the population and different
propensities to enter different depth of trial classes.

2.186   MESAK, H.I. AND W.M. MIKHAIL (1988), "Prelaunch
         Sales Forecasting of a New Industrial Product,"
         Omega, 16(1), 41-51.
     Presents a quantitative approach that aims principally at
forecasting sales of a new entrant, before its actual launch
in a competitive market of a recently introduced industrial
product. The research offers ways of operationalizing existing
first purchase and repeat purchase models together with am
entry market share model to actual limited historical data
about the diffusion process in a case study. The approach
should help a firm in making a sound strategic decision on
whether to enter a new business in the field of industrial
products.

2.187   NARASIMHAN, C. AND S.K. SEN (1983), "New Product
         Models for Test Market Data," Journal of Marketing,
         47 (Winter), 11-24.
     Compares test market models such as STEAM, SPRINTER,
NEWPROD, TRACKER, NEWS and others on dimensions of model
objective, number of stages modeled, level of complexity
handled, and likelihood of acceptance by product managers.
Very complete analysis, which identifies NEWS and TRACKER as
superior on the dimensions studied.

2.188   PARFITT, J.H. AND B.J.K. COLLINS (1968), "Use of
         Consumer Panels for Brandshare Prediction," Journal
         of Marketing Research, 5(5), 131-145.
     Uses panel data to forecast market shares. Long run share
is modeled as a function of ultimate penetration rate of the
brand, ultimate repeat-purchase rate and buying rate index of
repeat purchase of brand. Predictions can be made before
shares stabilize. In fact, they can be made as soon as
penetration curve and repeat purchase curve approach an
asymptotic value. So good predictions of long-run share may
be obtained early on in the product's life.

2.189   URBAN, G.L. (1970), "Sprinter Mod III: A Model for
the Analysis of New Frequently Purchased Consumer
Products," Operations Research, 18 (September-
October), 805-854.
A dynamic model for forecasting new product sales. Basic
versions model awareness-trial-repeat, which is dependent on
advertising dollars, appeal effectiveness and distribution
level. Measurements are obtained by questionnaires of ad
recall and intentions to purchase. The Mod III advanced
version explicitly incorporates more effects such as word-of-
mouth communication. Can be used in planning a test market,
charting early sales results, and projecting these results to
national sales levels.

2.190   URBAN, G.L. AND J.R. HAUSER (1980), Design and
Marketing of New Products, Englewood Cliffs, NJ:
Prentice-Hall (Textbook).

2.191   WIND, Y. (1981), Product Policy: Concepts, Methods
and Strategy, Reading, MA: Addison-Wesley (Textbook).

2.192   WIND, Y., V. MAHAJAN AND R. CARDOZO (1981), New
Product Forecasting, Lexington, MA: Lexington Books
(Textbook).

PRODUCT LAUNCH

Pioneering Advantages

2.193   CARPENTER, GREGORY S. AND KENT NAKAMOTO (1989),
"Consumer Preference Formation and Pioneering
Advantage," Journal of Marketing Research, 26(3),
285-298.
Pioneering advantage refers to the fact that market pioneers
often outsell later entrants, resulting in long-run market
share differences. This paper investigates the reasons for
pioneering advantage, and shows that it can arise from the
process by which consumers learn about brands and form their
preferences, not from entry barriers. Thus, if the preference
structure favors the pioneer it may be difficult for later
entrants to draw share, even if repositioning and switching
costs are minimal.

2.194   ELIASHBERG, JEHOSHUA AND THOMAS S. ROBERTSON (1988),
"New Product Preannouncing Behavior: A Market
Signaling Study," Journal of Marketing Research,
25(8), 282-292.
Exploratory empirical study of preannouncement of new
products. Premise: Preannouncement is a marketing
manifestation of signaling. Focus: Identify conditions that
will induce firms to preannounce new product introductions.
Preannouncement behavior can be explained by factors like:
market dominance, company size, attractiveness of competition,
environment, customer switching costs. Factors for
preannouncing firms: image enhancement, distribution
advantages, demand stimulation. Factors for non-preannouncing

firms: cannibalization, competitive reaction, inability to deliver, antitrust concern.

2.195   HAINES, DAVID W., RAJAN CHANDRAN AND ARVINDE PARKHE
        (1989), "Winning by Being the First to Market...Or
        Second?", Journal of Consumer Marketing (Winter), 63.
    Pioneering can lead to earning an entrenched position in consumers' minds; establishing an entry barrier in terms of quality, advertising and decision support; long-term market share advantages; etc. Disadvantages to pioneering can include difficulties in estimating market demand; entering seemingly promising markets that do not materialize; or uncertainties in which technology will eventually dominate the industry. The advantages to a follower strategy derive from lower costs and risks. Followers can also introduce superior manufacturing techniques or make improvements in the product design or in the marketing mix.

2.196   JONES, CHARLES (1985), "Strategic Issues in New
        Product Introductions," Journal of Advertising
        Research, 23 (April/May), 11-13.
    Presents success stories in the area of new product introductions. Provides a framework of strategy, organization and process for researchers who are involved with introducing new products to the market.

2.197   KALISH, SHLOMO, AND GARY L. LILIEN (1986), "A Market
        Entry Timing Model for New Technologies,"
        Management Science, 32(2), 194-205.
    A market diffusion model is developed that incorporates negative word-of-mouth associated with new product failure resulting from premature introduction. Analysis suggests that when introducing a new technology significant penalties may be associated with mistiming introduction.

2.198   MATTSON, BRUCE E. (1985), "Spotting a Market Gap for
        a New Product," Long Range Planning, 18(2), 87-93.
    Many new products and substitute technologies fail because they enter markets too late or with little price performance advantage. This paper is on locating and defining the boundaries of strategic entry windows for products/technologies. Strategic window is a dynamic time-projected view of the period of optimum fit between key requirements of the market and the competencies of the firm. Entry hurdles are distorted by the natural and systematic evolution of the market and its competitive environment (product cost and performance dimensions)--the firm's willingness and capability to surpass market-driven hurdles over the same period of time.

2.199   OLLEROS, FRANCESCO-JAVIER (1986), "Emerging
        Industries and the Burnout of Pioneers," Journal of
        Product Innovation Management, 3(1), 5-18.
    This study investigates why pioneering firms involved in radical product innovation often are fated to an early demise. The article discusses the merits and the limitations of technology-driven competitive strategies. Pioneer burnout can be caused by: a) externalities in the technical creation and

marketing creation process; b) high market uncertainty; c) high technological uncertainty.

2.200   SCHNAARS, STEPHEN P. (1986), "When Entering Growth Market, Are Pioneers Better Than Poachers?" *Business Horizons*, 29 (March/April), 27-36.

Discusses conditions under which pioneers, early entrants or later entrants have advantages in the market. Examines twelve well-publicized consumer growth markets such as Sony Walkman, disposable diapers and VCRs and shows that in about half of the cases, the pioneering brand ended up dominating the industry, and in the remaining cases, a later entrant proved to be dominant. Hence, both pioneering and "poaching" can have their risks.

2.201   URBAN, GLEN L., THERESE CARTER, STEVEN GASKIN, AND ZOFIA MUCHA (1986), "Market Share Rewards to Pioneering Brands: An Empirical Analysis and Strategic Implications," *Management Science*, 32(6), 645-659.

The authors present an empirical analysis of the relationship between brand order and market share, and find that there is an inverse relationship between the two. An initial sample of 82 brands across 24 categories was used to build the model and confirmation of the model was obtained via a holdout sample of 47 brands in 12 categories. Managerial implications for pioneers and later entrants are presented and discussed.

Policy Decision Issues

2.202   ANDREWS, KIRBY (1986), "Communication Imperatives for Products," *Journal of Advertising Research*, 26 (October/November), 29-32.

Reports on the results of Phase 1 analysis of television advertising for new products. Based on results, a list of nine communications imperatives for new product advertising are developed: capturing attention at beginning of commercial, building interest and involvement, communicating clearly, creating awareness of brand name, meeting advertisers' communication strategy, communication within a specified category, communication of some benefit of product difference, communication of support for product difference or benefit of product difference.

2.203   BASS, FRANK M. AND ALAIN V. BULTEZ (1982), "A Note on Optimal Strategic Pricing of Technological Innovation," *Marketing Science*, 1(4), 371-378.

A dynamic model of experience curve pricing. Optimal pricing policy depends on nature of dynamic demand and cost functions. Combines Bass (1980) demand function with experience curve cost function. Derives multiperiod pricing strategy.

2.204   BEARDEN, WILLIAM O. AND TERENCE A. SHIMP (1982), "The Use of Extrinsic Cues to Facilitate Product Adoption," *Journal of Marketing Research*, 19(2),

229-239.
Two field experiments conducted to explore effects of
varying levels of product warranty, manufacturer reputation
and price on consumer risk perceptions and affective responses
to new product concepts (tire and computerized jogging device).
Structural equation analysis revealed the important role of
warranties and other extrinsic cues in reducing consumers' risk
perceptions and enhancing their affective responses to
innovative product concepts.

2.205   DEAN, JOEL (1976), "Policies for New Products,"
         Harvard Business Review (November-December), 141.
Descriptively integrates pricing strategies to the dynamic
nature of new product's competitiveness cycle. Relates to
strategic position of product technologically and economically,
at different points in the new product's development cycle.
Discusses strategies and actions appropriate to Pioneering and
Maturity stages; discusses economic perspective and provides
many useful industrial examples.

2.206   JEULAND, ABEL P. AND ROBERT J. DOLAN (1982), "An
         Aspect of New Product Planning: Dynamic Pricing,"
         TIMS Studies in Management Sciences, 18, 1-21.
This study explores the dynamic relationship between demand
conditions and production costs and optimal product price
strategy. Popular theories of optimal price determination
largely ignore dynamic effects, despite the empirical evidence
suggesting that they should be considered. The article
presents a methodology for determining optimal pricing strategy
for the case where trial demand follows a diffusion process,
repeat purchasing is possible, and production costs are a
function of accumulated volume.

2.207   KALISH, SHLOMO (1983), "Monopolist Pricing with
         Dynamic Demand and Production Cost," Marketing
         Science, 2(2), 135-160.
Theoretical economics paper on monopolist pricing. Demand
and cost functions are dynamic, and optimal price changes as
new product diffuses. Determines price paths under varying
conditions of interest rate, saturation factors, learning curve
and word of mouth. Implications for policymaking are
discussed.

2.208   KARNANI, ANEEL (1984), "The Value of Market Share and
         the Product Life Cycle--a Game-Theoretic Model,"
         Management Science, 30(6), 696-712.
Presents a dynamic game-theoretic model of marketing
competition in an oligopoly in which firms sell differentiated
products.

2.209   MAHAJAN, VIJAY, SUBHASH SHARMA AND YORAM WIND (1985),
         "Assessing the Impact of Patent Infringement on New
         Product Sales," Technological Forecasting and Social
         Change, 28(1), 13-27.
In order to assess the impact of patent infringement on new
product sales, a model is developed through the intervention
model development process. Physical interpretations of model
parameters and determination of associated damages suggest that

the model can provide a sound basis for analyzing patent infringement disputes.

2.210   MONTGOMERY, DAVID B. (1975), "New Product
         Distribution: an Analysis of Supermarket Buyer
         Decisions," Journal of Marketing Research, 12
         (August), 255-264.
Explores relationship between 18 variables and a supermarket buyer's decision to accept or reject a new product. Multiple discriminant analysis and a hierarchical threshold model are used. Variables: promotion, company reputation, quality, newness, introductory allowances, competition, packaging, gross margin, advertising, private label, guarantee, distribution, broker, sales presentation, category volume and growth potential, shelf space, cost.

2.211   MOORE, WILLIAM B. AND DONALD R. LEHMANN (1982),
         "Effects of Usage and Name on Perceptions of New
         Products," Marketing Science, 1(4), 351-370.
Uses multidimensional scaling to test configural invariance hypothesis, i.e., perceptions of existing brands are not changed by introduction of new brands that are relatively different. Results: similarity judgments only stable for old brands. Similarity judgments for new brands more stable if descriptive names used. Consumption and information acquisition had little impact. Note: Types of bread (rye, pumpernickel) and not real "brands" were used.

2.212   SMITH, STEPHEN A. (1986), "New Product Pricing in
         Quality Sensitive Markets," Marketing Science, 5(1),
         70-87.
The article discusses pricing of a new product in a market having competing products of differing qualities and market penetration levels. Each customer type selects optimal product based on maximizing consumer surplus. Pricing policies for a new product determined for seller based on cumulative profit maximization.

2.213   TAUBER, EDWARD M. (1981), "Brand Franchise
         Extension: How Products Benefit from Existing Brand
         Names," Business Horizons, 24(2), 36-41.
Distinguishes how brand franchise extensions differ from other opportunities. Outlines their benefits and drawbacks, specifies some conditions under which they should be used, and provides an overview of a procedure for identifying and evaluating alternative extensions for a given brand name.

2.214   THOMAS, JOSEPH ANDREW AND PREM CHKABRIA (1975),
         "Bayesian Models for New Product Pricing," Decision
         Sciences, 6(1), 51-64.
Develops an information decision system for new product pricing based on Bayesian updating of prior estimates of demand distribution parameter values and on optimization by dynamic programming. The model considers the interaction of production and pricing decisions and emphasizes the simultaneous making of both decisions.

2.215   THOMPSON, GERALD R. AND JINN-TSAIR TENG (1984),

"Optimal Pricing and Advertising Policies for New
Product Oligopoly Models," Marketing Science, 3(2),
148-168.

Model of new product oligopoly. Contains: Bass demand
growth model, Vidale-Wolfe and Ozga advertising model,
production learning curve, exponential demand function, pricing
and advertising control variables are optimized. Theoretical
derivation of monopoly case provided. Then, oligopolistic
models are derived as non-zero-sum differential games.

2.216   WERNERFELT, BIRGER (1985), "The Dynamics of Prices
         and Market Share over the Product Life Cycle,"
         Management Science, 31(8), 928-939.
A mathematical representation of the Boston Consulting Group
(BCG) hypothesis. Analysis reconstructs BCG argument for early
growth maximization.   It is demonstrated that a firm may
growth-maximize early, but never late in life cycle. Only the
low price firm will pay for informative advertising, whereas
both firms in a duopoly will pay for persuasive advertising,
though less if their market shares are very different.

2.217   ZINKHAM, GEORGE M. AND CLAUDE R. MARTIN JR. (1987),
         "New Brand Names and Inferential Beliefs: Some
         Insights on Naming New Products," Journal of Business
         Research, 15(April), 157-172.
Consumers' attitudes toward names were studied and evidence
was   found   that   attitude   toward   a   brand   name   exists
independently of attitude toward a product or brand. A method
for measuring attitudes toward names is demonstrated.   In a
multiple regression setting, four predictor variables (number
of purchases, product interest, cognitive differentiation and
product experience) were found to explain up to 34% of the
variance associated with brand name attitudes.

2.218   ZUFRYDEN, FRED S. (1982), "A General Model of
         Assessing New Product Marketing Decisions and Market
         Performance," TIMS Studies in the Management
         Sciences, 18, 63-83.
The author proposes a generalized model for prediction of
market performance of new, frequently purchased consumer
brands. The model can run on data from either a pre-launch
test market or a short introductory sales period. Variables
that may be included in the model are pricing, promotion,
advertising media decisions, and product characteristics, and
also segmentation characteristics of target markets.

3

Product Diffusion Forecasting

INTRODUCTION

The forecasting of potential outcomes, whether sales, profit, or market share, occurs at every stage of the new product development process. At each stage, the firm must decide whether to continue or abandon development. Forecasts of future sales form the basis for much of this analysis. The forecast of adoption rates for a new product is undoubtedly a critical component of many new-product development decisions, yet it is often poorly done. Berenson and Schnaars (1986) presented several examples of wildly optimistic forecasts of market growth (as well as some accurate ones) and noted some of the reasons for mistaken forecasts. These included: relying on poor assumptions, failing to stress fundamentals (such as who the real customer for the new product would be), and being dazzled by new technology or the latest fad. Clearly, sales forecasting is not only a critical input to the new-product development process; it is also a difficult task.

Various classification schemes have been suggested for new-product forecasting models. Probably the most complete classification scheme was presented by Wind (1981) in the book New Product Forecasting. Classifications were based on eight sets of characteristics: purpose, type of products or services, unit and level of analysis, model format, dependent variable, independent variables, data requirements and analytical procedures. An alternative scheme was suggested in Assmus (1984): trial-repeat models and competitive structure models. In addition to the work of Assmus and Wind, several excellent review articles have provided comparative evaluations of these models (Mahajan and Muller, 1979; Geurts and Reinmuth, 1980; Tauber 1977; Easingwood, Mahajan, and Muller, 1983; Rao, 1985; and Mahajan and Wind, 1988). For a good overview of technological forecasting techniques, see Martino (1980), who described techniques such as cross-impact analysis, trend-impact analysis, and growth curves, in addition to models of forecasting. Alternate sources are Wheelwright and Makridakis (1980) who provided a survey of forecasting methods useful in technology forecasting, and Utterback (1979) who focused on methods for environmental forecasting.

(Note: This chapter focuses on models used in the forecasting of product adoption and diffusion. The Tauber, 1977; Assmus, 1984 and Mahajan and Wind, 1988 articles included discussions of pre-test-marketing and test-marketing models as well as product diffusion models. The reader interested in further information on these other kinds of forecasting models is directed to the stages in new product development chapter of this book.)

Most of the articles on new-product diffusion are technical in nature and formally present model specifications and assumptions. The majority of these articles were published in mathematically oriented journals such as Management Science and Marketing Science, and operations research and forecasting journals.

THE BASS DIFFUSION MODEL

Original Model and Extensions

According to Assmus (1984), diffusion models "explain trial purchases by forecasting the adoption and imitation process with the population of potential buyers" (p. 122). The most popular early diffusion model is the model of adoption of consumer durables proposed by Bass (1969). The model postulated that the adoption of an innovation depends upon a communication process. The new product is first adopted by a few innovators, who in turn generate word-of-mouth communication, influencing others to imitate their adoptive behavior.   The adoption process was modeled as an S-shaped curve (that is, slow initial growth, followed by rapid growth, finally slowing down as market sales approach potential). The model was designed to predict length of time to maturity and volume of yearly sales at maturity, based on a small number of early observations. These observations are used to estimate several parameters which characterize the nature of the diffusion process: the coefficient of external influence (imitation),   the   coefficient   of   internal   influence (innovation), and market potential.

Applications, extensions and variations of the Bass diffusion model have appeared in the subsequent literature. Heeler and Hustad (1980) applied the model to an international setting, noting several limitations to its use. Tigert and Farivar (1981) assessed its   performance in forecasting quarterly and annual sales of optical scanning equipment. Schmittlein and Mahajan (1982) compared two methods for estimating the parameters of the model, ordinary-least-squares and maximum likelihood, and showed the latter to provide more accurate forecasts. However, a follow-up study by Srinivasan and Mason (1986) suggested some problems with this approach. Norton and Bass (1987) further extended the model by including the effects of diffusion and substitution.

Refinements of Bass Model

An excellent review article, presenting a critique of these and several other diffusion models, was written by Mahajan, Muller, and Bass (1990). They traced the development of the diffusion modeling literature from the simplest models to extensions such as those described above. They discussed the data requirements of the Bass model in terms of the key parameters which must be estimated (coefficients of imitation, innovation, and market potential). Note that, in many cases of interest, no prior data will be available, and management judgment, or comparison to an analogous product, must be involved in the parameter estimation procedure.

Mahajan, Muller, and Bass (1990) succinctly summarized the major limiting assumptions of the original Bass (1969) model, which stimulated the refinements and extensions represented in the later articles. Nine key limitations exist:

Limitation 1. Market potential of the new product remains constant over time. There is no reason to believe this will always be the case, and several articles (Kalish, 1985, for example) have sought to incorporate a level of uncertainty or variability into the market potential estimate.

Limitation 2. Diffusion of an innovation is independent of all other innovations. Other innovations may stimulate the diffusion of a new product (for example, the rapid diffusion of compact discs increased the diffusion rate of CD players), or may slow it down or even cause it to stop abruptly (the success of VCR tapes and players hindered market acceptance of videodisc technology).

Limitation 3. The nature of an innovation does not change over time. The Bass (1969) model implied that the innovation is unchanging, whereas in high-technology product classes such as microcomputer software, several generations of product may be brought out over the diffusion period, each providing additional benefits and features. This may also affect the rate of diffusion: potential adopters who know Lotus 1-2-3, Version 3 is about to be launched may delay purchase of the Version 2 product. An additional twist in this scenario is that, if the long-awaited product does not live up to expectations, serious slowdowns in brand diffusion could be incurred (consider the failure of Osborne portable microcomputers).

Limitation 4. The geographic boundaries of the social system do not change over the diffusion process. The Bass (1969) and other later models did not adequately account for the diffusion of products in space as well as through time.

Limitation 5. The diffusion process is binary. The Bass (1969) model presumed each potential adopter is in one of two classes: adopts the innovation or does not adopt the innovation. The adoption process (A-T-R or some variant) is not explicitly contained in it. Several of the articles cited above have sought to incorporate a form of the adoption process into a diffusion model (Mahajan, Muller, and Kerin, 1984; Dodson and Muller, 1978; Kalish 1985). Dodson and Muller (1978) explicitly modeled the interaction between adopters and non-adopters of the product making certain assumptions about adopter behavior, and incorporated the influence of advertising on the process. Mahajan, Muller, and Kerin (1984) developed an introduction strategy for products which may be receiving either negative or positive word of mouth and also discussed implications for advertising policy.

Limitation 6. Diffusion is not influenced by marketing strategies. Numerous articles have sought to generalize the diffusion model by incorporating the effects of advertising, pricing and other policies controllable by the firm (De Palma, Droesbeke, Leflure, and Rosinski, 1986).

Several of these studies have examined the role of information sources such as advertising and word of mouth. Horsky and Simon (1983), in an empirical study of the adoption of telephone banking, showed that advertising accelerated the diffusion process. They also made practical recommendations to managers: advertising is most beneficial to the adoption process at early stages of introduction, and levels should be cut back as sales increase and the product progresses through the life cycle. Mahajan and Muller (1986) compared "pulsed" to uniform advertising policies and showed the effects of each on awareness levels (see also Mahajan, 1986). Optimal advertising policy during diffusion for a firm in a monopolistic market was discussed by Dockner and Jorgensen (1988).

Pricing, distribution, and other policies have been the subject of other generalizations of the diffusion model. Robinson and Lakhani (1975) solved for the optimum time path of price in a dynamic model of pricing policy for a new product. Berkowitz (1982) presented two models that were based on the concept that consumer purchase decisions reflect a reaction to the characteristics offered by a product. He illustrated his model with an application to residential solar heating in Canada. Kalish and Lilien (1983) modeled price subsidies and the effect of word of mouth on diffusion. Scott and Kaiser (1984) operationalized market acceptance as a function of price, product attributes and environmental factors. Kalish (1985) presented a model which incorporated dynamic pricing and advertising through time. Heeler (1986) studied the effects of distribution on the diffusion process. Diffusion acts both directly upon product adoption and indirectly as an interactive partner with advertising in generating awareness.

Another extension was presented by Wind, Robertson, and Fraser (1982). They recommended that diffusion patterns be forecast by market segment, which should lead to increased accuracy and greater effectiveness of the marketing effort. A method for modeling diffusion, market structure, and market power on either the buyer's or the seller's side was developed by Quirmbach (1986).

Limitation 7. Product and market characteristics do not influence diffusion patterns. It might be expected that product or market characteristics can affect the diffusion of an innovation. Mahajan, Muller, and Bass (1990) provided several examples of empirical studies which have shown this to be the case. However product and market characteristics are not explicitly modeled in the original Bass (1969) model nor in most of the extensions to this model.

Limitation 8. There are no supply restrictions. The Bass (1969) and subsequent models are models of demand and typically do not account for the case in which product diffusion is slowed by insufficient supply.

Limitation 9. There is only one adoption by an adopting unit. The Bass (1969) model was a model of first-time adoption and cannot model repeat or replacement purchases.   A few diffusion models have attempted to model this aspect of the diffusion process.   For example, Kamakura and Balasubramanian (1987) proposed a model that integrated two distinct components of demand for durable goods: adoption and replacement. Mahajan, Muller, and Bass (1990) provided examples of other studies exploring replacement as well as adoption.

OTHER DIFFUSION MODELS

Several authors have presented other models of product diffusion, and these are briefly reviewed here. Mahajan and Peterson (1978) examined the time pattern of the diffusion process using a dynamic model of diffusion. They presented several empirical examples, including the sales of washing machines in the United States.   Lilien (1980) developed a simple model that investigated the issue of control of the new product diffusion process. Infaseno (1986) compared consumer likelihood-of-purchase ratings to actual post-introduction purchase behavior, and used this information to develop and test a model for forecasting new-product sales. Sirinaovakul and Czajkiewicz (1988) investigated factors leading to the diffusion of an advanced manufacturing technology from region to region, using a spatial diffusion model.   Finally, Easingwood (1988) presented a generalized diffusion model which explained many very different diffusion paths.

DIRECTIONS FOR FUTURE RESEARCH

Mahajan, Muller and Bass (1990) provide a detailed guideline for future research in diffusion process modelling. They discuss five areas which are deserving of more attention:
1. Adoptions due to internal influence. Since adopters may be influenced by external or internal factors (the Bass 1969 model makes this explicit), can one distinguish between these two kinds of adopters? What are the characteristics of those adopters who are largely influenced by external sources?
2. Multiple adoptions.   Expecially in the case of industrial products, certain innovations will be adopted in multiple units by some customers (for example, a business firm may buy several microcomputers or copies of a new software application).   The equation driving the diffusion model must take into account multiple-unit adoption behavior of certain potential customers.
3. Effect of consumer expectations. Consumer expectations relative to price, performance, or other product aspects are likely to play an important role in the rate of diffusion. This has received scant attention up to now but ought to be addressed in future research.
4. Exploration of recent developments in hazard models. The "hazard rate" is simply the probability that an individual who is a nonadopter at time t will adopt in time t+1. Bass (1969) modeled this as a simple linear function. Over the past twenty years, much progress has been made in the statistical and related literature on the development of hazard models. There is room for improvement here; for example, advertising

and other marketing mix effects could be considered covariates having effects upon the hazard rate.   In fact, hazard modeling may be an interesting way to model marketing mix effects upon diffusion rates.

5. Understanding of diffusion processes at the micro (individual) level. The models presented above focus mostly on the macro, societal level of product diffusion.   More work needs to be done in modeling the patterns of social interaction at the individual level which affect the diffusion process.

In addition to these five areas for further research, Mahajan, Muller and Bass (1990) briefly discuss several other potential refinements to the Bass (1969) model. Many of these are related to the abovementioned limitations of the existing diffusion models.

PRODUCT DIFFUSION FORECASTING: ANNOTATED BIBLIOGRAPHY

INTRODUCTION

3.1   ASSMUS, GERT (1984), "New Product Forecasts," _Journal of Forecasting_, 3(2), 121-138.
Presents a review of new product forecasting techniques with an emphasis on the more recent developments in forecasting models.   Then, forecasting procedures are assessed by discussing their benefits and their costs.   The third part of the article discusses trends in new product forecasting.

3.2   BERENSON, C. AND S. SCHNAARS (1986), "Growth Market Forecasting Revisited," _California Management Review_, (Summer).
Growth market forecasts are often in error and sometimes wildly optimistic.   The authors present several examples of accurate and mistaken growth market forecasts and present several recommendations for improvements of forecasts.   These include: checking assumptions, stressing fundamentals (such as, 'who really are the customers for this product?'), avoiding euphoria and being dazzled by new technology, and staying flexible.

3.3   EASINGWOOD, CHRISTOPHER J., VIJAY MAHAJAN AND EITAN MULLER (1983), "A Nonuniform Influence Innovation Diffusion Model of New Product Acceptance," _Marketing Science_, 2(3), 273-295.
Excellent review of previous new product diffusion models: Bass, Mansfield, Gompertz curve, Floyd, Sharif-Kabir, Jeuland. Proposes NUI (Non-Uniform Influence) Innovation Model which overcomes three limitations of these models: 1) Allows word-of-mouth effect to systematically vary over time. 2) Allows diffusion curves to be nonsymmetrical (before and after location of maximum penetration rate). 3) Does not restrict location of inflection point for the diffusion curves. Empirical testing is presented for five consumer durables. Results are far superior to the Bass model.   Suggests that simple Bass model fist with some data and not with others because of the restrictive assumptions mentioned above.

3.4   GEURTS, MICHAEL D. AND JAMES E. REENMUTH (1980), "New
       Product Sales Forecasting Without Post Sales Data,"
       European Journal of Operations Research, 4(2),
       84-94.
Reviews various types of approaches to building forecasting
models that can be used to forecast sales prior to the product
introduction. Approaches covered: Bass, Massy, Assmus, Geurts,
others.

3.5   MAHAJAN, VIJAY AND EITAN MULLER (1979), "Innovation
       Diffusion and New Product Growth Models in
       Marketing," Journal of Marketing, 43(4), 55-68.
Review and assessment of diffusion models of new product
acceptance (first-purchase): Bass (1969), Fourt and Woodlock
(1961), Mansfield (1961), Gompertz curve (1972), Lekvall and
Wahlbin (1973). Extensions: Robinson and Lakhani (1975),
Horsky and Simon (1978), Lilien and Rao (1978), Bass (1978),
Peterson and Mahajan (1978), Mahajan and Peterson (1978),
Mahajan et al. (1979), Dodson and Muller (1978), Chow (1967),
Lockman (1978).

3.6   MAHAJAN, VIJAY AND YORAM WIND (1988), "New Product
       Forecasting Models: Directions for Research and
       Implementation," International Journal of
       Forecasting, 4(3), 341-358.
Evaluates strengths and weaknesses of new product
forecasting models and outlines a research agenda to enhance
their implementation and further development. Summarized eight
review articles including criteria used, specific models
included and a remarks section.

3.7   MARTINO, JOSEPH P. (1980), "Technological
       Forecasting: An Overview," Management Science, 28(1),
       28-33.
Overview of technological forecasting techniques. 1)
Modeling: most common means of technological forecasting; 2)
cross impact; 3) trend impact analysis; 4) growth curves; 5)
scoring model; 6) probabilistic system dynamics; 7)
technological progress function.

3.8   RAO, SANJAY-KUMAR (1985), "An Empirical Comparison of
       Sales Forecasting Models," Journal of Product
       Innovation Management, 2(4), 232-242.
Compares empirically the following forecasting models:
Mansfield, Martino, Bass, Non-uniform Influence (NUI) and
others. The NUI performed best overall and can accommodate
several kinds of symmetric and non-symmetric shapes. The
Martino model was almost as good as the NUI and was simpler to
estimate.

3.9   UTTERBACK, JAMES M. (1979), "Environmental Analysis
       and Forecasting," Strategic Management: A New View of
       Business Policy and Planning, Boston: Little, Brown.
This paper focuses on the firm's environment (the economics,
technological, social, political and institutional context
within which it operates), and on how firms have attempted to
analyze and forecast their environments as an input to the
process of accommodation of the firm to changes occurring in

the outside world.   Specific methods for environmental forecasting are discussed in detail including trend extension and Delphi probes.

3.10   WHEELWRIGHT, STEVEN C. AND SPYROS MAKRIDAKIS (1980), "Technological Forecasting," <u>Forecasting Methods for Management</u>, third edition, New York: Wiley, 267-288.
Technological forecasting is far from a science.   The authors discuss the importance of forecasting the technological future and survey the methods available for this purpose.

THE BASS DIFFUSION MODEL

Original Model and Extensions

3.11   BASS, FRANK M. (1969), "A New Product Growth Model for Consumer Durables," <u>Management Science</u>, 15(1), 215-227.
A significant model of the diffusion of innovations.   The adoption of a new consumer durable good is modeled as a communication process in which innovators are the first adopters, influencing others who imitate their adoptive behavior by word-of-mouth communication.   Several extensions and modifications have been presented in subsequent literature.

3.12   HEELER, ROGER M. AND THOMAS P. HUSTAD (1980), "Problems in Predicting New Product Growth for Consumer Durables," <u>Management Science</u>, 26(10), 1007-1020.
A popular model of new product diffusion (Bass') is applied in an international setting.   Several limitations on its use are noted: instability with limited data, environmental differences, and systematic underreporting of estimated time to attain peak level of first purchase sales.

3.13   MAHAJAN, VIJAY AND YORAM WIND (1986), <u>Innovation Diffusion Models of New Product Acceptance</u>, Cambridge, MA: Ballinger (Textbook).

3.14   MORE, ROGER A. AND BLAIR LITTLE (1980), "The Application of Discriminant Analysis to the Production of Sales Forecast Uncertainty in New Product Situations," <u>Journal of the Operations Research Society</u>, 31(1), 71-77.
Presents a conceptual model relating the error in the first year's sales forecast to marketing task similarity and marketing task complexity (which in turn was a function of buyer risk, distribution difficulty, and competitive advantage).   Data from 185 new product situations were collected by personal interview and self-administered questionnaire from 152 Canadian firms.   The discriminant function did somewhat better than chance in identifying the high risk introduction (over 20% error in unit sales) when tested in a hold-out sample.   This test was flawed because respondents knew the outcome.

3.15   NORTON, JOHN A. AND FRANK M. BASS (1987), "A
        Diffusion Theory Model of Adoption and Substitution
        for Successive Generations of High-Technology
        Products," Management Science, 33(9), 1069-1086.
This study deals with the dynamic sales behavior of
successful generations of high-tech products. Built upon the
Bass diffusion model. The paper develops a model which
encompasses both diffusion and substitution and demonstrates
forecasting properties of the model.

3.16   OREN, SHMUEL AND MICHAEL ROTHKOPF (1984), "A Market
        Dynamics Model for New Industrial Products and Its
        Application," Marketing Science, 2 (Summer),
        247-265.
New product planning models usually provide theoretical
market shares, based on consumer preferences under idealized
conditions, as output. This paper describes a class of models
that bridge the gap between theoretical market shares and
dynamic sales forecasts. Model accounts for differences in:
customer awareness for different products, product announcement
dates, product availability, marketing efforts, customer
inertia, customer purchasing delays. Example provided: high
speed non-impact computer printers.

3.17   OREN, SHMUEL S., MICHAEL H. ROTHKOPF, AND RICHARD G.
        SMALLWOOD (1980), "Evaluating a New Market: A
        Forecasting System for Nonimpact Computer Printers,"
        Interfaces, 10(6), 76-87.
Description of market-research-based forecasting system for
high speed computer printers developed at Xerox. Produced as
multi-stage forecasting model. Operations research scientists,
market researchers and planners worked together in the project.

3.18   SCHMITTLEIN, DAVID C. (1982), "Maximum Likelihood
        Estimation for an Innovation Diffusion Model of New
        Product Acceptance," Marketing Science, 1(1), 57-78.
Proposes maximum likelihood estimation for Bass model of
new product diffusion. Examples show that the maximum
likelihood forecasting provides more accurate forecasts than
ordinary least squares estimates. However, standard linear
regression cannot be used to estimate the model.

3.19   SRINIVASAN, V. AND CHARLOTTE H. MASON (1986),
        "Nonlinear Least Squares Estimations of New Product
        Diffusion Models," Marketing Science, 5(2), 169-178.
Followup to Schmittlein and Mahajan (1982) which improved
the Bass diffusion model by maximum likelihood estimation.
This paper argues that by looking only at sampling errors and
ignoring, for example, effects of excluded marketing variables,
Schmittlein and Mahajan seriously underestimated standard
errors of the estimated parameters. Proposes Nonlinear Least
Squares (NLS) approach which produces valid standard error
estimates. Fit and prediction validity of both approaches
comparable in an empirical analysis. NLS may also be
appropriate for other diffusion models.

3.20   TIGERT, DOUGLAS AND BEHROOZ FARIVAR (1981), "The
        Bass New Product Growth Model: A Sensitivity Analysis

for a High Technology Product," <u>Journal of Marketing</u>,
45(4), 81-90.

Assesses the performance of the Bass new product growth
model in forecasting quarterly and annual sales of optical
scanning equipment for supermarkets in U.S. Model is run with
both constrained and unconstrained estimates of market
potential. Bass model and modified analog of basic model
appeared to be robust under conditions of appropriate data from
the relevant time frames;models found to predict sales levels
correctly in subsequent time period.

3.21   WADE, BLACKMAN A., JR. (1986), "The Use of
        Innovation Diffusion Models in New Venture Planning
        and Evaluation," <u>Technological Forecasting and Social</u>
        <u>Change</u>, 29(2), 173-181.

A system for planning and evaluating new technology ventures
is presented and the role played by innovation diffusion models
is indicated. Deficiencies in the current state of the art of
diffusion models and the research needed to increase their
utility in new-venture decision making is discussed.

Refinements of Bass Model

3.22   BERKOWITZ, M.K. (1982), "Predicting Demand for
        Residential Solar Heating: An Attribute Model,"
        <u>Management Science</u>, 28(7), 717-727.

Presents two models which allow long run demand for a new
product to be estimated prior to any significant sales history.
Example used: residential solar heating in Canada. Models are
based on the concept that consumers react in their purchasing
decisions to the inherent packaging of characteristics in a
commodity. The use of survey information to enable specific
numerical estimates to be made is exemplified.

3.23   DEPALMA, A., F. DROESBEKE, CL. LEFLEURE, AND C.
        RASINSKI (1986), "Innovation Diffusion Models with
        Marketing Variables," <u>Belgium Journal of Operations</u>
        <u>Research, Statistics and Computer Science</u>, 26(4),
        37-72.

The authors of this paper examine extensions to the models
proposed for describing the diffusion of innovations in the
marketplace, many of which are generalizations of the Bass
model. The extensions examined here, in particular, include
the effects of marketing variables.

3.24   DOCKNER, ENGLEBERT AND STEFFEN JORGENSEN (1988),
        "Optimal Advertising Policies for Diffusion Models of
        New Product Innovations in Monopolistic Situations,"
        <u>Management Science</u>, 34(1), 114-130.

Deals with determination of optimal advertising strategies
for new product diffusion models. Considers the introduction
of a new consumer durable in a monopolistic market, the
evolution of sales is modeled by a flexible diffusion model.
Allows for discounting of future revenue streams and cost
learning curve.

3.25   DODSON, JOE A., JR. AND EITAN MULLER (1978), Models

of New Product Diffusion through Advertising and
Word-Of-Mouth," <u>Management Science</u>, 24(15),
1568-1578.
A model of the diffusion process is proposed which
incorporates interaction between adopters and non-adopters and
the influence of external information sources such as
advertising. The behavioral assumptions which support the
model are made explicit and the implications of these
assumptions for the shape of the new product growth curve are
derived.

3.26   GATIGNON, HUBERT AND THOMAS S. ROBERTSON (1989),
        "Technology Diffusion: An Empirical Test of
        Competitive Effects," <u>Journal of Marketing</u>, 53(1),
        35-49.
An empirical study of the factors accounting for the
adoption or rejection of a high-technology innovation is
reported. The results suggest that firms most receptive to
innovation are in concentrated industries with limited price
intensity and that supplier incentives and vertical links to
buyers are important in achieving adoption. Also, adopters
can be separated from non-adopters by their information
processing characteristics.

3.27   GREEN, PAUL E., ABBA M. KRIEGER AND ROBERT N. ZELNIO
        (1989), "A Componential Segmentation Model with
        Optimal Product Design Features," <u>Decision Sciences</u>,
        20(2), 221-238.
This paper presents a method for finding optimal market
segments for particular products, and vice versa. The model
is based on componential segmentation, in which the analyst
decomposes survey respondents' evaluations of conjoint-
designed product descriptions into separate contributions.

3.28   HEELER, ROGER M. (1986), "On the Awareness Effects of
        Mere Distribution," <u>Marketing Science</u>, 5(3), 273.
Awareness forecasting models are not complete unless they
take account of the awareness effects of mere distribution.
Distribution acts as both a main effect and as an interactive
partner with advertising in generating awareness. In turn,
awareness leads to distribution.

3.29   HORSKY, DAN AND LEONARD S. SIMON (1983), "Advertising
        and the Diffusion of New Products," <u>Marketing
        Science</u>, 2(1), 1-17.
Good econometric paper on new product diffusion in style of
Rogers and Bass. Assumes: advertising informs innovators,
word-of-mouth communication informs imitators. Empirical test
with good fit: telephone banking. Conclusions: Advertising
accelerates the diffusion process of new product.
Implications: Advertise heavily while product is introduced.
reduce level as sales increase and product moves through life
cycle (this is frequently done by firms).

3.30   KALISH, SHLOMO (1983), "Optimal Price Subsidy for
        Accelerating for Diffusion of Innovation," <u>Marketing
        Science</u>, 2(4), 407-420.
Examines social benefit of aiding introduction of alternate

energy sources into marketplace by government, and acceleration of market diffusion of these systems. Model investigates effects of price subsidy over time on rate of market diffusion. Considers word-of-mouth effects and learning curve cost declines. Market price closely related to diffusion effect (positive diffusion leads to price increases; market saturation leads to price decreases). Builds on Bass model.

3.31   KALISH, SHLOMO (1985), "A New Product Adoption Model with Price, Advertising and Uncertainty," Management Science, 31(12), 1569-1585.
This paper proposes a model of diffusion that incorporates price and advertising. It considers the importance of the two steps, awareness and adoption, in the diffusion process, as well as the reduction of uncertainty by information from early adopters. Awareness is modeled as an epidemic model, where information is spread by advertising and word-of-mouth. Adoption is conditional on awareness and depends on the perceived risk adjusted value and the selling price of the product. Preliminary results in one application are reported.

3.32   KAMAKURA, W.A. AND S.K. BALASUBRAMANIAN (1987), "Long Term Forecasting with Innovation Diffusion Models: The Impact of Replacement Purchases," Journal of Forecasting, 6(1), 1-19.
The model presented integrates two distinct components of the demand for durable goods: adoptions and replacements. Adoption is modeled as a diffusion process with the exogenous variables of price and population. Replacement rates depend on age of the owned unit and various other random factors. The integration of adoption and replacement demand components provides better sales forecasts, even under conditions where only limited data are available.

3.33   MAHAJAN, VIJAY (1986), "Reflections on Advertising Pulsing Policies for Generating Awareness for New Products," Marketing Science, 5(2), 110-111.
Rejoinder to Mahajan and Muller (1986).

3.34   MAHAJAN, VIJAY AND EITAN MULLER (1986), "Advertising Pulsing Policies for Generating Awareness for New Products," Marketing Science, 5(2), 89-106.
Comparison of pulsed to even advertising policy. Analytical model of this paper analyzes the impact of various pulsing and even policies on awareness. Application to Zielske's (1959) data on reprints of newspaper advertisements spaced out at different intervals.

3.35   MAHAJAN, VIJAY, EITAN MULLER AND FRANK M. BASS (1990), "New Product Diffusion Models in Marketing: A Review and Directions for Research," Journal of Marketing, 54(1), 1-26.
Dozens of extensions of the original Bass diffusion model have been published. This article provides a critical review of these models over the past two decades. The article also proposes a research agenda to make diffusion models theoretically more sound, and practically more effective and realistic.

3.36   MAHAJAN, VIJAY, EITAN MULLER AND ROGER A. KERIN
        (1984), "Introduction Strategy for New Products with
        Positive and Negative Word-Of-Mouth," Management
        Science, 30(12), 1389-1404.
Examines a diffusion model for products in which negative
information plays a dominant role, discusses its implications
for optimal advertising timing policy and presents an
application to forecast attendance for the movie 'Gandhi' in
the Dallas area.

3.37   MAMER, JOHN W. AND KEVIN F. MC CARDLE (1987),
        "Uncertainty, Competition and the Adoption of New
        Technology," Management Science, 33(2), 161-177.
This model helps a manager cope with uncertainty in a new
product's economic value or the extent of potential
competition. In particular, it considers the sequential
gathering of information on the product's economic value in a
Bayesian manner. The model permits a firm to account for
potential competition through a game-theory based analysis of
strategic considerations.

3.38   NASCIMENTO, FERNANDO AND WILFRIED R. VANHONACKER
        (1988), "Optimal Strategic Pricing of Reproducible
        Consumer Products," Management Science, 34(8), 921-
        937.
Paper investigates strategic pricing of consumer durables
which can be acquired through either purchase or reproduction
(e.g., computer software). Considers adverse effects of copy
piracy on profits. Uses a dual diffusion model which describes
sales and copying. Employing control theory methodology,
optimal price trajectories are derived for the period of
monopoly. The results indicate that skimming pricing is
optimal in absence of protection; and copy protection is
warranted only when sales diffuse much faster than copying and
protection does not significantly raise marginal production
costs.

3.39   QUIRMBACH, H.C. (1986), "The Diffusion of New
        Technology and the Market for an Innovation,"
        Rand Journal of Economics, 17(1), 33-47.
Shows that the diffusion of a capital-combined process
innovation results from a pattern of decreasing incremental
benefits and adoption costs for later adoption. A method is
developed for comparing diffusion rates for different market
structures in the capital equipment market. Author considers
cases with market power on seller's side of market, on buyer's
side, a case with no market power, and the welfare-optimal
case.

3.40   ROBINSON, BRUCE AND CHET LAKHANI (1975), "Dynamic
        Price Models for New-Product Planning," Management
        Science, 21(10), 1113-1122.
The authors present an extension of Bass's diffusion model
for the case of dynamic demand. They develop a model which
determines the shape of the optimal time path of price, given
rates of innovation and imitation in the market. Dynamic
programming is used to calculate numerically the optimal time

path.

3.41   SCOTT, JEROME E. AND STEPHEN K. KEISER (1984),
        "Forecasting Acceptance of New Industrial Products
        With Judgment Modeling," Journal of Marketing, 48(2).
        54-67.
Operational method for estimating quantitatively market
acceptance of new industrial products including estimates of
variations in likely market response as a function of price,
product attributes and environmental factors. Fundamental
premise is that the judgement process of potential adopters
can be modeled to gain valuable insights into the likelihood
of adoption, which varies as attributes of the product,
supplier, or decision environment are changed. Results from
two studies on solar energy systems demonstrate excellent
reliability and validity under field conditions.

3.42   TYEBJEE, TYZOON T. (1987), "Behavioral Biases in New
        Product Forecasting," International Journal of
        Forecasting, 3(4), 392-404.
The new product planning process generates an upward bias
in the forecast of a product's performance. Three sources of
such bias are discussed: 1) the post decision audit bias
reflects a regression-to-the-mean phenomenon since only those
products that are forecasted to do well, including those with
the most upward biased forecasts, are brought; 2) the advocacy
bias reflects the tendency of product planners to champion
their project by overpromising on forecasts; 3) the optimism
bias results from the act of participating in planning
activities. Role playing experiments found that persons who
were more deeply involved in a planning exercise were more
optimistic about the outcome. A third experiment demonstrated
that one reason for the optimism is that during the planning
process the illusion of control over environment leads planner
to change assumptions about uncontrollable events which can
affect outcome.

3.43   WIND, Y., T. ROBERTSON AND C. FRASER (1982),
        "Industrial Product Diffusion by Market Segment,"
        Industrial Marketing Management, 7(1), 1-8.
Focuses on the need to forecast diffusion patterns by market
segments.   The   usual   single   market   forecasts may be
inappropriate if the market is segmented. Evidence is offered
that diffusion pattern does vary by segment. The marketing of
new technologies can potentially be improved by planning and
forecasting on a segment by segment basis. This should lead
to more accurate forecasts and more effective sequencing of
marketing efforts such that segments most likely to achieve
rapid diffusion are targeted first.

OTHER DIFFUSION MODELS

3.44   BAYUS, BARRY L., SAMAN HONG AND RUSSELL P. LABE, JR.
        (1989), "Developing and Using Forecasting Models of
        Consumer Durables: The Case of Color Television,"
        Journal of Product Innovation Management, 6(1),
        5-19.

This paper presents the results of applying a forecasting model to color television industry sales for RCA's Consumer Electronics Division. In this application, a single model was inadequate to forecast sales accurately over the entire period under consideration. Econometric and simulation models are developed and described, and their performance and acceptability to management are discussed.

3.45   EASINGWOOD, C.J. (1988), "Product Life Cycle Patterns for New Industrial Products," R&D Management, 18(1), 23-32.
The author suggests the use of a diffusion model that is capable of tracking different diffusion patterns. Nine different diffusion classes are proposed. Actual data for a number of products confirm that the flexibility provided by this approach is necessary. That is, most classes are represented by at least one product. Possible explanations of class membership are proposed. More work is needed to confirm or refute these findings.

3.46   INFASENO, WILLIAMS J. (1986), "Forecasting New Product Sales from Likelihood of Purchase Ratings," Marketing Science, 5(4), 373-384.
Compares consumer likelihood of purchase ratings to actual purchase behavior after product introduction. Develops model for forecasting new product sales. Model is supported by empirical evidence and theoretical foundation.

3.47   LILIEN, GARY L. (1980), "The Implication of Diffusion Models for Accelerating the Diffusion of Innovation," Technological Forecasting and Social Change, 17(4), 339-351.
Explores the implications of a simple, yet robust model of innovation diffusion for developing insight into the problem of controlling the rate of new product diffusion. Some basic, theoretical results are developed using a simple model. Those results are shown to relate to optimal policies developed from a more complex model of innovation diffusion, developed for the Department of Energy's photo-voltaic program.

3.48   MAHAJAN, V. AND R.A. PETERSON (1978), "Innovation Diffusion in a Dynamic Potential Adapter Population," Management Science, 24(15), 1589-1597.
Presents a dynamic diffusion model to represent the time pattern of the diffusion process. Two examples used: membership in U.N. and sales of washing machines.

3.49   RAO, AMBAR G. AND MASATAKA YAMADA (1988), "Forecasting With a Repeat Purchase Diffusion Model," Management Science, 34(6), 734-752.
Presents a methodology for forecasting ethical drug sales as a function of marketing effort before sales data are available, and for updating the forecast with a few periods of sales data. Physicians' perceptions of the drug on several attributes are used for parameter estimation. The adoption process is conceptualized as a repeat purchase diffusion model where sales are expressed as a function of own and competitive marketing efforts and word-of-mouth.

3.50   SIRINAOVAKUL, B. AND Z. CZAJKIEWICZ (1988), "A
         Spatial Diffusion Model for Advanced Manufacturing
         Technology," <u>Technology Management I:</u> Proceedings of
         the First International Conference, 291-301.

The paper studies the variables which determine the
diffusion of advanced manufacturing technology. The authors
use a spatial diffusion model to explain this diffusion
process. Their model is composed of three parameters: the
absorptive capability; the innovation diffusivity; and the time
of innovation adoption.   The authors conclude with policy
guidelines for technologies, regions and planners.

4

The R&D-Marketing Interface

INTRODUCTION

This body of literature investigates an important issue encountered by innovating firms: how to manage the interface of the research and marketing departments. Earlier sections of this report indicated the fundamental importance of effective communication and integration of activity between these entities. This chapter examines the rather extensive literature on issues and dilemmas faced by firms seeking to integrate the activities of technical and marketing personnel, and on proposed solutions for better management of the interface.

Several authors have done exhaustive studies on this topic. The most notable are W. E. Souder and the team of Gupta, Raj, and Wilemon. These authors have been instrumental in proposing that productivity in new-product development can best be realized by a company's attaining a high level of cooperation between the technology-driven (technology-push) R&D department and the customer-oriented (market-pull) marketing department.

Souder and Chakrabarti (1978, 1988) and Souder (1980, 1981) identified several interface problems faced by firms. They included lack of communication, lack of appreciation, distrust, and departments being "too friendly" (leading to insufficient objective criticism across departments). He offered suggestions for improving the interface, including the development of a new-product committee for project steering, and the involvement of both parties early in the development process. In a later work, Souder (1987) developed a 12-cell matrix to help explain the different roles of R&D in interacting with customers. Only when levels of technical expertise are high for both R&D and customers should R&D play a dominant role in technology-driven new-product development, because only then would they not need the marketing area to "prepare" customers to accept the new products. As the sophistication level of customers declines, the demand for a productive R&D-marketing interface would increase. Also, Souder offered that the speed and flexibility which are critical for new-product development today cannot be achieved

by a sequential development approach: certain production and
marketing   activities ought to be performed in parallel.
Souder (1988) presented further evidence that harmonious
interaction between marketing and R&D   departments was
associated   with   improved   new-product   success   rates.
Personality conflicts and communication problems seemed to be
the major culprits in product failures. However, he cautioned
that the departments should not become too friendly.
Consistent with his earlier work, Souder's 1988 study
postulated that the challenging edge is lost when the two
departments feel too comfortable with each other.

Gupta, Raj, and Wilemon (1986) found that there were more
similarities than differences between the orientations of R&D
and   marketing.   Therefore, they reasoned that R&D and
marketing interface   problems were not simple "people"
problems; they suggested that improved interface may depend
as much upon organizational design factors   as interpersonal
factors. Gupta, Raj and Wilemon (1985a) also hypothesized four
characteristics found in effective R&D-marketing interfaces:
(1) early involvements of the R&D and marketing departments;
(2) an organizational structure conducive to   innovation; (3)
senior management support; and (4) organized new-product
activity as an integrated team approach.   (Note: a later
section of this   report discusses issues of organizational
structure.)   Further   implications about the level of
successful integration that can actually be achieved within
the organization are mentioned in the section on marketing and
technology integration. These authors have also done several
studies on personalities and on social barriers across the
interface.   These articles will be referenced and discussed
later in this section.

Other authors have produced studies with consistent
results and implications. Golden, Huerta, and Spivak (1985)
and Silva (1986) examined new-product development from the
team approach. Golden et al. suggested that there are three
team members critical to launching a new product successfully:
the product engineer; the sales and marketing person; and the
product technical manager. Their paper discussed the roles and
activities of each team member. Silva (1986) discussed how
to improve the interface using the team approach and provided
an example of its application. Crawford (1984) suggested the
use of a new-product protocol for minimizing conflicts and
misunderstandings between marketing and technical personnel.
In this view, both sides should agree on the technological
characteristics (benefits to be delivered) of the product and
also   its   market-related   attributes   (performance
specifications) prior to the development process. Marketing
and R&D would then both have a clear mandate of their required
tasks in the product development process.

Many of these studies show that organizational structure
and communication are important elements of the R&D-marketing
interface. In the ensuing discussion, the readings will not
focus on developing specific structural alignments as such,
but more on the management of those structures for successful
innovation and technology   transfer in the new-product
development process.

STRATEGIC IMPLICATIONS

Marketing and Technology Integration

Management of R&D and the R&D-marketing interface is critical to the successful management of the new-product development process. This interface should provide add value in terms of both the future marketability and engineering of a product, not just find a market for R&D's product (Bonnet, 1986). During product development, R&D must be involved in analyzing the product's quality, specifications, safe use, and disposal (European Industrial Research Management Association, 1982). Involving R&D in a product team can also shorten the lead time of entry. In their study of 23 new-product projects, Rabino and Moskowitz (1981) showed that most of the linkages between the two areas were only to find a market for the product. They pointed out that the interface should provide the means for improving the design of the product as well as its future marketability. Carroad and Carroad (1982) offered a simple model illustrating the strategic implications of the R&D-marketing interface. Their three-dimensional model consisted of the variables of production, marketing, and technology. Because the three axes meet at the origin, an innovation on any one of the dimensions is modeled as a movement away from the origin along that axis. The model implies that the other two dimensions must be linked. For instance, if the technology of manufacturing is known, but the product is targeted for a new market or if it is a new product, then the marketing and R&D departments must link up.

Marketing and technology strategies must be integrated to improve cooperation between these two departments (Nystrom 1985). Not only do the strategies need to be coordinated, but also, for a firm to sustain long-term growth, there must be a company-wide commitment for continual development and exploitation of the firm's resources. Therefore, integrating technological development in the overall strategic plan of the firm, and thus the overall marketing plan of the firm, is vital for survival. Some firms are more successful than others at carrying out this integration (Capon and Glazer, 1987). Gupta, Raj, and Wilemon (1986) suggested that how a firm perceives environmental uncertainty and other factors can influence recognition of the need for integration. Organizational structure, top managerial support, and socio-cultural differences between R&D and marketing managers all influence the level of integration attained. This study postulated that the gap between the level of integration needed and that achieved can influence innovative success.

R&D-Marketing Interface Integration with Company Policies

Many firms can no longer afford not to support some R&D. In the Capon and Glazer (1987) article discussed earlier, the authors stated that firms must form a policy based on the broadest possible asessment, development and exploration of its technology in order to sustain long-term corporate growth. Other strategic options for development such as external acquisitions are examined as alternatives to internal development (R&D). Moser and Plante (1987) advanced a model which linked R&D not only to functional activities but also to the overall strategic planning of the firm.   Brockhoff and Chakrabarti (1988) focused on R&D and marketing departments within the same business units in West German companies. In this study, it was found that the reasons for the failure of product innovation were complex and multidimensional, related to the fit between strategic behavior and the demands of the competitive environment.   The data did not show   any relationship between the technology and marketing strategies. However, if a company's corporate strategy is inappropriate, whatever the relationship between marketing and R&D departments, the strategy is likely to be ineffective.

Balancing the Pulls

Knowing how to balance the pulls of   marketing versus technology is critical to the success of a new product as well as to the strategic position of a firm.   Ramanujam and Mensch (1985)   and   Mensch   and   Ramanujam   (1986)   presented   a correspondence model which examined the impact of management goals and required effort on pressure to innovate. This study illustrated the balance required between technology and expansion of the market: the firm must know how far to allow science to take technology away from the   current market. Hooper (1985) furthered the idea of the need for management to balance five crucial elements for exploiting new technologies. They were the initiation of new-product ideas; development of enabling technologies; engineering for prototypes; the presence of suitable manufacturing capacity; and market knowledge and selling.   Kiel (1984) suggested that innovation may actually be stifled because of the confusion of science with technology. He indicated that the most innovative technology has a direct connection with the marketplace.

Structural considerations are important in the study of internal strategic interdependency within and among business units.   Harwitch and Thietart (1987) found that the types of interdependencies required for success hinged on the nature of the business and its environment. Also, interdependencies were influenced by the type of performance objective selected by the business. Finally, for a diversified firm to compete, the firm must have the capability to support concurrently multiple types of internal interdependencies and must be able to modify this set as the situation   warrants.   Having innovative strategies capable of handling routine competition may not be sufficient to sustain a firm over time. Firms also need to be able to handle major shifts in technology and the marketplace as they occur.   Gluck (1985) suggested that managers should not become too dependent on the various types of data that are increasingly easily available. Rather, they should   realize the need for creative people within the organization, foster   open communication flows between the executive and operating branches, and develop the view that change can be an opportunity.

Although studies have indicated that the R&D-marketing interface can be facilitated with organizational realignment, some aspects of disharmony may be inherent in an organization given the different strategic missions of groups within the firm (Link and Zmud, 1986). Szakonyi (1988) stated that inability of R&D to meet customers' future needs may stem from poor coordination between the R&D and marketing departments. Barriers to coordination and management of their interface is the subject of the next section.

BARRIERS TO EFFECTIVE INTERFACING

Organizational, Cultural and Communication Obstacles

Stefflre   (1985) examined how decisions are made and implemented within organizations.   His conclusions offer insight into potential organizational obstacles.   Innovative ideas have a greater chance of success in the following cases: when there are fewer links in the decision system; when the ideas involve a short time horizon; when there are fewer factions and the attitudes of those factions are not opposed to each other; and when decision making is centralized. Cultural differences may give rise to some of these barriers (Wiebecke, Tschirky, and Ulich 1987).

Crawford's product protocol (1984), discussed previously, is a concept designed to address these communication problems. A detailed description of product protocols, and how they can lead to more effective targeting of R&D and more reliable assessments of product success, is presented in Van Wyk (1988). Another model (Wilson and Ghingold, 1987) provided a marketing research technique for identifying and evaluating product features and suggested how to tailor them to meet market needs and to minimize manufacturing costs. The linking concept to be used is determined by the attitudes and behavior of the various departments.

Some of the most recent work on linkages across the organization looks beyond the R&D-marketing interface and considers the linking of all functional departments. A paper by Daugherty (1989) reports on an interesting in-depth study of several innovating firms. Daugherty concludes that different functional areas (marketing, planning, R&D and manufacturing) appear to exist in different "thought worlds." The departments view the linkage of technology and marketing differently and focus on different aspects of the interface problem. Having divergent views hinders interdepartmental communication.   To compound the problem, the firm's routine procedures for innovation reinforce these departmental separations and stifle the creativity necessary for successful innovative activity. The paper suggests that, while we have studied in depth the R&D-marketing R&D interface, we must not forget the key roles played by other functional areas and the difficulties in organizing the whole firm for productive results.

A strategic planning tool which has become popular in recent years in the United States is Quality Functional Deployment (QFD). It was originated in Japan in the early

1970s and was used successfully there for several years. Now, large American auto makers and other firms are using it to their advantage. It bears mention here because its implementation requires that marketing, production, and technical people must work together to design products that satisfy customer needs and also are feasible from an engineering standpoint. QFD requires the participants to translate customer preferences into product engineering characteristics and to recognize explicitly any design trade-offs that result (i.e., a motorized window in a car door may be preferred by customers, but it would make the door heavier and harder to close, which would not be preferred). Decisions on what characteristics to build into the product are made in light of costs, specifications, engineering capabilities, and comparison to competing products. The best short introduction to QFD is in a recent <u>Harvard Business Review</u> article by Hauser and Clausing (1988), but one should note that they have presented only one design matrix in detail. A full QFD plan may require several months of effort by a team of decision makers, and results in several more matrices, all representing other aspects of product design. Hauser and Clausing (1988) also show some of the early results indicating the benefits obtainable by careful application of QFD.

Personality and Social Obstacles

Lucas and Bush (1988) carried out an interesting study of personality factors involved in the R&D-marketing interface. Their research supported much of Souder's earlier research into personality disputes at the interface. Gupta, Raj, and Wilemon (1985a,b) delineated eight areas that act as barriers between interfacing individuals and,by extension, departments in an institution. Of these, three of the most critical center on personality characteristics. The eight areas were: (1) lack of communication; (2) insensitivity to others' points of view; (3) lack of support from the top; (4) personality differences; (5) lack of market knowledge; (6) organizational design problems; (7) managerial problems; and (8) cultural problems.

Lucas and Bush (1988) concentrated more on individual differences among people in various departments. They found that the nature of the interface and its problems may vary with the size of the firm. (Gupta, Raj, and Wilemon, 1985a, had previously found that size was not a factor in the amount of integration achieved.) Lucas and Bush (1988) also noted that there was no attempt to differentiate the relationship between the types of people involved in the two areas across a wide variety of industries. Thus, persons needed in marketing and R&D in the ethical drug industry may not be the same as those needed in, say, household products.

Gupta, Raj and Wilemon (1985a) found that the personality factors by themselves do not explain a large percentage of variability in the outcome variables. Other factors were suggested to have important impacts on the number and success rate of new products: the availability of financial resources and managerial and technological expertise, and the company's market position.

Lucas and Bush (1988) recommended the model of Gupta and Wilemon (1987, 1988) as a basis for important future research. This model looks at the credibility problem between the R&D and marketing divisions of engineering firms. The authors found that even though R&D managers may not have serious reservations about the qualifications of marketing managers as credible information sources, they may still question the quality of information provided by them. This credibility problem has implications for the improved practice of marketing research.

Hatch (1987), in a study of task characteristics and factors in interaction, found that there were physical barriers that one could impose or tear down. For example, the positioning of a desk was found to be a physical barrier that could always be negatively associated with reported interruptions. This study helps managers understand the interactive activity in a business and how the physical structure of that business may impede or assist innovative flows. Additional research is needed, however, to generalize these relationships to other jobs and firms.

ECONOMIC AND FINANCIAL ISSUES

Much evidence has suggested that "bean-counting" bureaucracies that are inflexible and tightly tied to financial performance goals do not understand the marketplace. By refusing to listen to market signals, they effectively stifle significant product innovation. They also are fairly short-sighted and thus unwilling to invest funds for projects that do not have immediate payoffs (Zimke and McCollum, 1987). As Mansfield (1982) suggested, there is a balance between the probabilities of technical completion and economic success. For ambitious R&D projects, the former may be low while the latter is high. His study discussed innovations in terms of their social rate of return (returns to society as a whole) and private rates of return (return to the company), and their resultant impact on managerial decisions. Lotspeich (1988) further discussed the economic analysis of R&D, suggesting that this area is one for further study.

MANAGERIAL R&D ISSUES

Strategy

As technology becomes more strategically important, R&D managers must think of the strategic management of their function, rather than just viewing it as a series of projects (Mitchell, 1985). Although creativeness has been shown to be stifled by too much structure, some strategic planning is in order. Mitchell's approach improves communication between management and technology through the formulation of a list of strategic technical attributes (STA). He suggested that management tends to think of technology as products or classes of products. R&D, on the other hand, thinks of technology as skills or disciplines that comprise the input from which

products evolve.   By identifying a set of STAs and allowing
different groups with varying responsibilities to make inputs
to the list, technology may be more effectively aimed toward
management goals.   Etienne (1981)   offered a model that
integrated product life cycles with the Utterback-Abernathy
dynamic model of innovation (discussed in the earlier section
on product innovation).   His model was designed to assist in
the   timing   decision   for   strategy   formulation and
implementation. He pointed out that a weakness of the firm
that can be tolerated at early stages of the cycle may be
catastrophic at later stages.

Group Characteristics

     Poor managerial policies within critical areas of R&D
may lead to new-product failure. Richardson (1985) suggested
five key reasons for these poor policies. First, there may be
little understanding of the needs and strategies of the
business.   Second, there may be no sponsor for an innovation
in the business.   Third, management may fail to respond within
the time frame demanded by the business or its environment.
Fourth, there may be poor project discipline and methodology.
Fifth, key technical personnel may be overloaded. He further
suggested that it is possible to overcome these problems by
developing sound managerial policies. He made the following
suggestions: research and development should not work in
isolation;   incentives should be present for firms to
innovate; and there should be   a corporate commitment to
developing and bringing new products to market.
     On a micro level, the success of R&D may be related to
the project groups within the R&D organization. Keller (1986)
showed that   group cohesiveness, physical distance, job
satisfaction, and innovation orientation were associated with
project performance.   Thus, the success   of the firm's
innovations is brought to the individual level. This study
revealed that group cohesiveness accounted for most of the
variance   in   tested   performance   criteria.   Innovation
orientation added   more value to projects and was a strong
success motivator, according to R&D group members.

The Japanese Influence

     Hull, Hage, and Azumi (1985) outlined differences between
American and Japanese approaches to R&D management   and
suggested future trends.   The Japanese invest comparatively
more in employer training, including group processes such as
quality circles,   and receive more suggestions for employer
innovation.   American firms   seem to emphasize quality
enhancement and cost reduction in   manufacturing, while
Japanese industry seems to increasingly emphasize new-product
development.   In another study, Pucik and Halvany (1983)
showed that American business can learn much about facilitating
commercialization of innovations from observing the Japanese
management   system, their culture, and their implementation
techniques. The Japanese integrate R&D with other critical
corporate functions and   develop a strong organizational

commitment towards innovation and technological support. Teamwork, open communication, competitive spirit, and the implementation process are factors of coordination. Their carefully built monitoring systems on the outside, high levels of interface coordination, and teamwork involving all those concerned with development, design and manufacturing lead to successful implementation. The Japanese research teams are stable since the relative lack of venture capital makes it difficult for R&D personnel to seek windfall profits as independent entrepreneurs. The steady feedback of market information to research personnel makes it more likely that research and development result in products that will meet market needs. Participation of production engineers in the development process increases the likelihood that the new product can be built efficiently with available or soon-to-be-available production technologies. The process is widely diffused throughout the organization, enlarging the strategic alternatives available to the firm.

THE R&D-MARKETING INTERFACE: ANNOTATED BIBLIOGRAPHY

INTRODUCTION

4.1   CRAWFORD, C. MERLE (1984), "Protocol: New Tool for
        Product Innovation," Journal of Product Innovation
        Management, 1(2), 85-91.
The new product development process is frequently hampered
by poor communication across the R&D-marketing interface.
Protocol is proposed by the author as a contract for improving
communication between R&D and marketing departments. A product
protocol lists benefits or performance specifications of the
new product, and development of the protocol is marked by
negotiation and bargaining between R&D and marketing.

4.2   DI BENEDETTO, C. ANTHONY AND ROGER J. CALANTONE
        (1990), "Effective Management of the R&D-Marketing
        Link for Improving New Product Success Rates,"
        Journal of Managerial Issues, 2(1).
Product innovation is essential for competitive firms in
today's business climate. This study examines previous
research into factors increasing the chances of success with
new products, and reports on recent work illustrating the link
between technology and marketing divisions in the new product
development process. The report presents ways by which a firm
can improve this link, and discusses implications for the
divisions and for top management.

4.3   EUROPEAN INDUSTRIAL RESEARCH MANAGEMENT ASSOCIATION
        (1982), "R&D and New Products," Research Management,
        15(4), 16-22.
This article is on R&D in the Design/Redesign and at the
Decline stages of the product life cycle. During new product
development, R&D must be involved with analyzing worth and
quality, setting specifications, conducting design reviews and
planning for eventual safe reuse or disposal of product.
Article deals with the role of R&D in quality assurance.

4.4   GOLDEN, S.L., J.M. HUERTA AND R.B. SPIVAK (1985),
        "New Product Marketing: A Team Approach," Simulation
        Profession, Proceedings of the Conference, 17-19.

This paper discusses the roles of three members of the new product development team: the product developer/engineer, the sales and marketing person and the product technical manager. The effectiveness of the team is tested when the firm customizes a sophisticated international forecasting system (whose R&D had been supported by clients) to satisfy a more general need.

4.5   GUPTA, A.K., S.P. RAJ AND DAVID WILEMON (1986), "R&D and Marketing Managers in High-Tech Companies: Are They Different?" IEEE Transactions on Engineering Management, EM-33(1) (February), 25-32.
Although many other studies suggest otherwise, the results of the empirical analysis presented here suggest that R&D and marketing managers in high-tech companies are not necessarily different in sociocultural outlook.   More similarities than differences were found. Thus, integration problems at the R&D-marketing interface may not be simple "people" problems, but may be due to difficulties with organization design.

4.6   GUPTA, ASHOK K., S.P. RAJ AND DAVID WILEMON (1987), "Managing the R&D-Marketing Interface," Research Management, 30(2), 38-43.
Four specific factors for effective R&D-marketing interfaces and successful product innovation: 1) Quality R&D-marketing integration (early involvement of both groups in the new product development process); 2) Organizational structure (clear role definition, decision autonomy); 3) Senior management support (commitment, interest and involvement); 4) Organized new product activity (integrated team structures). The study investigates 167 high-tech companies.

4.7   SILVA, DANIEL E. (1986), "R&D/Manufacturing Interface," Proceedings, First International Conference on Engineering Management.
Improvement of the R&D-manufacturing interface through the integrated team approach is discussed. An application of the method is described.

4.8   SOUDER, WILLIAM E. (1980), "Promoting an Effective R&D/Marketing Interface," Research Management 23(4), 10-15.
A study of 38 Industrial Research Institute member firms. Types of interface problems found were: lack of communication, lack of appreciation of each other's abilities, mutual distrust, and "too-good" friends (not enough objective criticism of each other's work). Numerous guidelines were offered for improving the interface, including: break down large projects to smaller units; open communication for everyone; appointment of a New Product Committee for steering; hiring highly qualified project managers; including both parties early on; etc.

4.9   SOUDER, WILLIAM E. (1981), "Disharmony Between R&D and Marketing," Industrial Marketing Management, 10, 67-73.
Many of the factors for disharmony found in the 1980 study were also found here. Practical suggestions for managing the

interface were offered, including: fostering harmony by keeping projects small; not permitting power and status differentials to arise; parties should challenge each other; set up two-person committee assignments, etc.

4.10   SOUDER, WILLIAM E. (1987), Managing New Product Innovations, Lexington, Mass.: Lexington Books (Textbook).

4.11   SOUDER, WILLIAM E. (1988), "Managing Relations Between R&D and Marketing in New Product Development," Journal of Product Innovation Management, 5(1), 6-19.

The author cautions against making R&D and marketing feel too comfortable with each other, since they might lose that challenging edge.   They should retain their identities and toughness but in better communication and cooperation.   Some of the results of the 1980 and 1981 articles by this author were supported.

4.12   SOUDER, WILLIAM E. AND ALOK K. CHAKRABARTI (1978), "The R&D/Marketing Interface: Results from an Empirical Study of Innovation Projects," IEEE Transactions on Engineering Management, 25(4), 88-93.

This paper examines organizational factors that characterize the interface between marketing and R&D.   The degree of collaboration or integration between functional units, such as marketing and R&D, influences the success or failure outcome of industrial innovation projects.   Several variables influencing the R&D-marketing interface are identified and related in an overall model which identifies actions that can be taken to improve the quality of the interface.

4.13   SOUDER, WILLIAM E. AND ALOK K. CHAKRABARTI (1980), "Managing the Coordination of Marketing and R&D in the Innovation Process," in B.V. Dean and J.L. Goldhar (eds.), Management of Research and Innovation, TIMS Studies in the Management Sciences, Vol. 15, 135-150.

This is an overview of the product innovation process in an industrial setting, focusing on the coordination of R&D and marketing efforts.   A review of the literature on intergroup conflict and organizational integration is provided and discussed as it relates to the marketing-R&D interface. Three different approaches to managing the interface between R&D and marketing are discussed.   1) The stage-dominant approach is appropriate when the technology and the market conditions are stable and well understood. 2) The process-dominant approach is most useful when the technology is not well understood.   3) The task-dominant approach is best used in those cases where both the technology and the market are not well understood.

4.14   SPENCER, WILLIAM J. AND DEBORAH H. TRIANT (1989), "Strengthening the Link Between R&D and Corporate Strategy," Journal of Business Strategy, 9(1), 38-42.

A report on strategic change at Xerox.   In order to improve

R&D accomplishments, the authors recommend coupling R&D activities more closely with overall corporate strategy. This does not mean abandoning basic for applied R&D. The trick is to protect the basic, but see that at least it builds on commercial opportunities and assure that the non-basic parts of the R&D program are closely tied to current strategic thinking. The key to achieving this is communication across departments.

STRATEGIC IMPLICATIONS

Marketing and Technology Integration

4.15   BONNET, D.C.L. (1986), "Nature of the R&D/Marketing Cooperation in the Design of Technologically Advanced New Industrial Products," R&D Management, 16(2), 117-126.
From a pilot study of 23 new product projects in 10 firms in U.K., it appears that firms are missing a fundamental issue in the R&D-marketing cooperation. Most of the time it is limited to an identification of general market need for a particular new product idea. The paper emphasizes that the interface should provide the means for an efficient product design procedure between R&D and marketing that should profit the engineering design of the product and its future marketability. The paper outlines the advantages and problems inherent in the exercise and proposes a framework for implementation.

4.16   CAPON, NOEL AND RASHI GLAZER (1987), "Marketing and Technology: A Strategic Co-Alignment," Journal of Marketing, 51(3), 1-14.
Examines issues associated with the management of technology. Highlights key factors involved in integrating technological considerations into overall strategic marketing plan. For a firm to sustain long-term corporate growth, it must do so from "a policy based on broadest possible valuation of, and continual development and exploitation of, firm's technology." Considers: 1) internal development vs. external acquisition; 2) selling the technology outright; 3) simultaneous exploiting and selling of the technology; 4) determining value of technology to firm and to others.

4.17   CARROAD, P. AND C. CARROAD (1982), "Strategic Interfacing of R&D and Marketing," Research Management, 25(1), 28-33.
A three-dimensional model for marketing and R&D to work together. A team or dyad approach seems to be best for interfacing. Each dimension (axis) in the model represents a type of innovation (product, technology or marketing). Any movement along an axis represents innovation in at least one area and implies need for interaction with the other areas.

4.18   GUPTA, ASHOK K., S.P. RAJ AND DAVID WILEMON (1986), A Model for Studying R&D-Marketing Interface in the Product Innovation Process," Journal of Marketing,

50(2), 7-17.

The integration of marketing and R&D in a firm is influenced by both the firm's strategy and its level of environmental uncertainty. Organizational design and senior management support, along with the sociocultural differences between R&D and marketing managers, can influence the level of integration achieved by an organization. The gap between the levels of integration needed and achieved is an influencing factor in innovation success.

4.19   NYSTROM, HARRY (1985), "Product Development Strategy: An Integration of Technology and Marketing," <u>Journal of Product Innovation Management</u>, 2(1), 25-33.

Better integration is required between marketing and technology strategy, just as it is required between marketing and technology people. The author proposes a framework for analyzing product development strategies integrating marketing and technology. Discusses the differences between "open" and "closed" product development strategies, differentiated by their technical orientation (external versus internal).

4.20   RABINO, SAMUEL AND H. MOSKOWITZ (1981), "The R&D Role in Bringing New Products to the Marketplace," <u>Journal of Business Strategy</u>, 1(4), 26-32.

The authors examined 23 new product projects and determined that most linkages at the R&D-marketing interface were established only to find a market for a product. They point out that the interface between R&D and marketing should provide the means for an efficient product design procedure that should improve the design of the product as well as its future marketability.

R&D-Marketing Interface Integration with Company Policies

4.21   BROCKHOFF, K. AND A.K. CHAKRABARTI (1988), "R&D/ Marketing Linkage and Innovation Strategy: Some West German Experience," <u>IEEE Transactions on Engineering Management</u>, 35(3) (August), 167-174.

The authors analyze data on the innovation success, causes of failure, marketing and technology strategy, and dynamics of the technological environment. The data were gathered using semistructured interview protocols. Marketing was mentioned as the most important cause for innovation failure; but the reasons for failure were interrelated in complex ways, related to the fit between strategic behavior and the demands of the competitive environment. Four different technology strategies were identified: defensive imitator, process developer, aggressive specialist, and aggressive innovator.   Four different marketing strategies were identified: defensive imitator, market defender, market penetrator, and innovative marketer.

4.22   MOSER, MARTIN R. AND MICHAEL S. PLANTE (1987), "Linking R&D with the Strategic Management Process of the Firm," <u>Engineering Management International</u>, 4(2), 127-132.

An examination of the problems associated with integrating R&D activities with the overall strategic planning process of the firm is presented. A model which links R&D to other functional activities as well as to strategic planning by a technical planning committee is proposed. The implementation of this process requires organizational, structural and communication adjustments.

4.23   QUELCH, JOHN A., PAUL W. FERRIS AND JAMES M. OLVER (1987), "The Product Management Audit," Harvard Business Review, 65(2), 30.
A simple presentation for a product manager's audit by top management. Focus groups work up inventory of product manager's tasks. Then seven elements (including such items as percent of time spent on activity and like/dislike of activity) are characterized by manager for each activity. Includes also suggestions to top management to help them do a better job.

Balancing the Pulls

4.24   GLUCK, FREDERICK W. (1985), 'Big Bang Management: Creative Innovation," The Mc Kinsey Quarterly (Spring), 49-59.
Many firms have product innovation strategies that are capable during routine times but cannot handle major shifts in industry or the marketplace when they occur. The author suggests the firm look at raw data, creative people and organization, top executives and workers' forums, and that management view change as an opportunity.

4.25   HOOPER, D.E. (1985), "New Technologies and Product Opportunities," IEE Colloquium on "From New Technologies to Profitable Products", 2, 1-4.
Five key elements for exploiting new technologies are identified: new product ideas, enabling technologies, engineering for prototypes, manufacturing capacity, and market intelligence and selling. The importance of balance between these elements and good management is discussed, as are issues of managing the investments.

4.26   HORWITCH, MEL AND RAYMOND THIETART (1987), "The Effect of Business Interdependencies on Product R&D-Intensive Business Performance," Management Science, 33(2), 178-197.
Firms must choose the appropriate level of internal strategic interdependency within and among business units. This study examines the efficacy of different structural linkages for achieving market share and ROI objectives in product R&D- intensive businesses. The interdependencies required for high performance are contingent upon the nature of the business and its environmental characteristics. For a given business type, high performance interdependencies are influenced by the type of performance objectives selected by the business. Also, a multi-business corporation which possesses a portfolio of product R&D-intensive businesses probably requires a more diverse set of interdependencies than mainstream centralized industrial R&D organizations or

independent entrepreneurial units.

4.27   KIEL, G. (1984), "Technology and Marketing: The Magic
         Mix?" Business Horizons, 27, 7-14.
     The author proposes that, as a result of the confusion of
science with technology, true product innovation may be
stifled.

4.28   LINK, ALBERT N. AND ROBERT W. ZMUD (1986),
         "Additional Evidence on the R&D/Marketing Interface,"
         IEEE Transactions on Engineering Management,
         EM-33(1) (February), 43-44.
     This article examines the managerial aspects of the R&D-
marketing interface.   The analysis of different factors
suggests that relationships in the interface can be improved
through organizational realignment, but some aspects of
disharmony may be inherent given the strategic mission of the
groups.

4.29   MENSCH, GERHARD O. AND VASUDEVAN RAMANUJAM (1986), "A
         Diagnostic Tool for Identifying Disharmonies Within
         Corporate Innovation Networks," Journal of Product
         Innovation Management, 3(1), 19-31.
     This article expands on the Correspondence Model article of
1985.   Examines mismatches and matches in the perceptions and
priorities of functional specialists, staff and line managers,
and senior managers (key participants in the innovation
management process).

4.30   RAMANUJAM, VASUDEVAN AND GERHARD O. MENSCH (1985),
         "Improving the Strategy-Innovation Link," Journal of
         Product Innovation Management, 2(4), 213-223.
     The authors propose a correspondence model of innovation.
The strategic formulation process by which processes are turned
into goals and efforts is subject to barriers to innovation
that exist throughout the process.   Pressures to innovate
include: high labor costs, new manufacturing systems, new
materials and components, shifts in demand, product
obsolescence, superior rival products, entrepreneurial needs,
product safety, shortages of skilled workers, and many others.
The empirical test of the model is limited to a sample from
northern Ohio.

4.31   SZAKONYI, ROBERT (1988), "Dealing With a Nonobvious
         Source of Problems Related to Selecting R&D to Meet
         Customers' Future Needs: Weaknesses Within an R&D
         Organization's and Within a Marketing Organization's
         Individual Operations," IEEE Transactions on
         Engineering Management, 35(1) (February), 37-41.
     Choosing R&D initiatives to meet customers' future needs
may be problematic.   These problems may stem from poor
coordination between a company's R&D organization and the
marketing organization.   Weaknesses of each type of
organization are discussed.

BARRIERS TO EFFECTIVE INTERFACING

Organizational, Cultural and Communication Obstacles

4.32   CLARK, KIM B. (1989), "Project Scope and Project
        Performance: The Effect of Parts Strategy and
        Supplier Involvement on Product Development,"
        Management Science, 35(10), 1247-1263.
This paper focuses on the relationship between product
development and project scope (the extent to which a new
product is based on unique parts developed in-house). Studies
of the automotive supplier industry suggest that different
structures and relationships exist in Japan, the U.S., and
Europe.   Little is known on how these differences, or
differences in parts strategies, affect development
performance. A distinctive approach to scope among Japanese
firms--high levels of unique parts, intensive supplier
involvement in engineering--accounts for a significant fraction
of their advantage in lead time and cost.

4.33   DOUGHERTY, DEBORAH (1989), "Interpretive Barriers to
        Successful Product Innovation," Marketing Science
        Institute, Report #89-114, Cambridge, MA: Marketing
        Science Institute.
Two major interpretive barriers to effective collaboration
across the specialized departments (marketing, planning, R&D
and manufacturing): 1. Departmental "thought worlds:" the
departments make sense of the technology-market linkages in
different ways (e.g. what issues are the most uncertain, what
facets of the market should be emphasized). 2. The firm's
routine procedures for product development tend not to include
the intense interactions and creative learning necessary to
produce innovation: instead they impose answers, cut off
questions, and reinforce departmental separation.

4.34   HAUSER, JOHN R. AND DON CLAUSING (1988), "The House
        of Quality," Harvard Business Review, 66 (May-June),
        63-73.
The House of Quality is the basic design tool of the
management approach known as Quality Function Deployment (QFD).
QFD emphasizes preproduction investment and minimizes the
amount of costly design changes after launch. Focus is on
translating customer attributes (CA) to engineering
characteristics (EC), using customer studies, managerial
judgment, etc. to account for the relationships between ECs
and CAs.   Helps management decide which ECs should be
concentrated on in order to improve customer satisfaction
efficiently.

4.35   KRANTZ, K. THEODOR (1989), "How Velcro Got Hooked on
        Quality," Harvard Business Review, 67 (September-
        October), 34-43.
Description of how Velcro learned how to manufacture quality
into their product. Rather than concentrating on quality
control and "inspecting" quality into Velcro fasteners, the
company made everyone responsible for quality.

4.36   MANSFIELD, EDWIN (1988), "The Speed and Cost of
        Industrial Innovation in Japan and the United States:
        External vs. Internal Technology," _Management_
        Science, 34(10), 1157-1168.
A comprehensive empirical investigation of the differences
between Japan and the United States in innovation cost and
time. Whereas the Japanese have substantial advantages in some
industries (e.g., machinery), they do not in others (e.g.,
chemicals). They have great advantage in carrying out
innovations based on external technology; not so for internal
technology. Japanese firms allocate a larger percentage of
total innovation cost to tooling and manufacturing equipment
and facilities, and a smaller percentage to marketing startup.
America's problem seems to stem from its inability to match
Japan as a quick and effective user ot external technology.

4.37   STEFFLRE, VOLNEY (1985), "Organizational Obstacles to
        Innovation: A Formulation of the Problem," _Journal of_
        Product Innovation Management, 2(1), 3-11.
Examines the main elements of decisions about innovations
and how they are handled. Discusses collective decisions:
the less factions and less negatively attitudes are correlated,
and the more centralized the decision, the higher the
probability chosen. Differences in what meets customer
expectations versus company's easiest path are also discussed.
If the decision is politically motivated by factions, the
innovation may be implemented in means counterproductive to the
firm's original intent.

4.38   VAN WYK, RIAS J. (1988), "Standard Framework for
        Product Protocols," _Technology Management I_:
        Proceedings of the First International Conference on
        Technology Management, Special Publication of the
        International Journal of Technology Management.
The paper describes the two parts of a product protocol.
First part of protocol: inherent technological characteristics
of a product. Second part: market related attributes. The
paper suggests that one can standardize the first part thus
facilitating the process of negotiation, contributing to more
effective targeting of R&D and improved product prognoses.

4.39   WIEBECKE, G., H. TSCHIRKY AND E. ULICH (1987),
        "Cultural Differences at the R&D/Marketing Interface:
        Explaining Inter-Divisional Communication Barriers,"
        Proceedings, IEEE Conference on Management and
        Technology: Management of Evolving Systems, 94-101.
The results of an empirical study of communication barriers
between R&D and marketing are presented. These barriers are
related to cultural differences between the departments
involved. The departmental subcultures of R&D and marketing
are different in their basic assumptions about time scales, the
firm's overall relationship to the environment, and the nature
of reality as a basis for decisions. A framework for an
interface design is developed, and managerial and scientific
implications are discussed.

4.40   WILSON, DAVID J. AND MORRY GHINGOLD (1987), "Linking

R&D to Market Needs," Industrial Marketing Management, 16, 207-214.

A market research technique for identifying and evaluating the more important product features and service aspects of new industrial products is described. The method helps tailor product design and performance aspects to market needs and manufacturing costs. The linking concept used is rooted in attitude/behavior theory.

Personality and Social Obstacles

4.41   GUPTA, ASHOK K., S.P. RAJ AND DAVID L. WILEMON (1985a), "R&D and Marketing Dialogue in High-Tech Firms," Industrial Marketing Management, 14, 289-300.

An empirical study of 200 R&D managers in high-tech companies.   Conclusions of the study were as follows: 1)consensus between R&D and marketing managers on importance of areas requiring integrated efforts is essential. 2)Companies successful in their new product programs achieve a significantly greater degree of R&D-marketing integration.   3) Company size does not affect level of integration achieved. 4) Companies that achieve a high degree of integration do so by concentrating on all key areas (for example, setting new product goals, budgets, and schedules); generating and screening ideas, market information, test marketing results and modification of products).

4.42   GUPTA, ASHOK K., S.P. RAJ AND DAVID WILEMON (1985b), "The R&D-Marketing Interface in High-Technology Firms," Journal of Product Innovation Management, 2(1), 12-24.

Examines three product failures: RCA Selectavision, Nimslo 3-dimensional camera and Pringle's Potato Chips. Investigates the degree of R&D-marketing integration required and achieved as perceived by R&D and marketing managers.   These are different on many key variables: a perceptual gap exists in six of the ten areas where integration is viewed as being most important.   Implications: Marketing thinks it is doing an adequate job providing information on customer requirements, test-marketing results, competitive strategies, commercial applications of ideas; R&D disagrees. Also, R&D wants to get more involved with marketing than vice-versa.   Senior management should implement a joint reward system as a means of encouraging competition.

4.43   GUPTA, ASHOK AND DAVID WILEMON (1987), "Credibility Problem at the R&D-Marketing Interface," Proceedings, IEEE Conference on Management and Technology: Management of Evolving Systems.

A credibility problem exists between R&D and marketing divisions in engineering firms.   R&D questions the quality of information provided by marketing, and/or the marketing managers as credible sources of information, based on their behavioral traits.   R&D managers have reservations about the quality of marketing information but less reservation with marketing managers as credible sources of information.

Implications for marketing manager selection and training, and marketing research practices, are discussed.

4.44   GUPTA, ASHOK K. AND DAVID WILEMON (1988), "The Credibility-Cooperation Connection at the R&D-Marketing Interface," Journal of Product Innovation Management, 5(1), 20-31.

R&D managers' perceptions of marketing information and managers are analyzed from the point of view of information and source credibility. These perceptions were found to differ significantly in high and low integration companies, and were influenced by various organizational practices. Cooperation across the interface was highest where organizational practices were supportive of cooperation and R&D perceived marketing input as credible. The authors discuss ways in which a corporate climate conducive to interfunctional cooperation can be stimulated.

4.45   HATCH, MARY JO (1987), "Physical Barriers, Task Characteristics, and Interaction Activity in R&D Firms," Administrative Sciences Quarterly, 32(3), 387-399.

Several types of interactions are associated with physical barriers, independent of their association with task characteristics and individual differences. Additional research is needed to generalize these relationships to other jobs and firms. The desk is the only physical barrier negatively associated with reported interruptions. The study aids in the understanding of the relationship between interaction activity relationships and physical structure.

4.46   LUCAS, GEORGE H., JR. AND ALAN G. BUSH (1988), "The Marketing-R&D Interface: Do Personality Factors Have an Impact?" Journal of Product Innovation Management, 5(4), 257-268.

This interface is a most critical part of the new product development process. This study examines the question over which one should dominate product development. Paper investigates individual differences, particularly personality differences, as an influence on the integration of the two and the resultant new product success level. Provides suggestions to management on how to maximize positive outcomes from this critical business process.

ECONOMIC AND FINANCIAL ISSUES

4.47   LOTSPEICH, RICHARD (1988), "Economics of Research and Development," Resources and Energy 10(2), 185-189.

Economic analysis of R&D provides a valuable guide for public and private decisions on allocating resources to R&D efforts that support technological innovation. Addresses issues regarding the liming of R&D investment and uncertainty in the outcome. Also suggests directions for areas in the economics of R&D concerning further research.

4.48   MANSFIELD, EDWIN (1982), "How Economists See R&D,"

Research Management, 15(4), 23-29.
What makes for commercial success? The author lists two factors: 1) linkage between R&D and marketing; 2) balance or tradeoff between probabilities of technical completion and economic success (given commercialization). For ambitious R&D projects, the former may be low but the latter is likely to be high. The paper studies 37 innovations and discusses their social (returns to society as a whole) and private (return to investing company) rates of return.

4.49   ZIMKE, M. CARL AND JAMES K. MC COLLUM (1987), "A
         Message to Detroit -- Bridge the Gap in Mechanical
         Innovation," Sloan Management Review (Spring),
         49-54.
Article criticizes "bean-counting" bureaucracies that don't understand the marketplace, and do a great job of stifling product innovation by refusing to listen to market signals.

MANAGERIAL R&D ISSUES

Strategy

4.50   ETIENNE, E. CELSE (1981), "Interactions Between
         Product   R&D   and   Process   Technology,"   Research
         Management, 24(1), 22-27.
Integrates product life cycle and Utterback-Abernathy model. Examines timing question in strategy formulation and implementation. Weaknesses of a firm may be tolerated at early stages, but may be catastrophic at later ones.

4.51   MITCHELL, GRAHAM R. (1985), "New Approaches for the
         Strategy Management of Technology," Technology in
         Society, 227-239.
As technology becomes more strategically important, R&D managers must think of the strategic management of their functions rather than just projects. The new approach combines in one perspective that management "hears" technology and thinks of products or classes of products. Technology hears the term and thinks of skills or disciplines that comprise the input from which products come.

Group Characteristics

4.52   KELLER, ROBERT T. (1986), "Predictors of the
         Performance of Project Groups in R&D Organizations,"
         Academy of Management Journal, 22(4), 715-726.
Results from 22 project groups in large R&D organizations showed that group cohesiveness, physical distance, job satisfaction and innovation orientation were associated with project performance.

4.53   RICHARDSON, PETER R. (1985), "Managing Research and
         Development for Results," Journal of Product
         Innovation Management, 2(2), 75-87.
R&D occasionally fails because of R&D management.   Poor

policies within critical areas of R&D lead to failure to deliver.   Key reasons: 1) poor understanding of needs and strategies of business, 2) absence of sponsor in business system, 3) failure to respond in time frame demanded by business, 4) absence of good project discipline and methodology, and 5) overloading of key technical personnel. The firm should overcome these problems by developing sound management policies within R&D.   Institutional roadblocks to innovation are identified: 1) isolation of R&D; 2) lack of incentives for operations to innovate; 3) lack of corporate commitment to commercialization.

The Japanese Influence

4.54   HULL, FRANK M., JERALD HAGE AND KOYA AZUMI (1985), "R&D Management Strategies: America Versus Japan," IEEE Transactions on Engineering Management, EM-32(2) (May), 78-83.
   The article outlines differences between American and Japanese approaches to R&D management and suggests future trends.   Data from a comparative study of U.S. and Japanese factories are used to assess the extent of these differences. Japanese factories were found to invest comparatively more in employee training, including group processes such as quality circles, and receive more suggestions per employee. Innovation is also evaluated slightly higher in Japanese plants.   There also appears to be a slight convergence in R&D management strategies;   American industry appears to be placing greater emphasis on quality enhancement and cost reduction in manufacturing and Japanese industry seems to increasingly emphasize new product development.

4.55   PUCIK, VLADIMIR AND NINA HATVANY (1983), "Management Practices in Japan and Their Impact on Business Strategy," Advances in Strategic Management, 1, 103-131.
   Japanese management system facilitates the commercialization of innovations and assures the integration of R&D with other critical corporate functions.   The article discusses strategies, techniques for implementation and implications for American business.

5

Organizational Structure

Organizational structure is the alignment of a company's resources for the attainment of company goals. A review of the literature on organizational structure as it relates to the new product development process reveals the necessity of deliberate structuring of the organization to accommodate product innovation as an overall goal. Considerations that apply to a firm's overall configuration are reviewed in this chapter. This chapter will include some technology transfer issues, but that subject will be treated more completely in Chapter 6.

AN INNOVATIVE ORGANIZATIONAL DESIGN

Basic Configurations

General organizational configurations and/or characteristics for innovative or entrepreneurial firms are widely discussed in the literature. Most of these readings build on a body of knowledge obtained from management journals such as Harvard Business Review, Journal of Business Strategy, Business Horizons, and Management Science. Several books are also relevant to both the general and innovative context (Mintzberg, 1979, 1983; Jelinek, 1986). The management literature readings may not always discuss new-product development or innovation specifically, but they are included here because they lay out important concepts, terminology, and groundwork for understanding and designing an appropriate company configuration for innovation.

Mintzberg (1979, 1980, 1981) lists five natural organizational configurations that tend to emerge: simple structure, machine bureaucracy, professional bureaucracy, divisionalized form and the adhocracy (a term coined by Mintzberg to refer to a firm with a dynamic, organic structure and an automated technical system). This literature is a good starting point for those who are not knowledgeable of organizational structures for the overall firm. For a more complete discussion of the configurations, Mintzberg (1983) offered an entire book on the subject. According to

Mintzberg, the harmony between the fit of each of these structures with its technology and environment is a key to the firm's organizational success. He pointed out each structure's limitations or advantages. These include such factors as a structure's flexibility and its ability to monitor environmental trends. Several of these basic configurations are likely to have the common characteristics found in firms that are innovative or able to implement innovation. Further, through an understanding of the limitations of the various structures, managers and others can pinpoint problem areas within their own company that may impede the new-product development process or innovation.

Johne (1984) carried out a study of innovating firms. He showed that firms in an industry where innovation is of great importance for competitive reasons pursue organizational structures that aid the process of getting new products to the market efficiently. The types of strategy variables he examined were specialization, formalization, standardization, centralization, and stratification. The reader may note that Mintzberg's organizational structures are somewhat implied in these different strategies. A firm might pursue an offensive or defensive strategy depending on the nature and likely actions of competitors. Another important observation was that leading firms spend on the average three times as much on R&D as less successful firms. Finally the last group of variables he examined were the implementation and initiation of innovation. He found that firms tend to adopt an organic, flexible product innovation process that adapts to the specific context.

Innovative Firm Characteristics

General organizational characteristics that facilitate innovation can be found in the literature from a variety of sources. Characteristics such as flexibility, concentration of power, access to technical competence, and direct attention of those in the implementation process and strategic areas were most often mentioned by respondents in Huchsinger and Bagby's research (1987).

Another study done by Pearson (1988) characterized the firm slightly differently. He proposed five key activities for successful innovating firms. First, the firm should create a supportive environment. Second, it should be structured loosely around its goal. Third, it should define clearly its strategic focus for innovative ideas. Fourth, it should know where to look for ideas and how to leverage them. Finally, the firm ought to seek good ideas at full speed. Innovation, he pointed out, may be unsettling, but it is a constant challenge that builds momentum and possible market leadership.

Most of the literature in this area concludes that there are basic features shared by innovative firms, although the successful specific implementation details of a concept vary from one company to another (Nord and Tucker, 1987). Various features they found that were common in the different contexts were: organizational flexibility, concentration of power, access to technical competence, and direct attention by management to those in the implementation process. This study also posed interesting conceptual problems that should be considered when undertaking a study on innovation. These included: What sense does it make to define something as innovative independent of how it is perceived by the adopting system? If an innovative process or product is not perceived as innovative by the company, then it may not receive the attention it needs for support, or it may be more easily adapted within the system. If a product is considered innovative, then it may meet with implementation barriers (because it is new) or it may be treated much more cautiously than if it did not involve innovation. Why should one distinguish between the adoption of innovation and the process of innovation? The adoption of an innovation is more a problem of managing organizational change. However, the ability to innovate implies a different level of expertise and problems.

Integration of Characteristic and Configuration Theory into Structure

Mintzberg (1979, 1980, 1981) forwarded the idea that some basic structural configurations are better than others for innovation. Although he did not deal with specific alignments within overall structures for product development, other studies in the literature do. Larson and Gobeli (1988), after concluding a study of 540 development projects, assessed the effectiveness of five different project management structures. These structures are basic to the study of innovation in general, so they will be briefly characterized. In the first structure, the functional organization, the development project is divided into segments and assigned to relevant functional units, with each functional group responsible for its segment of the project. Then the parts are assembled into the whole. In a venture team, a separate project manager oversees a group of professionals operating outside the normal boundaries of the organization with responsibility for the project as a whole. Between these two opposites there are a variety of matrix structure types, in which the normal vertical hierarchy is overlaid by a lateral project management system. A functional matrix has a project manager who coordinates the efforts of the functional groups. Functional managers are responsible within their discipline. In a project matrix the project manager has direct authority to make decisions about personnel and work-flow activities. Functional managers are limited to providing resources and advisory support. In the balanced matrix, the project manager is responsible for defining what needs to be done, and the functional managers are concerned with how it will be accomplished. Both parties work together and jointly approve work-flow decisions.

Galbraith (1971) presented an early study of matrix organization designs. An in-depth study of matrix organizations by Knight (1976) explored the advantages and problems inherent in these structures. He further outlined possible resolutions for the problems, and pointed out various synergies and methods for ensuring that they occur. Matrix organizations were shown to be related to new product success (Kolodny, 1980). Quinn (1980) outlined a variety of specific implementations of configurations or alignments of resources that some companies have chosen for product development. For example, there are IBM's overlapping project teams, Hewlett-Packard's series of small, discrete, freestanding units, and Intel's flexible applied technology groups that work close to the marketplace.

Several other articles deal with accessing the impacts of manpower flows and interdependencies in matrix structures within an innovative process (Harwitch and Thietart, 1987; Ettlie, 1985). The Harwitch and Thietart article was referred to in the R&D-marketing interface section, while the study by Ettlie is more fully developed in the technological transfer section.

MANAGERIAL FRAMEWORKS FOR EVALUATING STRUCTURE

Some of these organizational characteristics and structures have been fully developed and are capable of providing frameworks from which managers can develop organizational structures conducive to new-product development. Foster and Pryor (1986) identified basic principles of innovation management that were not dependent on specific company characteristics. They found that companies first began with a careful analysis of their resources, opportunities, and challenges. They then designed a vision; organized managerial support, structures, and environment around that vision; implemented the vision while giving careful attention to the knowledge of obstacles to implementation; and then continually reviewed and reassessed the situation.

Other articles in this section identified problems at different stages of product development. Henry and Vinson (1984) offered two suggestions for improving the effectiveness of new-product development at all stages. First, one should have a realistic concept of product quality. Second, one should develop a structure linking customer wants, design logic, and steps in the development process.

Another type of framework was offered in a paper by Pierce and Delbecq (1977) after they conducted a comprehensive study of organizational variables that may affect innovation. The authors derived descriptive regression models that identified many of the important organizational concerns for each of the three stages of innovation: initiation, adoption, and implementation. Each one was evaluated in terms of organizational context, structure, and member attitudes. Although the models were not tested, they offered a comprehensive list of variables that could be considered in the formulation and implementation of organizational strategies for innovation. Variables such as the existence of work groups, the number of employees in a work group, and the types of employees within the work groups can be examined throughout the various stages of innovation within the different contexts.

MANAGERIAL CONSIDERATIONS

Strategies

In the formulation, conceptualization, and implementation of a new-product strategy, a firm's configuration or technology and the type of strategy chosen could affect the success of the new venture. In an article cited earlier in this report, Cooper and Schendel (1976) discussed strategic responses to technological threats. They suggested that, in order to survive, firms must improve upon the old technology but also make a commitment to develop products utilizing the new technology. What balance is chosen between old and new technologies depends on the pattern of substitution in the market. For example, there may be a rapid diffusion of a new product in the market or it may follow an S-shaped growth curve (slow initial growth, followed by rapid growth, which eventually slows down). Or, the technological innovation may have limited immediate application but great potential within the industry. The growth pattern in turn will determine the response strategy, which determines the resource allocation.

A group of articles viewed this strategy process from the managerial perspective. McGinnis and Ackelsbery (1983) identified how managers can affect organizational issues to improve strategic planning by using a model of important variables for innovation management. General organizational variables in the model are (1) goals and processes that are initially ambiguous, (2) open organizational structure (not tightly structured), (3) good working relationships between departments, (4) meaningful consideration of other points of view, and (5) perceived value of innovation.

Several authors (Roberts, 1980; Romanelde, 1987; Kazanjian, 1988) examined the nature of new ventures, its problems, and various strategies. Roberts (1980) took a detailed view of new ventures. He identified reasons why companies would want to take on new ventures: traditional markets may not be able to sustain further growth; the firm may want to develop a new product or enter an untapped foreign market; or the company may want to take advantage of a good economic opportunity. He further looked at venture strategies and categorized them according to corporate involvement. 3M was provided as an illustrative case study. Key lessons to be learned from the study were that a firm must have long-term persistence while striving to emulate entrepreneurial behavior. Kazanjian (1988) looked at growth patterns of new ventures and the problems associated with the stages and found that there was some correlation between the two. For instance, in an early stage of a new venture there are conceptual and developmental problems. At a later stage, growth may be a major problem. Romanelde (1987), in his study of early venture strategies, found that once a choice has been made regarding a strategy for exploiting resources, firms do best if they concentrate on making those strategies work rather than on trying to change the strategy.

Other strategy-oriented articles address topics such as portfolio management (Kamm, 1986), and the suppression of technology as a strategy for controlling resource dependency for managerial consideration   (Dunford, 1987).

The Japanese Influence

There has been keen interest in the management practices
of Japanese firms and their impact on innovation   and
integration of R&D with other critical corporate functions.
MacDowall (1984), examining the Japanese culture and its impact
on innovation, paid special attention to characteristics of
Japanese industry, government, and universities. Innovative
activity within the Japanese industrial system was found to
possess certain characteristics: R&D programs were carried out
in central research   laboratories, product development
engineering occurred at production plants, and high feedback
levels existed between customers and engineers.
     Pucik and   Hatvany (1983) reviewed the Japanese
strategies,   techniques of implementation, and their
implications for American business. Some of the techniques
identified were open communication, job   rotation, slow
promotion, internal training, and emphasis on work groups.
They also identified some of the cultural characteristics of
the Japanese economy (emphasis on market share, internal
growth, and aggressive innovation) and their implications for
the American economy.
     Seven factors tied to successful innovation were outlined
in a study by Gerstenfeld and Sumiyoshi (1980). They included
the Japanese   propensity to risk taking; their reward
structures; their   organizational designs; their workers'
philosophy; group consensus making; the cooperation between
government, business, and banks; and the   collectiveness of
their culture.

IMPLEMENTATION AND ASSIMILATION OF INNOVATION

A Conducive Approach

One of the most difficult and most critical tasks for
managers is the assimilation of an innovation or new product
strategy into the organization. Chapter 6 of this paper is
devoted to technology transfer in the R&D-marketing interface
literature. A few of the studies are worth mentioning here
as well, as they offer basic approaches or studies from which
managers can gain insight.
     In the development of a new product, the depth and breadth
of the integration will affect the success of the new product
development process (Quinn, 1981).   Benson and Barclay (1987)
offered a selection of methodologies that allow companies to
develop the attributes associated with new-product success. Two
different approaches to the implementation of innovation are
described: rule-bound (each step has a standard or rule for
evaluation of completeness or correctness of implementation)
and autonomous (implementation is not bound by rules but rather
from feedback at the point of delivery). It was found that
autonomous approaches are more effective because individuals
take the initiative and use their delivery skills and expertise

more effectively than in a rule-bound system, and because of the timeliness of the feedback process and the flexibility gained from this approach (Marcus, 1988). An analysis by Maeyer and Goes (1988) advanced a model that suggests that organizational assimilation of technological innovations is determined by contextual (environmental, organizational, and leadership) attributes, innovation attributes, and attributes arising from the interaction of the other two types. Each of these contexts was examined and the most effective mix of characteristics was suggested. For further comments on these articles, see the technology transfer section.

Management Roles: Supervising and Product Championing

A variety of sources provided literature on management roles in innovation. Several articles dealt in particular with R&D management and how to develop organizational configurations that were successful. Gluck and Foster (1978) created a whimsical scenario illustrating top management's role in overseeing technological advancements in product lines. Negative and positive management factors affecting technological change were found to include: allocation of time by the CEO for the project, personal oversight, ability of the CEO to affect strategy, isolation of the CEO from the projects, the creation of an innovative spirit, and the lack of evaluation of the project. Richardson (1985) examined why R&D departments fail to produce. Key reasons included an absence of a sponsor in the base system, an absence of good project discipline and methodology, and overloading of technical personnel.

Other articles further discussed the importance of a sponsor or product champion in new products (e.g., Calish and Gamache, 1984). The product champion is not necessarily employed among existing management, since top managers by nature are often risk averse. The product champion can offer protection of the new product from financial and managerial restraints imposed on the venture by corporate managers. The champion thus sponsors the venture and may offer special financial incentives to the corporate entrepreneur for developing the new venture within the business. Chakrabarti (1974) explored the role of the product champion in the innovation process. Qualities of a successful product champion were examined as well as organizational factors conducive to innovation.

Political Power Issues

Related to this issue is the literature that deals with the power and politics of the new-product process. Some of these issues will also be further developed under the technology transfer section, but a few articles will be mentioned here. In these articles it is clear that success in new-product development depends on having support of the elite power holders. Further, managers should expect conflict and learn how to diffuse it before it happens if they wish to see their project become successful (Lilien, 1983).

Miller and Droge (1986) did an interesting study that included a mathematical model of the relationship between an organization's structure and the personality of the chief executive officer. They found that in smaller organizations this is indeed an important variable. As the size of the company increases, this becomes less important, but the relationship continues to have an effect on strategy formulation.

Entrepreneurship and Intrapreneurship

Quinn (1979) indicated that an effective entrepreneurship strategy within a company can facilitate the successful implementation of large-scale innovations, help to develop innovative strategies, and make the firm capable of responding to rapid change. Much of the literature on managing change has supported this study by indicating that entrepreneurial activity is conducive to successful innovation. In a study of corporate innovation and entrepreneurship, Knight (1987) showed that entrepreneurial firms were good at implementing innovation, and that innovative and entrepreneurial firms had a great deal in common with one another. They tended to have similar corporate environments, to allow similar emphasis on the role of champion, to have similar resource allocations and financial policies, and so on.

In recent years, much attention has been devoted to how the firm can stimulate an entrepreneurial climate, or foster "intrapreneurship," in which entrepreneurial-type activity by company personnel is encouraged and supported. In the Roberts (1977) article included in the innovation section of this paper, the way in which 3M has fostered corporate innovation is outlined. This firm has a strong commitment to internal new-product development and identifying new businesses, and to that end has set up an opportunities analysis group designed to study market and global business opportunities. Recent "intrapreneurial" successes such as Post-It Notes attest to the success of 3M's approach. By contrast, Dow Chemical uses venture capital investment and technology acquired from outside to build new businesses, and Exxon uses venture capital and internally derived R&D results in combination with venture capital as its key to success (Roberts, 1977). Drucker (1985) pointed out that the management of innovation required policies and practices in four areas: organizational culture, performance measures, organizational structure policies, and "don'ts" policies. His study also had structural implications and is further discussed under structure. Burgelman (1983) conceptually integrated entrepreneurial and administrative economic activity through the idea of "corporate entrepreneurship." McGinnis and Verny (1987) described organizational characteristics that facilitate innovation and foster a higher level of intrapreneurship. Further evidence that intrapreneurship is a valuable competitive edge was presented by Rule and Irwin (1988).

OTHER AREAS FOR MANAGERIAL CONSIDERATION

Gerace (1988) developed an organizational analysis matrix to help companies establish an R&D department that could provide new products faster and less expensively. Some of the areas in the matrix are staff management and marketing; R&D department planning, structure and controls; R&D department innovation and creativity, manufacturing quality issues; and financial operations.

Several academic managerial literature sources, particularly Academy of Management Journal and Administrative Science Quarterly, offer managers assessment models by which they can gauge the appropriateness of the levels of their company's organizational variables. Several of the articles try to measure the fit between technology and organizational structure (e.g., Alexander and Randolph, 1985). Their model suggests a method of measuring the fit between technology and structure. An organizational lag model provides not only a basis for further study, but also some interesting insight into the management of innovation. The model implies that there should be a balance in the implementation of administration and technical innovations so that the equilibrium between the social and technical systems can be maintained (Damanpour and Evan, 1984).

Several articles discussed the degree of "fit" between a company's structure and its external environment. As viewed by Hutchinson (1976), organizational form evolves as the goals and environment of the organization change. Cawood (1984) identified interlocking concepts that need to be balanced as innovation and a dynamic environment increase risk and change. These concepts included the corporate mission, corporate focus, flexibility, commitment, trust, and communication. This acceptance of the need for ongoing change is also discussed in McTavish (1984), who implied that ongoing dynamic change may be the only way to ensure needed organizational diversity.

Rousseau (1979) developed an open system framework for investigating relationships between the environment and technology, and between technology and structure. To operationalize successfully the technological issues at each stage of development requires also an integration of policies. However, the policies that need operationalization come from a variety of areas. The ability of technology to deliver innovation, the managerial policies concerning the innovation, financial policies, marketing plans, and integration patterns within a firm will all affect the structural configuration employed by the company. Thus one cannot isolate the study of structure for innovation from the process of innovation and all that it entails. The integration of company policies in the implementation of innovation is further developed in the chapter on technology transfer.

The literature to this point has had one issue in common. All authors commented on the lack of easily available means of measurement in such issues as the need for boundary roles; the fit between technology and organizational configuration; and the fit between the organization and the environment. Perhaps as some of the literature suggests, rather than finding a specific fit for each case, managers should strive to understand the basic concerns and issues of innovation.

NEW APPROACHES AND GAPS IN THE LITERATURE

In recent issues of <u>Administrative Science Quarterly</u> and <u>Academy of Management Review</u>, some readings appear that offer different perspectives for further consideration.   Tushman and Anderson (1986) explored the technical-environmental link by considering not only technological change but also important social, political, and legal change.   Bailey (1986) further stated that researchers need to integrate the study of social action and the study of social form when examining the innovation process.   Both articles brought to light the importance of the individuals and their interrelationships in the new-product development process.

Some articles have identified gaps in the organizational structure literature to date.   Clark (1988) pointed out three underexplored areas in current innovative studies in his recent book.   First, he   remarked that there is a neglect of innovation in organizational studies.   Second, he stated that studies have had too narrow a focus (that is, a focus on profits and not products) and that this narrowness blocks innovation. Finally, he noted that there is a weakness of cross-cultural analysis in relation to the transfer of innovation.

Crisp (1984) pointed out that the inadequacies of the educational programs for those who would manage the process of technological   innovation relate to the nature of management. He stated that managers need to learn how to motivate people to accomplish particular goals. Most of the emphasis in business schools is on hard data analysis and synthesis. Strategies are formulated and the most appropriate structures for success can be developed.   However, the inadequacy of education comes in the transfer of the information to the practicality of the real world situation. In less-than-favorable conditions, the ability of a manager to obtain support for the process,   to motivate and group individuals together for success, and to maintain flexibility and focus is not and perhaps cannot be taught in today's business schools.

ORGANIZATIONAL STRUCTURE: ANNOTATED BIBLIOGRAPHY

AN INNOVATIVE ORGANIZATIONAL DESIGN

Basic Configurations

5.1   JELINEK, MARIANN (1986), Organizations by Design:
        Theory and Practice, second edition, Plano, TX:
        Business Publications (Textbook).

5.2   JOHNE, FREDERICK A. (1984), "How Experienced Product
        Innovators Organize," Journal of Product Innovation
        Management, 1(4), 210-223.
   A sample of active innovating firms is studied. It was
found that a small number of firms, in an industry where
innovation is an important competitive factor, choose
organizational practices which are valuable for getting new
technically advanced products to market efficiently. Structural
variables examined include: specialization, formalization,
standardization, centralization, stratification.

5.3   JOHNE, F.A. (1984), "The Organization of High-
        Technology Product Innovation," European Journal of
        Marketing, 18 (6/7), 55-71.
   Examines best current product innovation practice; describes
organizational arrangements currently used by firms which are
regular   product   innovators.   Dependent   measure   used:
differences in firm's product innovation performance.
Independent variables: 1) strategy (explicit or implicit); 2)
resources and 3) structure used for product innovation task.
Conclusions: 1) Leaders want to read competition in terms of
product innovation; 2) Leader firms spend on average three
times as much sales revenue on R&D; 3) Leader firms do not
adopt a single, clearly defined organizational format to handle
all the complications of product innovation.

5.4   JOHNE, F.A. (1985), Industrial Product Innovation:
        Organization and Management, Beckenham, Kent,
        England: Croom Helm.
   This book discusses organizational designs and structures,

then presents detailed case histories of current practice. Highlighted are current organizational practices in two main types of firms: active and experienced product innovator firms and less innovative firms.

5.5   MINTZBERG, HENRY (1979), The Structuring of Organizations, Englewood Cliffs, NJ: Prentice-Hall (Textbook).

5.6   MINTZBERG, HENRY (1980), "Structure in 5's: A Synthesis of the Research on Organization Design," Management Science 26(3), 322-341.
    Typology of five basic configurations is presented: Simple Structure, Machine Bureaucracy, Professional Bureaucracy, Divisionalized Form, and Adhocracy. Elements of these configurations are: the basic parts of the organization (operating core, strategic apex, middle line, technostructure, and support staff). the basic mechanisms of coordination, design parameters and contingency factors.

5.7   MINTZBERG, HENRY (1981), "Organization Design: Fashion or Fit?" Harvard Business Review, 59 (January-February), 103.
    Elements in organizational design should be well suited to task the firm wishes to accomplish. The author lists five natural configurations of certain elements of structure and environment. Harmony among the parts may be the key to organizational success.

5.8   MINTZBERG, HENRY (1983), Structure in Fives: Designing Effective Organizations, Englewood Cliffs, NJ: Prentice-Hall (Textbook).

Innovative Firm Characteristics

5.9   BART, CHRISTOPHER K. (1988), "Organizing for New Product Development," Journal of Business Strategy, 9(4), 34-38.
    New venture units should emerge as one of the keys to enhancing the new product process in large, diversified firms. They offer the promise of pursuing simultaneously two strategic missions: new products and efficiency in the operation of historical, existing businesses.

5.10   LAMB, WARREN (1985), "Building Balanced Innovation Teams," Journal of Product Innovation Management, 2(2), 93-100.
    Action Profile Technique: how managers allocate their initiatives across the decision-making stages over the long run. The measure employed uses observation and categorization of body movements and rhythms; assesses natural ability of people, and suggests how to build balanced innovation teams.

5.11   LUCHSINGER, VINCE AND D. RAY BAGBY (1987), "Entrepreneurship and Intrapreneurship: Behaviors, Comparisons, and Contrast," SAM Advanced Management Journal, 52 (Summer), 10.

Companies that foster intrapreneurship are characterized by: 1) practicing enlightened management principles; 2) adopting an entrepreneurial style that avoids bureaucratic barriers and fosters an innovative climate; 3) encourage intrapreneurship and innovation among the work force. To do this, the firm should 1) focus on results and teamwork; 2) reward innovation and risk taking; 3) tolerate and learn from mistakes; 4) remain flexible and change-oriented.

5.12   NORD, WALTER R. AND SHARON TUCKER (1988),
        "Implementing Routine and Radical Innovations,"
        <u>Administrative Science Quarterly</u>, 33(2).
An exhaustive review of the literature. Conclusions: 1) One cannot define innovation independent of how it is perceived by the adopting system. 2) One must distinguish between the process of innovation and organizational learning. 3) One must also distinguish between the process of adoption of innovation and the process of innovating.

5.13   PEARSON, ANDRALL E. (1988), "Tough-Minded Ways to Get
        Innovative," <u>Harvard Business Review</u>, 66 (May-June),
        99-106.
An in-depth discussion of five key activities that make some competitors outstanding innovators: 1) they create supportive environment; 2) they structure loosely; 3) they define a clearly strategic focus for innovative ideas; 4) they know where to look for ideas and how to leverage them; 5) they go after good ideas at full speed. Innovation may be unsettling but it is a constant challenge that builds momentum and possible market leadership.

Integration of Characteristic and Configuration Theory into Structure

5.14   GALBRAITH, JAY R. (1971), "Matrix Organization
        Designs," <u>Business Horizons</u>, 14, 29-40.
Illustration of the transition of Standard Products Inc. from a functional company to a pure matrix form. Focuses on forming functional and project teams. Author describes alternatives with matrix forms, and factors that help determine choices (product technology, economics, interdependence etc.) since not all organizations need a pure matrix.

5.15   GALBRAITH, JAY (1982), "Designing the Innovative
        Organization," <u>Organizational Dynamics</u> (Winter),
        5-25.
Innovation requires of an organization that structure, processes, rewards and people must be combined in a special way: designed to do something for the first time. Their components are completely different from those designed to do something well for the millionth time. If ideas produced are to be implemented then a transition process to transfer ideas from the innovative areas to the operating parts need to be i place. Offers excellent ideas concerning the key processes that need to be established for integration.

5.16   GOBELI, DAVID H. AND ERIK W. LARSON (1986), "Matrix

Management: More than a Fad," Engineering Management International, 4, 71-76.

115 managers from 62 different companies were asked to classify their new product development structure into one of five categories: functional, functional matrix, balanced matrix, project matrix, project team. In spite of widespread criticism of matrix structures, the results showed that matrix structures were the most popular. Generally speaking, most respondents said they would use the same structures as before. In sum, the matrix structure is not dead or dying, but at the same time that does not imply it is easy.

5.17   KNIGHT, KENNETH (1976), "Matrix Organization: A Review," Journal of Management Studies, 13(2), 111-130.

A review paper on matrix structures, centered around five basic questions: (a) What does the term "matrix organization" mean? (b) What reasons are there for introducing such structures? (c) What advantages are claimed by them? (d) What problems do they encounter? (e) How can they be made to work effectively?

5.18   KOLODNY, HARVEY F. (1980), "Matrix Organization Designs and New Program Success," Research Management, 23(5), 29-33.

The article shows that matrix organizations often have high rates of new product innovation.

5.19   LARSON, ERIK W. AND DAVID H. GOBELI (1988), "Organizing for Product Development Projects," Journal of Product Innovation Management, 5(3), 180-190.

How to organize to support development of new products. Five basic structures are discussed: functional, functional matrix, balanced matrix, project matrix, and project team. These are approximately in order of decreasing emphasis placed on function and increasing emphasis on product project.

5.20   SANDS, S. (1983), "Problems of Organizing for Effective New Product Development," European Journal of Marketing, 17(4), 18-33.

Identifies nine possible choices for new product development organization, and discusses the characteristics of each: 1. New product group located in marketing; 2. Product manager handling new products; 3. New product manager; 4. New product group located in technical division; 5. New product department (line); 6. New product department (staff); 7. Task forces and venture groups; 8. New product committees; 9. Integrative new product organization.

MANAGERIAL FRAMEWORKS FOR EVALUATING STRUCTURE

5.21   FOSTER, WILLIAM K. AND AUSTIN K. PRYOR (1986), "The Strategic Management of Innovation," Journal of Business Strategy, 7(1), 38-42.

Large corporations realize that medium-to-small and start-up businesses generate most of the growth in GNP. They are looking for some fundamental ways to become more innovative and entrepreneurial. Basic underlying principles of innovation management, not specific of other companies, need to be understood. To be truly innovative, the first major task is to discover the company's resources, opportunities and challenges. A plan for innovation consists of: 1) design a vision; 2) organize means, support structures and environment to achieve vision; 3) implementation and obstacle analysis; 4) reassess and review.

5.22   HENRY, DONALD F. AND WILLIAM D. VINSON (1984), "A
        Fresh Look at New Product Development," Journal of
        Business Strategy, 5 (Fall), 22-31.
Three possible dilemmas in the new product process are: 1) development is serial; 2) it is hard to define business versus technical goals; 3) firm must develop business plan emphasizing the linkage between operating work and business performance. How to improve effectiveness as a process: 1) get a realistic concept of product quality; 2) develop a structure linking customer wants, design logic, and steps in the process (documentation of a new product should cover all of the above inputs).

5.23   PIERCE, JON AND ANDRE DELBECQ (1977), "Organizational
        Structure, Individual Attitudes and Innovation,"
        Academy of Management Review, 2(1), 27-37.
Innovation (initiation, adoption and implementation of new ideas or activities in an organizational setting) is viewed in terms of organization content, structure, and member attitudes. Three predictive models for each phase of innovation are derived and are presented as directions for future research and theory construction. Organic structure more innovative, best in overall innovativeness and particularly at initiation stage. Adoption stage needs strong centralized formal decision making.

MANAGERIAL CONSIDERATIONS

Strategies

5.24   BINGHAM, FRANK G. AND CHARLES J. QUIGLEY, JR. (1989),
        "Venture Team Application to New Product
        Development," Journal of Business and Industrial
        Marketing, 4(2), 49-59.
Presents a new product implementation model designed to reduce the risk inherent in new product ventures in the industrial marketplace. The model describes a process that gives the industrial firm the ability to exert greater control over internal and external factors critical to successful new product implementation.

5.25   BRUNO, ALBERT V. AND JOEL K. LEIDECKER (1988),
        "Causes of New Venture Failure: 1960s vs. 1980s,"
        Business Horizons, 31 (November-December), 51-56.
The authors examined Silicon Valley firms founded in the 1960s and the 1980s and determined a list of reasons for venture failure: 1. product market reasons: product timing,

product design, inappropriate distribution or selling strategies, unclear business definition, overreliance on one customer. 2. Financial reasons: initial undercapitalization, assuming a debt investment too early, venture capital relationship. 3. Managerial/key employee reasons: ineffective team, personal problems, one-track thinking, cultural/social factors.

5.26   DUNFORD, RICHARD (1987), "The Suppression of
        Technology as a Strategy for Controlling Resource
        Dependency," Administrative Science Quarterly, 32(4),
        512-525.
This study utilizes and extends the resource dependence perspective of a strategy that the suppression of a technology is one used to control. Specific tactics and their characteristics are identified along with their objectives and the processes by which these may be achieved.

5.27   KAMM, JUDITH B. (1986), "The Portfolio Approach to
        Divisional Innovation Strategy," Journal of Business
        Strategy, 7(1), 25-36.
Application and use of portfolio strategy by general managers can be instrumental in achieving broader objectives and economic goals despite drawbacks of uncertainty expense and inefficiency that are often associated with innovation. This paper shows how the portfolio strategy can be used, points out its strengths and weaknesses and implications for the innovative process.

5.28   KAZANJIAN, ROBERT K. (1988), "Relation of Dominant
        Problems to Stages of Growth in Technology-Based
        New Ventures," Academy of Management Journal, 31(2),
        257-279.
Two studies investigating growth patterns of new ventures are presented. The first study theorized a stage of growth model to apply specifically to technology-based new ventures. Stages are described as responses of organizational design variables to a firm's response to sets of dominant problems it faces at sequential times. The second study explored relationships between stages of growth and theorized pattern of dominant problems using data base of 105 firms. Life and maturity of venture may be characterized by stages: concept and development; commercialization; growth; stability.

5.29   MC GINNIS, MICHAEL A. AND M. ROBERT ACKELSBERG
        (1983), "Effective Innovation Management: Missing
        Link in Strategic Planning?" Journal of Business
        Strategy, 4(1), 59-66.
A well-written survey of literature on variables affecting innovation in an organizational context. Develops a model of important variables and how a manager can affect these organizational issues to improve strategic planning. Top managers should set goals and processes (maybe initially ambiguous), foster an open organizational structure and good working relationships between departments, and meaningfully consider other points of view. Finally, the organization must perceive the value of the innovation.

5.30   MEYERS, PATRICIA W. AND DAVID WILEMON (1989),
          "Learning in New Technology Development Teams,"
          Journal of Product Innovation Management, 6(2),
          79-88.
This study investigates the ways in which new product
development teams learn in technology-based organizations.
Factors examined: learning modes employed by teams, conditions
blocking team learning which create errors, learning transfer
among teams.   Methods for improving the learning climate and
managerial implications are presented.

5.31   ROBERTS, EDWARD B. (1980), "New Ventures for
          Corporate Growth," Harvard Business Review, 58 (July-
          August), 134.
The article explores the nature of ventures. Reasons to
undertake ventures are: 1) traditional markets cannot sustain
further growth; 2) develop a new product; 3) enter an untapped
foreign market; 4) take advantage of an economic opportunity.
Venture strategies depend on corporate involvement and include:
providing venture capital, venture nurturing, venture spinoff,
new style joint venture, venture merging, internal ventures.
The article deals particularly with New Style Joint Venturing
and its advantages and disadvantages. Key lessons: for venture
success a firm must combine long-term persistence with
entrepreneurial behavior.

5.32   ROMANERLE, ELAINE (1987), "New Venture Strategies in
          the Minicomputer Industry," California Management
          Review, 30 (Fall), 160.
Examines how early strategies of 108 firms in the
minicomputer industry influenced both early survival and later
capacities and directions for change over the period 1957 -
1981.   Strategic activity patterns of firms that survived their
early years are examined and compared with those of firms that
failed.   Once a choice has been made regarding a strategy for
exploiting resources, firms do best if they concentrate on
making those strategies work as opposed to trying to change the
strategy itself.

5.33   TYEBJEE, TYZOON T. (1988), "A Typology of Joint
          Ventures: Japanese Strategies in the United States,"
          California Management Review, 31(1), 75-86.
Recent Japanese-American joint ventures have been of four
types: 1. A Japanese firm acquiring an equity position in an
entrepreneurial high-tech company that requires expansion
financing; 2. A Japanese firm assumes an equity position in an
ailing division of a large American firm; 3. Two parents spawn
together a new separate entity, typically a venture in some
incipient market; 4. A joint venture evolves from a buyer-
supplier relationship.

     The Japanese Influence

5.34   GERSTENFELD, ARTHUR AND KEYI SUMIYOSHI (1980), "The
          Management of Innovation in Japan: Seven Forces that
          Make the DIfference," Research Management, 23(1), 30-
          34.

1) Japanese companies have more propensity to risk (less conservative). 2) Reward structure is different: lower engineer salaries but potentially high bonuses. 3) Organizational design at the marketing-R&D interface (integration and differentiation recognized as necessary for effective organizations.) 4)Workers in Japan are less anti-innovation. Unions actually often encourage innovation there. 5) Group consensus decision making is common. 6) Government-industry cooperation prevalent. 7) Cultural issues: collectiveness oriented, high integration, homogeneity, enthusiasm and loyalty associated with lifetime employment.

5.35   MAC DOWALL, JOSEPH (1984), "The Technology
         Innovation System in Japan," _Journal of Product
         Innovation Management_, 1(3), 165-172.
    Sketches characteristics of Japanese culture and impact on innovation.   1) Industry: social attitudes, competition, paternalism, employees, management style, attitude toward risk in innovation. 2) Government and Universities: Japanese education and technology base. 3) Industrial innovation system. Foci of innovative activity are 1) R&D programs of a central research laboratory; 2) product development engineering in production plants; 3) feedback between customer contact and engineers; 4) production engineering development and innovation from quality control activity.

IMPLEMENTATION AND ASSIMILATION OF INNOVATION

A Conducive Approach

5.36   BENSON, MARK H. AND IAN BARCLAY (1987), "Improving
         New Product Success Through Organization
         Development," _Proceedings_, IEEE Conference on
         Management and Technology: Management of Evolving
         Systems.
    The authors discuss the need for improvement in the new product development process, via a planned organization development process is discussed. Methodologies allowing companies to develop attributes that lead to successful new product development are presented.

5.37   MARCUS, ALFRED A. (1988), "Implementing Externally
         Induced Innovations: A Comparison of Rule-Bound and
         Autonomous Approaches," _Academy of Management
         Journal_, 31(2), 235.
    Research analyzed now nuclear power plants implemented safety review innovations after Three Mile Island. Power plants with relatively poor safety standards tended to respond in rule bound manner that perpetuated their poor performance (usually because of record they were allowed no "zone of discretion" for implementing innovations). Power plants which had autonomous approaches to implementation achieved better success.   This appears to be due to the idea that the autonomous approach is closer to the point of delivery. They can thus rely on feedback information from project, encourage individual initiation, and take advantage of delivery skills,

knowledge and expertise.

Management Roles: Supervising and Product Championing

5.38   CALISH, IRVING G. AND R. DONALD GAMACHE (1984),
        "Wizards and Champions: The Kingdom of New Venture
        Management," Journal of Product Innovation Management
        1(4), 238-241.
Champion: a "true entrepreneur"; not from existing corporate
management, since in most cases, successful corporate managers
are risk-averse.   Further, corporate managers are often
hampered from becoming a champion because of corporate culture.
Wizard: offers the champion protection from unrealistic
financial and managerial restraints and bottom line and market
share measurements.   The wizard is thus a sponsor.   Chalice:
special incentives to the champion for developing the new
venture into a profitable business.

5.39   CHAKRABARTI, A.K. (1974), "The Role of Champion in
        Product Innovation," California Management Review,
        17(2), 58-62.
Supported by data from 45 cases of product development with
varying degrees of success, the concept of product champion and
his role in the innovation process is explored.   Problems as
well as the desirable qualities of a successful product
champion are examined and organizational factors conducive to
innovation are identified.

5.40   GLUCK, FREDERICK W. AND RICHARD FOSTER (1978),
        "Managing Technological Change: A Box of Cigars for
        Brad," Harvard Business Review, 56 (September-
        October), 139.
The CEO of Diversified Manufacturing Corporation learns a
lesson in overseeing technological advance in a product line.
A whimsical article describing the activities of a new Vice
President for development as he goes through correspondence
with the CEO about management concerns for advancing technology
and change.   Concerns include: 1) time allocation of CEO and
his ability to affect strategy; 2) the isolation of CEO from
the company; 3) future innovative spirit lacking; 4) lack of
personal oversight. 5) lack of evaluation of project.

5.41   MAIDIQUE, M.A. (1980), "Entrepreneurs, Champions and
        Technological Innovation," Sloan Management Review,
        21(2), 59-76.
This article highlights the important role of the
entrepreneur or product champion in radical product innovation.
The role differs, however, according to the developmental stage
reached by the firm.   Top managerial support for the
entrepreneur is essential to successful product innovation.

5.42   ROBERTS, E.B. AND A.R. FUSFIELD (1981), "Staffing the
        Innovative Technology-Based Organization," Sloan
        Management Review, 22(3), 19-34.
This paper studies the behavior roles involved in the
technology-based innovation process. Five different roles are
needed for successful innovation: 1. Idea Generation; 2.

Entrepreneur or Champion; 3. Project Leader; 4. Gatekeeper; 5. Sponsor or Coach. "Ideal" profiles of the characteristics and activities are developed from empirical findings.

Political Power Issues

5.43   LILIEN, GARY L. (1983), "If the President Likes a New Product a Model Won't Kill It," _Interfaces_, 13(3), 54-58.
An anecdotal article about a new entry into an established market.   The product failed model-based pre-test-market analysis, and the firm failed to change existing advertising campaign as a result.

5.44   MILLER, DANNY AND CORNELIA DROGE (1986), "Psychological and Traditional Determinants of Structure," _Administrative Science Quarterly_, 31(4), 539-560.
A study of the relationship between an organization's structure and the personality of the chief executive officer. Not related to new product success and relation to organization, except that in small organizations CEO's personality and ideas will be more important.

Entrepreneurship and Intrapreneurship

5.45   BURGELMAN, ROBERT A. (1983), "Corporate Entrepreneurship and Strategic Management: Insights from a Process Study," _Management Science_, 29(12), 1349-1364.
Presents a model of the strategic process concerning entrepreneurial activity in large, complex organizations. Provides a conceptual integration of entrepreneurial and administrated economic activity through the idea of "corporate entrepreneurship."

5.46   DRUCKER, PETER (1985), _Innovation and Entrepreneurship_, New York: Harper and Row, Ch. 13, 147-176.
Entrepreneurship management requires policies and practices in four areas: 1) culture of organization to create climate; 2) measure performance; 3) policies geared to certain organizational   structure;   4)   "don'ts"   policies. Recommendations for structures: 1) put new venture elsewhere in old structure; 2) set up as new venture to product managers (project teams); 3) all 'infant' groups should report to one main group; 4) keep it away from burdens it cannot handle (different policies or rules); 5) carefully manage rewards and compensation.

5.47   KNIGHT, RUSSELL M. (1987), "Corporate Innovation and Entrepreneurship: A Canadian Study," _Journal of Product Innovation Management_, 4(4), 284-297.
Discusses   the   practices   of   the   more   successful entrepreneurial firms.   Recommends how firms should organize to explore, develop and produce new innovative ventures.

Discusses role of intrapreneur as product champion.

5.48   Mc GINNIS, MICHAEL A. AND THOMAS P. VERNEY (1987),
        "Innovation Management and Intrapreneurship," SAM
        Advanced Management Journal, 52 (Summer), 19.
Describes individual and organizational characteristics that
facilitate innovation and foster a higher level of
intrapreneurship within a firm.

5.49   MORRIS, MICHAEL AND DUANE DAVIS (1988), "Attitudes
        Toward Corporate Entrepreneurship: Marketers Versus
        Non-Marketers," Proceedings, 1988 Conference on the
        Marketing-Entrepreneurship Interface, 139-150.
Entrepreneurship is viewed as an organizational process
consisting of three dimensions: innovativeness, risk-taking
and proactiveness. Marketing and non-marketing managers are
compared on their opinions on the importance of entrepreneurial
orientation. The results suggest marketing managers may be
less entrepreneurial than non-marketing managers.

5.50   MORRIS, MICHAEL H., DUANE L. DAVIS AND JANE EWING
        (1988), "The Role of Entrepreneurship in Industrial
        Marketing Activities," Industrial Marketing
        Management, 17, 337-346.
Entrepreneurship: an organizational process consisting of
innovativeness, proactiveness and risk-taking. Study reports
results from a survey of marketing managers regarding
perceptions of entrepreneurship, its importance in their firms,
marketing management areas where entrepreneurship is most
critical, and obstacles to encouraging entrepreneurship within
the marketing function. Marketers see their own activities as
fairly entrepreneurial.

5.51   MORRIS, MICHAEL H. AND GORDON W. PAUL (1987), "The
        Relationship Between Entrepreneurship and Marketing
        in Established Firms," Journal of Business Venturing,
        2, 247-259.
Describes the relationship between entrepreneurial and
marketing orientations of a firm. The hypotheses that
entrepreneurial firms tend to be more marketing oriented, and
that marketing provides a vehicle for achieving
entrepreneurship within the organization, were supported.
Dimensions of entrepreneurial orientation are innovativeness,
risk taking and proactiveness. Dimensions of marketing
orientation are investment in marketing activities and people,
and adoption of the marketing concept.

5.52   QUINN, JAMES BRIAN (1979), "Technological Innovation,
        Entrepreneurship, and Strategy," Sloan Management
        Review, 20(3), 19-30.
Details factors that have made entrepreneurial system so
effective and outlines the current shortcomings of large
institutions with respect to those factors. Draws on the
author's experience with major enterprises that have
successfully undertaken large-scale innovations and develops
strategies to respond to enormous challenges ahead.

5.53   RULE, ERIK G. AND DONALD W. IRWIN (1988), "Fostering

Intrapreneurship: The New Competitive Edge,"
Journal of Business Strategy 9(3), 44-47.
Covers several keys to successful intrapreneurship: 1)
Generate new ideas; 2) Screen new ideas; 3) Support middle
managers;   4)   Support   idea   development;   5)   Encourage
flexibility; 6) Reward contributors; 7) Provide leadership.
Many people value innovation but few know how to achieve it.
Article lists 33 ways to encourage intrapreneurship, including
activities such as in house market research, monitoring trade
shows, liaison with universities and customer focus groups.

5.54   SOUDER, W.E. (1981), "Encouraging Entrepreneurship
        in Large Corporations," R&D Management, 11(2),
        18-22.
Empirical study of 50 successes and 50 failures in new
product development. Six factors were identified that related
to innovative managerial activity: 1. Early identification of
potential   entrepreneurs   by   management   and   allocation   of
projects to them. 2. Give entrepreneurs formal licance to carry
out the function. 3. Networking encourages innovation and
creativity. 4. Provide entrepreneurs with sponsorship. 5. Give
them the right level of authority. 6. Provide discretionary
powers.

OTHER AREAS FOR MANAGERIAL CONSIDERATION

5.55   BAILEY, STEPHEN R. (1986), "Technology as an Occasion
        for Structuring: Evidence from Observations of CT
        Scanners and the Social Order of Radiology
        Departments," Administrative Sciences Quarterly,
        31(1), 78-108.
New   medical   imaging   devices   may   actually   alter   the
organizational and occupational structure of radiologic work.
The article found that technologies do influence organizational
structures in orderly ways, but their influence depends on the
specific historical process in which they are embedded.

5.56   DAMANPOUR, FARIBORZ AND WILLIAM M. EVAN (1984),
        "Organizational Innovation and Performance: The
        Problem of 'Organizational Lag,'" Administrative
        Science Quarterly, 29(3), 392-409.
Organizational lag model: a time lag exists between rates
of adoption of technical and administrative innovations. This
model is applied to study the impact of adoption of types of
innovation   on   organizational   performance.   Uncertainty   or
change in environment affect strategy and/or structure of
organization, which in turn leads to the implementation of
innovations.   There   needs   to   be   a   balance   between
implementation of administrative and technical innovations
which helps maintain equilibrium between the social and
technical systems, which lead to high performance.

5.57   GERACE, MICHAEL J. (1988), "Improving Product
        Development Using Organizational Analysis,"
        Adhesives Age, 31(1), 28-30.
Proposes an organizational analysis matrix to help companies
establish an R&D program that provides new products faster and

less expensively.   The author discusses staff management and marketing; R&D department planning, structure and controls; R&D department innovation and creativity; and manufacturing quality and financial operations.

5.58   JELINEK, MARIANN (1977), "Technology, Organizations and Contingency," Academy of Management Review, 2(1), 17-26.
A   survey   of   studies   of   technology,   environment   and organizational contingency to construct a synthesis of theory and   suggest   further   research.   A   multiple-environment, multiple-technology model of the firm is proposed. Intervening technologies   and   elaborated   structure   protect   the   core technology and mediate fit among parts of the organization and between organization and environment.

5.59   ROUSSEAU, DENISE M. (1979), "Assessment of Technology in Organizations: Closed versus Open Systems Approaches," Academy of Management Review, 4, 531-542.
An   open   systems   framework   for   assessing   technology   is derived at three technology levels.   This will allow better research   facility   to   assess   technological   studies,   to investigate relations between environment and technology.   It will also provide a basis for research evaluating relationship of technology to environment, and technology to structure.

5.60   TUSHMAN, MICHAEL AND PHILIP ANDERSON (1986), "Technological Discontinuities and Organizational Environments," Administrative Sciences Quarterly, 31(3), 439-465.
This paper focuses on patterns of technological change and on the impact of technological breakthroughs on environmental conditions.   The authors demonstrate that technology evolves through   periods   of   incremental   change   punctuated   by technological breakthroughs that either exhaust or destroy the competence of firms in an industry.   These breakthroughs or discontinuities   significantly   increase   environmental uncertainty and munificence.

5.61   WALKER, GORDON (1985), "Network Position and Cognition in a Computer Software Firm," Administrative Sciences Quarterly, 30(1), 103-130.
This study examines the network structure of one entire organization, and how the position of the firm within the network structure affects its judgment of specific, theoretical outcomes.   Examines   interrelationships   and   how   they   might affect the firm's view of themselves, the environment, the industry, or competition.

NEW APPROACHES AND GAPS IN THE LITERATURE

5.62   ALEXANDER, JUDITH W. AND W. ALAN RANDOLPH (1985), "The Fit Between Technology and Structure as a Predictor of Performance in Nursing Subunits," Academy of Management Journal, 28(4), 844-859.
Study of 27 units in the Southeast.   Results indicate that

a fit between technology and structure has potential for enhancing unit design related to unit performance. Suggested fit techniques that require further study to be validated.

5.63   CAWOOD, DAVID (1984), "Managing Innovation: Military
        Strategy in Business," Business Horizons, 27(6), 62-
        66.
Author has six interlocking concepts that need to be reweighed and balanced as innovation, and a dynamic environment, increase risk and change. These are: corporate mission, corporate focus, flexibility, commitment, trust and communication.

5.64   CLARK, PETER A. (1988), Anglo-American Innovation,
        Berlin: De Gruyter.
Points out that technical innovation is good. Emphasizes necessity of conceptualizing technical innovation as shaped by organizational and cultural factors. Points out three problems or lacking areas in current innovation and organizational studies: 1) neglect of innovation in organizational studies; 2) blockages to innovation because of too narrow focus; 3) weakness of cross-cultural analysis in relation to transfer of innovation.

5.65   CRISP, JOHN D.C. (1984), "The Neglect of Technology
        Management," Journal of Product Innovation
        Management, 1(4), 267-272.
A commentary on the inadequacies of educational programs for those who plan to manage the process of technological innovation.

5.66   HUTCHINSON, JOHN (1976), "Evolving Organizational
        Forms," Columbia Journal of World Business, 11(2).
The article shows that organizational structure is evolving and changing as a company changes the focus of its goals and as the environment changes.

5.67   MC TAVISH, RONALD (1984), "Approaching the New
        Product Organization Problem: Favor Flexibility and
        Variety of Attack," European Journal of Marketing,
        18(6/7), 30-42.
A case study illustration of the practical problems faced by companies in organizing new product activities in industrial markets. The implication of the study is that a 'best' organizational solution may be in acceptance of the necessity for regular adaptation and experimentation: on-going dynamic change may be the only way to ensure needed organizational diversity.

6

Technological Transfer

INTRODUCTION

The last two chapters have discussed the importance of the roles of the interface between R&D and marketing, and of the appropriate organizational structure, in stimulating successful innovation. In a way, these are both really means to an end, the end being effective transfer of technology, both within the firm and between the firm and its environment. Effective technology transfer requires internal interdependencies such as the R&D-marketing interface, and external interdependencies such as the organization-external environment interface and the organization-technology interface. It also requires an environment conducive to innovation. Technological transfer, then, can be thought of as effective management for an end goal.

Miles et al. (1978) interrelated corporate structure with the environment. This article categorized main problems facing all firms into three classes: entrepreneurial, engineering and administrative. Depending on the nature of the business, the different strategies for dealing with these basic problems would lead to effective structuring. Firms could be characterized by their informational or environmental stances (defenders, analyzers, prospectors). Much of the early integrative material was related to understanding organizational configurations. However, achieving innovativeness and adequate levels of technological transfer entails much more than proper selection of structural configurations.

Some studies have begun to take this broader integrative approach. In an article discussed in Chapter 4, Nystrom (1985) realized that it was obvious that new-product development strategy must be able to form an effective link between the R&D and marketing divisions of a firm. However, unlike many previous researchers, Nystrom noted that this does not happen in a vacuum. Most recently a study done by Meyer and Goes (1988) examined the assimilation of innovations into organizations. Their model suggested that organizational assimilation of technological innovations is determined by three types of attributes. They are attributes of context, of innovation, and of the interaction of the two. Thus, between situations, the attributes and assimilation will vary.

There has been a series of books that discuss issues of technological transfer. Most of them examine obstacles and opportunities of technology transfer, how to manage success, and how to address policy issues. Davis and associates (1986) took a multi-disciplinary approach to the study of how dissemination and adoption of innovations can be facilitated. They pointed out important historical lessons for managers for obtaining productivity gains. Foster's (1986) book focuses on understanding the institutional biases that underlie a company's use of technology.   He postulated that technological product improvements follow a characteristic pattern of adoption in an organization. He suggested that R&D managers should learn from experience and study the pattern of innovation within their company to understand their company's biases. Leslie (1983) presented a view of Kettering's clarity of perception of the systemic nature of innovation in his organization, General Motors. The author implies that today's managers will gain important insights by reading about others' management styles. Kettering understood how the effect of technological change radiated outward from the lab to touch the work of many organizational units. Without the support of these other units, even the best science would fail to show commercial success. This is consistent with Foster (1986). Kettering also believed that mass production methods are opposed to those essential to R&D. Managers should keep this in mind and help the units involved understand the problems as well. The ideas that inherent barriers need to be torn down and that incentives are needed to improve technological transfer are not new.

Wasserman (1985) looked at the implementation of telephone transmission at the turn of the century. He pointed out that in technically based firms there is a strong temptation to overlook the ways in which innovation might interact with what is already in place. R&D and management must therefore be able to focus on well-defined problems and contemplate the complications of mixing old technology with new. He also proposed that innovation is a social and political process that needs to be well understood to be effectively managed.

ORGANIZATIONAL TRANSFER AND STRUCTURE ASPECTS

Several studies have examined organizational aspects that enhance technological transfer. One such approach, the gatekeeper approach, is most relevant to companies involved in product development in a dynamic environment (Davis and Wilkof, 1988). In this approach, the organization's structure and the processes that are implemented will influence how scientific and technical information are transferred as well as the quality of the information that is disseminated and used. Thus improving the context in which transfer takes place may be more effective than changing the efficiency of existing transfer procedures. A related model (Gillespie and Mileti, 1977) examined the interrelationships between technology, behavior, and structure.

Morone and Ivins (1982) examined the transfer of

technology from national laboratory to industry. They found that certain factors were critical in improving the process: there needed to be an interaction between industry, laboratory, marketing, and engineering throughout the process; spinoffs should be nurtured; labs that would have commercial markets needed to possess special technical capabilities; and lab development projects should be focused to meet industrial goals. In Bitondo's (1988) study of technology transfer in a decentralized corporation, it was found that the probability of successful implementation of research is improved when the research has been focused on the long-range divisional goals and when marketing, manufacturing, and engineering division personnel are involved in the formulation of research strategy and plans. Also, the probability of successful implementation was improved when the company has created a favorable environment for innovation expectations.

INTERFACES AND BARRIERS

Other studies have looked at the various interfaces within a large firm and at the factors that enhance technological transfer. Burt and Soukup (1985) investigated the engineering and purchasing interface, and its ability to incorporate information flows concerning new-product development. Vendors can give valuable feedback on which specifications are realistic, supply constraints, and costs added to product that might be overlooked. Purchasers can provide information that help monitor the environment, identify strengths and weaknesses of new products, and provide focus for future research. Therefore, management should make sure these channels of feedback are established and cultivated. Ginn and Rubenstein (1986) forwarded the idea that all interfaces are potentially fundamental barriers. They found that projects that had greater technical and commercial success tended to have higher levels of conflict among organizational divisions. Therefore they reasoned that by increasing compatibility of goals among participating groups the relationships at one of the fundamental barriers can be improved.

Souder (1977) looked at several group decision-making processes and found that consensus and collaboration problems at the R&D-marketing interface may be best alleviated by a combined nominal-interacting process. Thorn (1987) also studied problem solving for innovation. He supported the belief that creative problem solving can be taught. He offered two methods through which this process could take place. One entailed professional brainstorming, and the other, called Synectics, involved a series of meetings. He forwarded several key factors that are vital if any problem solving is to take place: a clear problem statement; a commitment to solving the problem; experienced people in the area; the use of a combination of approaches; and capable leadership.

MANAGEMENT AND ORGANIZATIONAL ISSUES

Literature on managing transition is useful for those who must implement innovations in house. Quinn (1982) proposed a list of strategies that managers need to consider when managing a transition. Whenever an innovation is being implemented there will be some organizational resistance. Managers need to know how to minimize that resistance. Quinn suggested that they should build organizational awareness, lead the formal information systems, build credibility, legitimize new viewpoints, and structure for flexibility. He also felt that managers would be responsible for tactical strategic shifts and would need to create pockets for commitment, to crystallize the focus, to formalize commitments, and to integrate innovative ideas.

As Omsen and Ekestrom (1987) pointed out in their study, often there is no one in charge of evaluating unsolicited product ideas. When most companies are approached with a new idea, they are either unreceptive or unsure of how to handle it. Thus a company should develop a program to maximize these potential areas as they represent potential opportunities at a reduced development cost.

There may also be an inherent difficulty in getting management to take seriously and make decisions in a timely fashion for a business opportunity from the R&D community (Graham, 1986). Knowing how and when to apply pressure on research-dependent projects is important to their success. When the strategic goals of the company are not clearly and consistently translated into terms that give direction to the R&D effort, two problems occur. Political conflicts arise as technical disputes arise; and without top direction, R&D managers become the de facto strategists (Graham, 1986). Another essay further develops the point. Rosenbloom (1985) pointed out that the unwillingness or inability to formulate a clear vision of necessary technical effort is what paralyzes effort and turns potential commercial victory into defeat. Without a coherent and consistent strategy to serve, R&D does nothing more than tread water. Thus, the real obstacle to innovation implementation lies in the shaping of strategy at the executive level. The Wise (1985) book on the role of R&D leadership, referenced in Chapter 4, is also appropriate reading here.

Managers can handle conflict in an effective or ineffective manner. Barker, Tjoswold, and Andrews (1988) studied various methods for dealing with conflict and the implications this had for technology transfer. Four techniques were studied: cooperation, confirming, competition, and avoidance. They found that cooperation (positively linked goals) and, to a lesser extent, confirmatory techniques were more effective and offered constructive conflicts. Competition and avoidance techniques were mostly ineffective and unsuccessful. Thus, choosing the right method of dealing with conflict, managers can encourage technological transfer.

In concluding the discussion of technology transfer, it is helpful to point out some suggestions for managers. Vandermerwe (1987) made several points that help to improve the receptiveness and implementation of new ideas. This study found that lack of receptiveness is frequently found to be due

to an organizational factor. Firms may have to devote more
effort to internal diffusion of new technology: possibly as
much   as   is   devoted   to   external   diffusion   (into   the
marketplace). Several barriers must be overcome to make this
possible: it may be difficult to   communicate observable
benefits to concerned parties; the risks involved may be seen
as too high; or the idea may meet with interdepartmental
resistance, or with political or psychological barriers.

TECHNOLOGICAL TRANSFER: ANNOTATED BIBLIOGRAPHY

INTRODUCTION

6.1   DAVIS, DONALD A. AND ASSOCIATES (1986), <u>Managing</u>
        <u>Technological Innovation: Organizational Strategies</u>
        <u>for Implementing Advanced Manufacturing Technologies</u>,
        San Francisco, Jossey-Bass.
The book is a collection of papers taking a multi-
disciplinary approach to the study of: 1) how can the
dissemination and adoption of advanced manufacturing
technologies be facilitated; 2) once adapted, how can
innovative technologies be implemented and managed to obtain
maximum productivity gains.   Chapters are arranged in three
parts: 1) Innovation in Organizations: Obstacles and
Opportunities; 2) Managing the Implementation of Advanced
Technologies; and 3) Strategic Planning and Business Policy
Issues.

6.2   FOSTER, RICHARD N. (1986), <u>Innovation: The Attacker's</u>
        <u>Advantage</u>, New York: Summit.
This book deals with understanding the institutional biases
that underlie a company's use of technology.   The author
believes that the ability of any technology to improve a
product's performance in ways significant to customers follows
a characteristic pattern.   R&D managers do not pay enough
attention to studying the past and lessons learned.   A
defensive action is to improve the current product, but that
is often a failure in new threats.   Having alternative
technologies in the wings is not a bad idea.

6.3   LESLIE, STUART W. (1983), <u>Boss Kettering: Wizard of</u>
        <u>G.M.</u>, New York: Columbia University Press.
Kettering kept up a personal involvement in actual R&D
technical work.   His greatest contribution lay in the clarity
of his perception of the systemic nature of innovation in large
organizations making complex products. He understood how the
effects of technical change radiated outward from the
laboratory to touch the work of many other organizational
units. Without their support, even the best science would fail
to show commercial value.   Procedures of mass production are

opposed to those essential to development and early production of a new product.

6.4   MEYER, ALAN D. AND JAMES B. GOES (1988),
        "Organizational Assimilation of Innovations: A
        Multilevel Contextual Analysis," Academy of
        Management Journal, 31(4), 897-923.
This study examined the assimilation of innovations into organizations, a process unfolding in a series of decisions to evaluate, adopt and implement new technologies. A model is advanced that suggests that organizational assimilation of technological innovations is determined by three classes of antecedents: contextual attributes, innovation attributes and attributes arising from the interaction of the other two.

6.5   MILES, RAYMOND E., CHARLES C. SNOW, ALAN D. MEYER AND
        HENRY J. COLEMAN, JR. (1978), "Organizational
        Strategy, Structure and Process," Academy of
        Management Review, July 1978.
This article is on maintaining an effective alignment with the environment while managing internal interdependencies. Discusses entrepreneurial, engineering, and administrative problems.

6.6   REICH, LEONARD S. (1985), The Making of American
        Industrial Research: Science and Business at GE and
        Bell, 1876-1926, New York: Cambridge University
        Press.
The development of national markets and sophisticated products put a new kind of pressure on the industrial uses of the R&D knowledge base. The book examines history of development of R&D and marketing scope of business since late 19th and early 20th century. Since there has been a push in this direction it has profoundly altered the concerns of managers. While past answers to problems may not be relevant to current context, the study expands repertoire of manager's responses and complications of size do not distort or mask the underlying issues. It does not offer universal prescriptive advice, but represents lessons through history.

6.7   WASSERMAN, NEIL H. (1985), From Invention to
        Innovation: Long-Distance Telephone Transmission at
        the Turn of the Century, Baltimore, MD: Johns
        Hopkins University Press.
This is case study of the process by which a technical solution to the problems of long-distance telephone communication was implemented. In a technical based company there is a temptation to overlook the ways in which innovation might interact with what is already in place. R&D management must know when and how to direct focus to well-defined problems, and be able to contemplate the complications of mixing the old with the new. Shows also how innovation is a social and political process.

ORGANIZATIONAL TRANSFER AND STRUCTURE ASPECTS

6.8   BITONDO, DOMENIC (1988), "Technology Transfer in a

Decentralized Corporation," <u>Technology Management I</u>:
Proceedings of the First International Conference on
Technology Management: Special Publication of the
International Journal of Technology Management.

This paper discusses the flow of technology transfer from
laboratory to client divisions. Successful use of research
results by the adopting organization is improved when the
research focuses on long-range divisional needs and when
personnel from various functions (marketing, manufacturing and
engineering) are involved in developing research strategy and
plans.   Another factor conducive to successful implementation
is management "forcing functions"; that is, setting up a risk-
reward system to stimulate technology transfer.

6.9   DAVIS, P. AND M. WILKOF (1988), "Scientific and
       Technical Information Transfer for High Technology:
       Keeping the Figure in its Ground," <u>R&D Management</u>,
       18(1), 45-59.

The gatekeeper approach to the management of scientific and
technical information (STI) is most relevant to firms
developing products in a dynamic technological environment.
Authors argue that these companies have a choice of how to
effectively organize.   The organizational structure of
processes they implement will have major effects on how STI is
transferred as well as the quality of the STI that is
disseminated and used.   Hence, changing the context within
which STI is transferred may be much more effective than
improving the efficiency of existing transfer procedures.

6.10   GILLESPIE, DAVID AND DENNIS MILETI (1977),
       "Technology and the Study of Organization: An
       Overview," <u>Academy of Management Review</u>, 2(1), 7-16.

A heuristic scheme for study of technology and
organizations.   Discussion suggests variable theoretical
statuses, different levels of organizational study, application
to product and service types of organizations, and a proposed
means of identifying technological effects.   Scheme has three
variables: Technology, Structure and Behavior.

6.11   MORONE, JOSEPH AND RICHARD IVINS (1982), "Problems
       and Opportunities in Technological Transfer from the
       National Laboratories to Industry," <u>Research
       Management</u>, 25(3), 35-44.

Government, national laboratories and industry must make
changes for effective technological transfer from government
labs to industry.   Changes needed: 1) for transfer of
technology to spinoff applications: interactions between
industry and lab should be actively promoted; labs should act
as suppliers of goods and services;   spinoffs should be
nurtured; patent practices should make it easier for large
firms to obtain exclusive licenses.   2) For transfer of
technology intended for market: development of technology
intended for market should be assigned to labs only when they
possess special technical capabilities;   lab development
projects should be contingent upon industry interest.

INTERFACES AND BARRIERS

6.12   BURT, DAVID N., AND WILLIAM R. SOUKUP (1985),
        "Purchasing's Role in New Product Development,"
        Harvard Business Review, 63 (September-October), 90.

Engineering and purchasing must forge a relationship that incorporates the flow of information in the new product development process. Vendor can provide realistic specifications and supply constraints. Purchaser can monitor environment and identify strengths and weaknesses. Purchaser's information flows should be tied to new product development process and with engineering. May determine success of new product.

6.13   GINN, MARTIN E. AND ALBERT RUBENSTEIN (1986), "The
        R&D/Production Interface: A Case Study of New Product
        Commercialization," Journal of Product Innovation
        Management 3(3), 158-170.

Region of intensity of R&D-production interface: between Development to Introduction to Growth of revenues and profits. Article discusses transfer of technology across this interface. Two case histories are presented illustrating high and low imperatives (pressure for quick launch, difficult to manufacture, scaled up concurrently with a new processing technology). Interface is a key focus for interpersonal conflict. Projects which were greater technical and commercial successes tended to have higher levels of conflict and more superordinate goals than others. The firm can improve interface relations by increasing compatibility of goals among participating groups (a fundamental barrier at the interface).

6.14   SOUDER, WILLIAM E. (1977), "Effectiveness of Nominal
        and Interacting Group Decision Processes for
        Integrating R&D and Marketing," Management Science,
        23(6), 595-605.

The properties of three group decision-making processes (nominal, interacting and nominal-interacting) were tested by nine strategic planning teams each composed of R&D and marketing personnel. Results indicated that consensus and collaboration problems between R&D and marketing may be alleviated by a combined nominal-interacting process.

6.15   THORN, DICK (1987), "Problem Solving for Innovation
        in Industry," Journal of Creative Behavior (second
        quarter), 92-108.

Develops and fine tunes a creative problem solving process. Believes problem solving can be taught and begins discussion with two most common methods: 1) Asborn-Parnes: University of Buffalo Creative Problem Solving Institute (professionally applied brainstorming); 2) Synectics: involves a series of meetings.

MANAGEMENT AND ORGANIZATIONAL ISSUES

6.16   ALLAIRE, YVAN AND MIHAELA FIRSIROTU (1985), "How to
        Implement Radical Strategies in Large Organizations,"
        Sloan Management Review, (Spring), 19-34.

Success or failure of corporate reform hinges on management's ability to change driving culture in time with required changes in strategies, structures and management systems. The paper gives a clear discussion to add meaning to radical change and the paucity of modes to guide management. Nothing can replace intuition, experience, or skills. But they are better supported by a clear understanding of how to transform a social system and how an organization can be radically changed.

6.17   BARKER, JEFFREY, DEAN TJOSWOLD AND ROBERT ANDREWS (1986), "Conflict Approaches of Effective and Ineffective Project Managers: A Field Study in a Matrix Organization," Journal of Management Studies, (March), 167-178.

Four techniques studied: cooperation, confirming, competition and avoidance. Competition and avoidance were the most ineffective and unsuccessful techniques. Cooperative and confirmatory were effective for management and constructive conflict.

6.18   GARTNER, JOSEPH AND CHARLES S. NAIMAN (1978), "Making Technology Transfer Happen," Research Management, 21(3), 34-38.

Discusses how technological transfer can be improved at all levels: firm must eliminate inherent barriers and introduce incentives. For example: if technology is appropriate in a university lab but not economic for in-plant use, incorporate data to achieve optimum yield for the industrial site; all the components in the lab center are not needed for the industrial environment.

6.19   GRAHAM, MARGARET B.W. (1986), RCA and the Videodisc: the Business of Research, New York: Columbia University Press.

Author reconstructs the inherent difficulty in getting management to take seriously and in a timely fashion the definition of a business opportunity that came from the R&D community. Knowing how and when to apply pressure on research dependent projects is an important managerial consideration for the success of the project. When strategic goals of the company are not clearly and consistently translated into terms that give direction to the R&D effort, problems occur. Political conflicts arise as technical disputes. When there is no top direction, R&D and management become the de facto strategists.

6.20   KELLEY, GEORGE (1976), "Seducing the Elites: The Politics of Decision Making and Innovation in Organizational Networks," Academy of Management Review, 1(3), 66-74.

The success or failure of innovative ventures depends largely upon gaining and holding support of organizational elites. Presents analysis and strategies to elicit elite support initially, and develop a means to maintain support for venture until implementation. 1) How is innovation viewed in organization's theoretical policy framework" Who is the innovator, what is his view of the 'big picture?' 2) Expect conflict and learn how to diffuse it within group and organization. Know the elite and their different power bases.

6.21   MC INTYRE, SHELBY AND MEIR STATMAN (1982), "Managing
         the Risk of New Product Development," Business
         Horizons, 25(3), 51-55.
This is a practitioner-oriented view on managerial and organzational issues related to successful new product development.

6.22   OMSEN, ARNE H. AND SWEN EKESTROM (1987), "Implanting
         New Organizational Product Ideas into Operating
         Companies," Technovation, (December), 23-37.
Selling outside ideas is difficult. Most often, there is no one in charge of evaluating unsolicited product ideas. Then, the firms are either unreceptive or unsure of how to handle them, if they are introduced to them. Internal ideas in general do not meet with this resistance. If (untested) outside ideas represent potential opportunities, then the company should have programs to maximize these potential areas.

6.23   PIERCY, NIGEL (1981), "Marketing Information:
         Bridging the Quicksand Between Technology and
         Decision Making," Quarterly Review of Marketing,
         7(1), 1-15.
This article shows empirically that the use of management information systems by firms improved the companies' marketing performance on new products.

6.24   QUINN, JAMES BRIAN (1982), "Managing Strategies
         Incrementally," Omega, 10(6), 613.
Suggestions for managing transitions: 1) lead formal Information System; 2) build organizational awareness; 3) build credibility; 4) legitimize new viewpoints; 5) seek tactical shifts and partial solutions; 6) broaden political support; 7) overcome opposition; 8) structure for flexibility; 9) create pockets of commitment; 10) crystallize focus; 11) formalize commitment. Manage integration by 1) concentrating on a few thrusts; 2) coalition management.

6.25   ROSENBLOOM, RICHARD S. AND KAREN J. FREEZE (1985),
         "Ampex Corporation and Video Innovation," in Richard
         S. Rosenbloom (ed.), Research on Technological
         Innovation, Management and Policy, Vol. 2, Greenwich,
         CT: JAI Press.
This essay drives home the point that top management's inability or unwillingness to formulate a clear vision of necessary technical effort is what paralyzes effort or turns commercial victory into defeat. Without a coherent and consistent strategy to serve, no R&D lab can do more than just tread water. This lab with excellent resources failed to capitalize on them. The real obstacle to the innovation implementation lies in the shaping of strategy at the executive level.

6.26   VANDERMERWE, SANDRA (1987), "Diffusing New Ideas In-
         House," Journal of Product Innovation Management,
         4(4), 256-264.

Study of senior executives concerning their attempts to introduce new ideas and gain support for them in their firm. Alert to organizational resistance, why it occurred, and how it could have been avoided. How to improve receptiveness of new ideas was addressed. Problems most often can be traced to some organizational dimension. New technical ideas may by their nature be slow movers. Firms may need to put more conscious effort to internal diffusion activity as they do externally in the marketplace. Requires new skills and a new role for originating individuals.

6.27   VAN DE VEN, ANDREW H. (1986), "Central Problems in the Management of Innovation," Management Science, 32(5), 590-607.

A general management perspective in innovation: key problems confronting general managers and examination of the effects of how these problems are addressed on innovation effectiveness.

6.28   WISE, GEORGE (1985), Willis R. Whitney, General Electric, and the Origins of U.S. Industrial Research, New York: Columbia University Press.

The book points out there is no single best way to organize the R&D director's task, nor is there any one most effective personal style for an R&D leader. Whitney's greatest contribution was to legitimize, in the minds of general managers, the value of doing serious research, and the value of linking their research for commercial applications. Whitney believed in the publication of scientific results, except for the immediate publication of clearly commercial significance, to gain the respect of professional peers. His laboratory was designed as a "career" facility.

7

Observations and Conclusions

In conclusion, we would like to integrate our findings and present some observations which, we hope, will initiate more original research in this field. We seek to be thought provoking and relatively brief in our conclusions, rather than exhaustive. First, we offer some observations and conclusions specific to the chapters and topics in this review. Then we will conclude with remarks of a more general nature, addressing the current state of research and suggesting future directions.

OBSERVATIONS ON PRODUCT INNOVATION

Chapter 1 of this review examined the broad topic of product innovation. In particular, we discussed how models of the innovative process have revealed patterns in innovation, and how the process could be improved. The Utterback and Abernathy and related papers took a macro perspective (that is, sought to build a general, dynamic model of product innovation), relying on cross-sectional data from innovating companies to find partial support for the model. These studies found support for some relationships which are potentially of great use to product managers and R&D planners. Several notions should be particularly thought provoking for managers: (1) some kinds of innovations appeared to be more appropriate than others for firms to invest in, depending upon the firm's technical autonomy, size, and so on; (2) each type of innovation calls for a specific type of management strategy and organizational structures; (3) certain industries may be "ripe" for revolutionary attack, and defending firms ought to anticipate and plan for such an attack. However, these kinds of statements ought to be tested with longitudinal data collected over several years or decades. For the most part, only cross-sectional "snapshot" data were used in the studies cited in Chapter 1; thus the authors can point only to tendencies in directions predicted by the Utterback-Abernathy model and claim only partial support.

Despite this difficulty, this literature has much to offer the firm and the manager involved in product innovation. Certainly, the innovativeness of American industry has become a focus of attention in recent years, as America competes in an increasingly global marketplace. Business giants such as 3M, IBM, and Procter & Gamble are examples of firms which have consistently developed successful new products based on innovative ideas. Not all firms have the resources or the abilities in marketing, production, or development to keep pace with these giants, however. These firms must not only be more selective in their investments in order to spend efficiently; they must also seek alternatives to internal innovation and development which complement the skills and resources they do possess. Merger (and acquisition) mania is still strong, yet not all mergers or acquisitions live up to expectations. Managers can thus ask: For what firms, and in what circumstances, is it unwise to invest very much in in-house product development? And what are the wisest alternatives? Here is clearly an area of business where corporate managers have potentially much to learn from their counterparts in academia.

There is evidence that American corporations reduced their commitment to R&D in the late 1980s. Ten years earlier, investments in advertising and promotion had been rising proportionally to investments in research and development, a statistic blamed by some on overcommitment to (or misunderstanding of) the marketing concept (see discussion in Chapter 1). This pattern began to change in the early 1980s, as renewed interest and investment in R&D was evident. Companies such as Ford saw commitment to quality products as the only way to maintain a strong American presence in the world market. Recent reports in the business press, however, are showing that commitment to R&D has begun to falter again. (See the "R&D Scoreboard" sections of Business Week, June 22, 1987 and June 20, 1988.) Some firms, perhaps impatient with the lack of quick returns to R&D investments, have begun asking that all-too-familiar question, "What has R&D done for us lately?" and have justified R&D cutbacks as a result. Possibly they should have been asking another question: "How can we reallocate the money we are spending on R&D more efficiently?" As is well known by now, American industry certainly cannot ignore the global competitive market. Rather than cutting back on R&D spending and compromising future innovative success, firms should learn from the mistakes of the 1970s and 1980s and invest more wisely.

A related point concerns the issue of government support for innovation. Several authors cited the key role of government, most recognizing that what economists have long said is correct: promoting competition, financing risky projects, and lowering entry barriers improves the innovative process. With the U.S.-Canada free-trade pact already being implemented, the possibility of a North American economic community being developed (including Mexico), and the imminent European economic community emergence (referred to as Europe 1992), government involvement in private business and the likely effects on innovativeness are currently very hot topics. As Alan Blinder pointed out in his book, Hard Heads, Soft Hearts, what economists say is best for a nation's economic welfare is not always welcomed with open arms by business or by the general public. The controversy over the U.S.-Canada free trade deal is a good example. The 1988 Canadian national election was fought over this deal. The Europe 1992 negotiations have not always been smooth, either. Reactions are needed in the literature to Japanese government "targeting" of specific industries. The paybacks to immense Japanese government-sponsored and/or supported research and development expenditures are well known. How such investment has affected global competition is unknown. It is not in the scope of this book to say what should or should not be done in these cases. Issues of national independence and pride, cultural sovereignty, and fears of unemployment and other social repercussions are involved in addition to strictly economic issues. Although we do not investigate them here, we at least recognize some of the difficult questions which arise at the mention of government's role in private enterprise, especially R&D, and note that there often are no easy answers. Even so, the answers would be more evident if business researchers became involved in these discussions.

OBSERVATIONS ON NEW-PRODUCT DEVELOPMENT AND FORECASTING

Managers involved in product development are playing in a high-stakes game. Millions of dollars may ride on a GO/NO GO decision; the dollar amounts that the big failures lose for their companies are frighteningly high. So it is quite astute of von Hippel and others to suggest that we (as firms conducting market research) have become very good at understanding the perceptions, needs, and intentions of individuals, but maybe these are not the individuals we ought to be studying. Do market researchers sometimes ask the right questions of the wrong people?

Given the successful application of numerous test-market and pre-test-market models (of the kind discussed in Chapter 2), one can conclude that market researchers do what they do well. Still, we wonder about the long-term effect of focusing research on current heavy users of a product. More effort should be concentrated on identifying and studying the market segments that von Hippel calls the "lead users," especially for truly innovative product concepts.

It is heartening to see the level of expertise that has been achieved by marketing academics and consultants in the area of new-product development and forecasting. Wind, Mahajan, and Cardozo's book, New Product Forecasting, demonstrates the scope of approaches available to the practitioner. They list conjoint and multiattribute approaches to concept testing; ASSESSOR, COMP, and the Yankelovich, Skelly and White LTM procedure, among others, for pre-test-market analysis; TRACKER and other approaches for studying repeat purchase behavior via consumer panels for test-market-based forecasting; and several diffusion models used for early-sales-based forecasting, including that of Bass. The review articles of Assmus, Shocker and Hall, and others clearly indicate the usefulness of these approaches to product developers. Our abilities to test new products and develop supporting promotional campaigns seem to increase daily. A recent Business Week article, "Stalking the New Consumer" (August 28, 1989) examined the resulting effect in consumer markets: product line extension to meet the needs of smaller segments even more precisely (the Business Week article calls this "micro marketing").

There is, inevitably, room for improvement. The goal, of course, is not to eliminate all product failures at any cost. Such a strategy would inevitably result in ultra-conservative product development and too many missed opportunities. The goal is rather to manage the process to eliminate the obvious losers and take reasonable risks with the others, always being ready to make adjustments (including possibly making a KILL decision if necessary) during the process. To manage the development process effectively, the manager must rely on the best available market information. But, despite the level of sophistication attained by present-day market researchers, misleading, questionable, or just plain wrong information is still generated and presented to managers for their use. One of the best discussions on this topic is by G. Lavidge in his article, "Nine Tested Ways to Mislead Product Planners" (Journal of Product Innovation Management, 1(2), 1984, pp. 101-105). He notes that, in practice, products are often tested under unrealistic conditions; inadequate experimental controls are set up; the wrong individuals may be tested; and the researcher presents the manager with an incomprehensible sea of numbers rather than hard recommendations. (Note also the Feldman and Page article mentioned in Chapter 2, which comments on how "real-life" product development processes are often far less rigorous than the textbook ideal.) It appears that both the product manager and the market analyst have made great strides in recent times, yet they still have some improvements to make in their respective roles in new-product development. In their book, Wind, Mahajan and Cardozo note that the more sophisticated forecasting models are not necessarily more accurate: practitioners can improve their forecasting by selecting one of the commercially available, relatively simple models, perhaps tailoring it to fit the product type and market characteristics.

OBSERVATIONS ON INTERFACING AND ORGANIZATION

A hot topic in both the business and engineering literature is the R&D-marketing interface. Chapter 4 discussed numerous recent articles on this topic. In this age of increasing global competition, it is hardly surprising that this linkage has received so much attention. There is a natural duality to the new-product development process in firms. The process requires adequate coordination and cooperation between business and engineering functions. This parallelism is found at several stages through the development process: ideas can be market driven or technology driven; preliminary prototype feasibility is just as important as preliminary market assessment; technical as well as management and marketing skills and resources are required to bring the idea to fruition. Crawford's product protocol article clearly illustrates how difficult it can be to coordinate the activities of these functional areas. The series of articles by Souder and by Gupta, Raj, and Wilemon explore some of the reasons for weak interfacing between marketing and R&D: factors range from distrust and lack of appreciation to misunderstanding of each other's role perceptions and expectations. Indeed, the Crawford article implies that the interface <u>needs</u> to be managed.   A natural, cooperative interface apparently does not just happen but requires hard commitments from both sides (in the form of a mutually agreed upon protocol). Top management, having undoubtedly had both good and bad experiences with the R&D-marketing interface, may quickly zero in on this as a major area of improvement in the product development process. The success of Quality Functional Deployment in several Japanese and American companies indicates that this method can substantially improve communication across functions, with better-designed products as a result.

The issue of interfunctional linkages has implications for organizational structure as well. Firms such as IBM and Hewlett-Packard have successfully experimented with project teams and other structures that bring together individuals from different functional areas within the organization.   Much recent work has shown certain kinds of matrix structures to be particularly suited to new-product development. Other firms such as 3M encourage and support intrapreneurial activities and have been quite successful.

The practitioner-oriented publications have provided several recent case histories of successful organizational innovations, such as 3M's Post-It Notes. Entrepreneurship and intrapreneurship have also been the topics of several recent business books in the popular press. The academic work of Crawford, Souder, Gupta, et al., and others, complements popular sources to the advantage of the practitioner. First, these academic studies point out that real organizational obstacles do exist. Second, and perhaps more important, they shed light on the nature of these obstacles. With a better understanding of the difficulties that exist at the R&D-marketing interface, management can begin to take action (such as insisting on written protocols) that leads to more effective interfacing. In addition, we cannot forget the need for the effective interfacing of management with planning and manufacturing. Dougherty's article suggested that the main functional areas recognize similar problems, but each area views an issue from its own perspective (or "thought world"). No wonder, then, that communication across departments is sometimes garbled, especially in light of the fact that current organizational structures tend to encourage high walls between departments. There is great opportunity for improvement in the areas of organzation and interdepartmental communication for more effective innovation.

SOME FINAL OBSERVATIONS ON THE LITERATURE AND FUTURE DIRECTIONS

This concluding section presents a brief critique of the state of the literature, in terms of areas covered (product, process, R&D, and diffusion) and the scenarios investigated (macro and micro). Figure 1 is provided as a framework for the ensuing discussion.

In synthesizing and integrating the literature, we have found that some topics in product development and innovation have been over-covered.   By this we are referring to unnecessary repetition of similar research on the same topic at the same stage of development, either in a journal or within a discipline.   There has been excessive coverage of certain topic areas in cells V and VII of Figure 1, that is, in the areas of products and R&D.   We are referring to some of the product screening and R&D-marketing interface literature. Some of the articles reviewed under these topic headings were repetitious of earlier articles and did not contribute much new information to either the practitioner or the academic.

On the other hand, all of the topic areas of Figure 1 are covered to one extent or another.   In deficient areas, the problem did not appear to be one of under-coverage.   More typically, the problem was one of knowledge transfer between engineering   and   marketing/management,   and   also   between practitioner and academic. The blame for inadequate knowledge transfer   must   be   shared   by   the   participants.   Sometimes academics start looking for solutions to problems long after they are recognized by practitioners.   Consider, for example, that very little work was done in product failure before 1972, and that prior to this time no published studies were done that compared   successes   to   failures   empirically.   Also, organizational issues, R&D-marketing interface (cell VII), and technological transfer (cell IV) have emerged only recently as desirable   areas   in   the   academic   literature   (although,   of course,   important earlier work had been done in each area). Academic   investigations   seemingly   lagged   the   managerial importance   of   each   of   these   topics.   Organizing   for   the encouragement of innovation and technological transfer seems to have been attended to in the marketing/management literature before much work was published in the engineering literature.

FIGURE 1:   FRAMEWORK OF TOPIC AREAS IN LITERATURE

EFFECTS OR SCENARIOS

AREAS COVERED IN THE LITERATURE	Macro	Micro
Products	I	V
Processes	II	VI
R & D	III	VII
Diffusion	IV	VIII

Indisputably, academic researchers have made important advances in several practical areas related to new-product development. Concept testing, pre-test-market modeling, and test marketing come to mind. But, as is clear from the discussion earlier in this section, practitioners such as market researchers and consultants still make mistakes in applying the advanced methodologies available to them. In his article on misleading product planners, Lavidge felt obliged to warn the market researcher not to conduct product tests under unrealistic conditions, and not to rely exclusively on focus group results for assessing consumer reaction to new-product offerings. We can assume that these and related cautions are well known to academics who teach and do research in new product development. It appears that practitioners could do a better job of integrating certain aspects of the academic knowledge base to improve their practice. Of course the converse can also be true: academics may not be as effective as they think in communicating their techniques to managers. John Little recommended that we try to bridge the gap of understanding between the manager and the analyst as far back as 1970. Perhaps both sides still have some distance to go in order to close this gap. Academics may be producing elegant solutions to difficult practical problems, yet one may still question the utility of some of the literature to managers.

As a further example of this, consider cells V and VI (micro aspects of product and process innovation). Marketers have become adept at identifying market needs and making required product and process improvements, and much literature supports the methods and techniques of conducting customer research. However, technology-push innovation is, for some firms, at least as or even more important than market-pull innovation. In the brief discussion of the lead user concept earlier in this conclusion, we raised the question of whether marketers have become adept at eliciting information from the wrong people, especially regarding innovative idea scanning. When is this the case, and how indeed can the market researcher know when he or she is being misled by wrong choice of a respondent sample? Academics have recognized this problem and have begun suggesting ways in which the practice could be improved. It is now up to them to communicate both the dangers and the remedies to the practitioner community. Likewise the practitioners must be responsive to suggestions and not fall back to the tried-and-true techniques just because they are easy to use.

The literature can be criticized for being nonconvergent in many areas. The problem is not necessarily contradictory or inconsistent findings. In some cells (notably cell V, product innovation), there has not been much of an effort on the part of the contributing authors to look for convergent concepts. In some cases, the contributions of other researchers are relatively neglected, although they could potentially be used as bases from which to build. (A case in point is the scattered literature on product success and failure.) If managers are to use the reported results, the results should be available to them in the form of broad, reliable conclusions.   Internal consistency with previous published work by the same author is not enough.   What is needed is proven high convergent external validity with other ideas.   These authors recommend meta-analyses of heavily-researched topic areas, which will definitively draw together the scattered findings to develop comprehensive and implementable conclusions and identify inconsistencies. Relatively few attempts have been made at integrating previous research in Cells V and VI.   Crawford, in his 1987 textbook, reported a meta-analysis of the few articles that reported success and failure rates of new products, and Johne and Snelson (<u>Journal of Product Innovation Management</u>, 5(2), 1988, pp. 114-128) presented a literature review of selected articles on product success factors.

By contrast, cell VIII (diffusion of an idea through a population) has received much more attention in this regard. A number of good review articles on new-product forecasting, diffusion, and test-market models are available and have been cited earlier in this review.

We conclude by noting that certain areas seem to require more research, and that a good place to start to identify these areas is to turn to the business community.   Academics interested in increasing the store of knowledge in product innovation and development should identify the topics with the highest leverage value within business firms.   That is, they should determine what issues are most crucial to managers. The topics they identify as candidates for future research can be validated by discussing them with top business academics in the area of new product management.

Author Index

Please note: This index lists <u>entry numbers</u> as found in the annotated bibliography sections for easy reference.

Subject Index

Please note: this index lists <u>page numbers</u>.

About the Compilers

ROGER J. CALANTONE is a Professor of Marketing and Decision Sciences. He will be joining the academic staff of Michigan State University in 1991. He has written articles for various journals, including *Management Science, Journal of Marketing,* and *Journal of Marketing Research,* among others.

C. ANTHONY DI BENEDETTO is Assistant Professor of Marketing in the School of Business and Management at Temple University in Philadelphia. His articles have appeared in numerous journals, including *R&D Management, Journal of Product Innovation Management,* and *Industrial Marketing Management.*